W9-AFI-160

Schools for Tomorrow

To my husband Frank

Schools for Tomorrow
Building Walls or Building Bridges

Edited by

Bernadette O'Keeffe

LIBRARY

 The Falmer Press

(A member of the Taylor & Francis Group)
London • New York • Philadelphia

UK   The Falmer Press, Falmer House, Barcombe, Lewes, East Sussex, BN8 5DL

USA The Falmer Press, Taylor & Francis Inc., 242 Cherry Street, Philadelphia, PA 19106-1906

© Selection and editorial material copyright B. O'Keeffe 1988

All rights reserved. No part of this publication may be reproduced, stored in a retrieval system, or transmitted in any form or by any means, electronic, mechanical, photocopying, recording or otherwise, without permission in writing from the Publisher.

First published 1988

Library of Congress Cataloging-in-Publication Data

Schools for tomorrow : building walls or building bridges / edited by Bernadette O'Keeffe.
   p.   cm.
   Bibliography: p.
   Includes index.
   ISBN 1–85000–287–8
   ISBN 1–85000–288–6   (pbk.)
   1. Minorities—Education—Great Britain.
   2. Pluralism (Social sciences)—Great Britain.
   3. Ethnicity—Great Britain.   4. Church and education—Great Britain.   I. O'Keeffe, Bernadette.
   LC3736.G6S43 1988
   370.19'34'0941—dc19   87–36019
                                                CIP

Jacket design by Caroline Archer

Typeset in 11/13 Bembo by
Imago Publishing Ltd, Thame, Oxon.

Printed and bound in Great Britain by
Redwood Burn Limited, Trowbridge, Wiltshire

LC
3736
.G6
S43
1988

Contents

Contents

Introduction

As a stimulus for change in British society few factors outweigh in importance the demographic shift which has taken place in Britain since the end of the Second World War. Formerly secular, although subtly underpinned by a Christian heritage, society is now increasingly viewed as being multicultural, multifaith and multiethnic. Thus, the emergence of pluralism, with religious, cultural and spiritual dimensions, carries with it a challenge for, and a challenge to, our liberal traditions. One area of challenge lies in the need to promote approaches to education which are capable of responding to the social change that has occurred and also an effective curriculum which reflects our differentiated society. Will school structures reflect pupils from all backgrounds who one day will be required to take their place in society and to contribute to its values in their diverse ways? Will all pupils be made aware of the rich diversity around them and be encouraged to contribute in a positive way?

The mere setting of goals will not ensure their successful completion. Demands for greater accountability and for measurements of effectiveness increase day by day. Public examination results provide one yardstick for measurement. The need for accountability and for some measurement of results have frequently focus on public examination results. A second measure (far harder to quantify but nevertheless essential) is the degree to which pupils leave school feeling confident members of their society. The extent to which schools successfully promote for all pupils a sense of positive self-image is becoming increasingly available for public scrutiny.

The Inner London Education Authority (ILEA) has broken new ground with a recent publication[1] of its analysis of public examination performance by ethnic background. The 1986 figures show that Indian, Pakistani, South-East Asian, Greek, African, 'other European', and 'other white groups' achieve well above the fifth year average. Within this group children from Asian, South-East Asian, Indian and Pakistani backgrounds achieve the best GCE 'O' level and CSE results. On most measures however, the achievement of pupils from Bangladeshi, Turkish and Caribbean family backgrounds were below average. The contrasting results in performance between Bangladeshi and other Asian groups is important additionally in illustrating that Asian pupils cannot be treated as one undifferentiated group.

Explanations of the differential outcomes of pupils are frequently set out in terms of group characteristics. In particular, language and family organization and the level of support it provides are identified as key factors in arriving at explanations for different children's individual success.

In looking to factors outside schools to explain levels of achievement, particularly for causes of underachievement, it must be acknowledged that such emphasis must not allow schools the possibility to absolve themselves of the rigours of an examination of their structures, processes and practices. Looking beyond the ILEA research findings we must raise questions (which must not be ignored) as to whether some families have been more successful than others in achieving, for their children, a balance between their two sources of identity. The twin springs of identity combine that sense of identity which is rooted in the past with that aspect of identity which is future-orientated. The sense of identity which comes essentially from the past provides what Bellah refers to as the 'given' of social existence[2]. It is not just a territorial matter but an heritage from the past which is 'the real essence of one's personality everywhere in the world'. On the other hand, looking forward, there is the sense of identity which is future-orientated which relates to aspirations and to a commitment to the country one lives in.

That family organization and background are contributory factors to success, using both academic and positive image measurements, are confirmed in the findings of a study of Hindu family life in East London. Generally speaking, Hindus are very conscious and proud of their cultural heritage and religious and traditional patterns of thought and behaviour help to shape their lives. Geographical change is not seen as destructive to their religious and cultural values. For many families work is linked to religious beliefs and values together with their obligations within British society.[3] Thus, the Hindu family provides and sustains identity. It is a supportive system providing economic, soical and emotional security.

The same study illustrates how all parents interviewed, regardless

of their socioeconomic groups, place a major emphasis on the importance of education for their children who are encouraged to study. The
values and attitudes displayed can be summed up in Kahl's term —
'getting ahead' or aspiring families.[4] Education is seen as the key to
success and children are encouraged to utilize fully their educational
opportunities and to achieve higher standards of living than their
parents enjoyed. A lack of educational qualifications is seen as a chief
barrier to upward mobility. Looking to the future, Hindu children are
seen by their community as the future 'lights' of Hinduism.

The findings of this study help us to reflect on the centrality of
the child's identity in its maturation. The starting points as in so many
other areas are not equal. For some children a sense of identity which
is in balance provides a source of strength — for others not so
fortunate identity is confused and their sense of positive self-image
impaired.

Clearly, the interplay of factors contributing to the differential
outcomes of education for the different ethnic groups are complex.
The Swann Report[5] identified a network of socioeconomic and educational variables in attempting to provide answers to achievement dis-
parities. For some observers the important key factors are the ability
and motivation of pupils, their self-image together with socioeconomic
factors such as family background and the aspirations of parents and
their occupational status. Others emphasize or take as their starting
point those structures and processes of the educational system which
disadvantage minority groups. Further research is needed to ascertain
which set of variables weigh more heavily, those relating to school
factors, or to family factors, in furthering our understanding of the
roots of underachievement and lack of positive self image.

There is mounting evidence to show how our educational system
has failed to come to terms with the differential needs of pupils from
diverse backgrounds. I have argued elsewhere that the wide variety of
programmes established under the guise of multicultural education
may, indeed, reflect an unwillingness to grapple seriously with the
reality of differentiation which finds expression in the multifaith,
multicultural and multiethnic nature of our society. A procrustean
approach to education emerges to ensure that differentiated needs will
be subsumed on the basis that 'we know best'.[6]

For Gibson, schools are 'one of the pillars of institutional
racism'.[7] For a significant number of children from West Indian backgrounds, schools have failed to provide the means to encourage personal attainment and the building up of self-esteem. Gibson notes that
children from West Indian homes suffer from an identity crisis which

has in turn undermined their confidence. Schools in perpetuating the *status quo* consistently fail to meet the needs of West Indian children. They experience 'the stress of living in a society that devalues them because of their skin colour'. Their stress is manifested in a lack of confidence, low self-esteem and low aspirations. The disillusionment experienced by these children further saps their confidence. Gibson's study makes it clear that a significant number of pupils from West Indian homes are adrift in an uncomprehending society.

Further evidence is provided by the Archbishop of Canterbury's Commission which draws attention to the grievances of parents from minority groups regarding aspects of the school curriculum and the inability of the educational system to provide an education which is sensitive to the tradition and faith of their children.[8] A recent all-party Commons Committee found that 74 per cent of 15-year-old Bangladeshi pupils cannot speak English fluently. They referred to the education of this group as 'an educational and social disaster'.[9]

While the Muslim community and other religious groups voice their concern about the quality of education being provided and the detrimental consequences for their children, official responses continue along the lines of 'we know what is best for your children'. The Swann Report considered to the requests of Muslims for an extension of the dual system to establish their own voluntary aided schools. Having evaluated the concerns of Muslims and other religious groups the majority of the Swann Committee concluded that 'we do not believe that such "separate" schools would be in the long term interests of ethnic minority communities'. Its response exhibits a singular unwillingness to accept structural change and a failure to grasp opportunities which have the potential to promote diverse approaches to education.

Preservation of cultural identity and the achievement of social integration are two widely accepted educational goals. While the latter is primarily concerned with the need to maintain social stability and social cohesion, the former objective is justified in terms of human rights and social justice. Craft has indicated the tension arising from educating for diversity and educating for social cohesion. The 'problem' is one of 'deciding on the *minimum* level of acculturation necessary for full participation in society and the *maximum* extent to which diversity might be encouraged'.[10] Disagreements at all levels of theory and practice are evident between those who stress social cohesion at the expense of social diversity.

The Swann Committee, in discussing the inadequate educational responses of schools in the past and in seeking to work through its educational philosophy, proposes a concept of 'education for all'. It calls for an approach to education which will help prepare all pupils whatever their backgrounds to understand the 'shared values' of a democratic pluralist society. The Swann Committee sees a democratic pluralist society as:

> seeking to achieve a balance between, on the one hand, the maintenance and active support of the essential elements of the cultures and life-styles of all the ethnic groups within it, and, on the other, the acceptance by all groups of a set of shared values distinctive of the society as a whole. This then is our view of a genuinely pluralist society, as both socially cohesive and culturally diverse. (p. 6)

In formulating educational policy the Swann Report concentrates on ethnicity. It seeks to develop appropriate ways of integrating all pupils into an all embracing pluralist culture. To this end it adopts a mainly secular outlook which views religion as a cultural phenomenon and principally a private matter. It misses the significance of, and fails consequently to give due recognition to, religious differentiation. From a Muslim point of view:

> it failed miserably to understand or accept a basic principle of differentiation between the essential foundations of humanity which are divinely sanctioned and the temporary changing rules and regulations constructed by man.[11]

The secular basis of their priorities and the application of secular ideas to support all areas of knowledge is seen by Muslims to undermine concepts of education which are central to Islamic thought. The Swann concept of 'integrational pluralism' is thus rejected as a means of developing cultural pluralism rooted as it is in 'a secular approach to religion and all religious communities'.[12] As Ashraf observes, 'Their hope is that in two or three generations the "education for all" will integrate all their religious communities by brainwashing them and by systematically drawing them away intellectually and emotionally from their different religious backgrounds'.[13]

For Muslims, education is a process which aids the balanced growth of the total personality. The maintenance and strengthening of spiritual values and the fostering of a sound religious belief is a central task. For them religion must have a central place in education and the understanding of all phenomena must take place within a religious framework.

From the Muslim point of view, state education places an undue emphasis upon reason and rationality and underemphasizes the spiritual dimension. Muslim children are felt to be vulnerable in state schools arising from the secular, anti-religious ethos believed to be prevalent in an increasing number of schools. As Asraf points out 'Muslims want their children to grow up as good Muslims and they find the secularist state schools creating non-believers in spite of religious education. Children are encouraged to be critical of their own tradition and values and even their faith'.[14]

I have described in detail elsewhere the ways in which religion has become marginalized in many county schools.[15] It is frequently the case that for all pupils in county schools their religious beliefs and practices have become a private affair without formal expression within the school. On the other hand, Christian pupils in church schools are enabled to express their Christian faith within the school environment. The faith needs of children of other faiths who attend church schools are not catered for; for them religion is invariably a private matter.

The Swann Committee received evidence of the failure of schools to give equal treatment to religious groups. Religious education provided in schools was often criticized in terms of the approaches adopted, content and its generally low status. Nevertheless, the Committee believes that 'religious education can play a central role in preparing all pupils for life in today's multi-racial Britain, and can also lead them to a greater understanding of the diversity of the global community' (p. 496). In setting goals for religious education a phenomenological approach is recommended '. . . as the only response that accords with the fundamental principles underlying the ideal of cultural pluralism' (p. 475). From a Muslim perspective this approach is firmly rejected '. . . from the point of view of the harmonious growth of children, this appoach is going create conflict in their mihds based as it is on an educational approach which is nothing but a secularist dogmatic approach to religion'.[16]

A crucial task today for all those responsible for education lies in determining and going down the most promising avenues leading towards rapprochement in diversity. For this to become a reality there must be a continuous interpretation of the suitability of what is 'on offer'. In a society such as Britain there is considerable scope for developing the capacity for imaginative and inventive thinking and in working out positive steps towards such a goal. I have identified a number of factors which actively work against developing a rapprochement — a hidden curriculum which suppresses diversity, policy makers living under the illusion of a consensus on what constitutes good education and a failure to identify suitable ways of arbitrating between conflicting views of what constitutes 'good education'.

It is time to reflect seriously about issues of underachievement, the growing alienation of some pupils, an end process which has been described as 'an educational and social disaster' and the urgent need to close the gap between educational and societal realities and democratic ideals. We need to explore the ambiguities and contradictions in educational thinking, policies and practices. For in these ambiguities may be found the seeds of change with the potential to place rapprochement as a central platform in education for a multifaith, multicultural and multiethnic society.

In a world of shrinking boundaries where the consequences of confrontation become more hazardous and where the need for rapprochement at all levels becomes increasingly more evident this book sets out to discuss some of the issues involved.

This volume develops a number of themes crucial to educational provision in a multifaith, multicultural and multiethnic society. A number of the contributors draw on an exploratory study undertaken at King's College London and published under the title *Faith, Culture and the Dual System; A Comparative study of Church and County Schools'.*[17] From that study emerged a number of issues and challenges which face schools as they respond to religious and cultural diversity. The different contributors to this volume reflect the dilemmas and contradictions of educational provision as they discuss the need for a more flexible approach which will meet the needs of a differentiated society.

Ball describes the failure of the comprehensive system to meet educational and social goals which to begin with emphasized equality of opportunity, parity of prestige between schools and an ease of pupil transfer. He points to the failture of church schools to reflect their local community in their pupil intake.

Ball's examination of comprehensive provision, characterized by a lack of agreed definition, of conflicting goals and objectives, and the absence of agreement as to where values begin, echoes MacIntyre's perceptive analysis.[18] For MacIntyre the absence of a vocabulary of consensus in the language of discourse has undermined shared intentions as the link between beginnings and ends.

In exploring the themes of openness, diversity and belonging, Aspin traces the complexities underlying the education debate. Looking to the future we see that participation is the key. Participation in theory and in practice, in structure and in value provides a base where 'we can nevertheless all stand as equals in an ethic of community belonging'.

Hobbs, in looking at the progress of multicultural education, illustrates how little attitudes have changed, even among teachers over the last decades. He addresses the question of how governors, teachers and administrators may address the urgent situation which has arisen as a result of schools and policy makers failing to provide an education which enables all pupils to develop a sense of belonging. Convinced that all have an important contribution to make to the well-being and harmony of British society, Hobbs maintains that a positive effort must be made to undertake a reorientation of the curriculum to enable schools to do more than merely reflect society. There must be a purposeful direction in all school activities which works towards the 'formation of citizens' for a 'just harmonious plural democracy'. For Hobbs such a goal cannot be achieved without teachers working to that end and directing their professional activities toward realizing that goal. He assigns a pivotal role to teachers and by extending a concept of multicultural education which is sufficiently broad to command the support of teachers, parents and pupils in all schools wherever they are situated he posits that a common purpose greater than the transmission of knowledge may emerge. For teachers it would 'offer them at a time of confusion and conflict a unifying vision of society of which they, in common with their pupils, are citizens'.

Ashraf, in providing an Islamic perspective on education, recognizes the attempts of educationalists and policy makers to come to terms with racism. Nevertheless the 'education for all' policy advocated in the Swann Report gives rise to serious misgivings, both on a theoretical and practical level. Noting that as long as culture is separated from religion in addressing educational issues and in the formulation of education policy he asserts that there can never be a genuine understanding and appreciation of the needs and requirements of Muslim children. For Ashraf, education must be guided by a religious approach to life, instead of an approach dominated by concepts which stress rationality at the expense of faith.

Anwar tells us that while policy makers have slowly recognized that the presence of ethnic minority groups have implications for state education as a whole there is much that needs to be done for the educational needs of the Muslim community and Muslim children. Practical ways in which state schools can respond to the different needs of the Muslim community are outlined, including the availability of places at single-sex schools for both boys and girls, the teaching of mother tongue, their religion, culture and that history which is a central part of their identity.

The next two chapters address two important curriculum areas —

school worship and religious education. There is today increasing pressure to amend the 1944 Education Act which requires the school day to begin with a collective act of worship on the part of all pupils. Recent ministerial signals point to government action in this respect in the near future. The multiplicity of beliefs to be found in schools is frequently cited as a major reason for change in the satutory requirements for collective worship and religious education in maintained schools.

Watson focuses on the place of school worship and provides guidelines for constructing an educational rationale for its inclusion in the school curriculum. Starting with the needs of pupils Watson develops five characteristics which would enable all schools, whatever the diversity of pupil's background to be a 'worship-enabling community'.

The Swann Report sets the scene for Cole in discussing the approach to, and the content of religious education. In discussing the changes which have occurred in the teaching of religious education and the direction in which it is moving Cole is firmly of the opinion that the only justification for the teaching of religion in education must be an educational one. Attention is drawn to the ways in which thematic approaches to religious education have practical applications both for multifaith schools or 'monocultural, all white schools'.

Looking at the role of church schools Duncan develops the theme of service to the community. He points to a growing awareness that church schools should seek ways of becoming more socially responsive. Recognizing that church schools are on 'the borders of experimentation' and have the potential for innovation, Duncan explores ways in which the Church of England school can develop a rationale which will enable it to hold in creative tension its dual roles of responding to the needs of the Christian community and providing a service for the nation's children.

Burgess focuses on the extent to which church schools with a voluntary-aided status have a greater degree of autonomy than county schools thereby being enabled to determine management procedures, pupil and staff appointments and a greater say in curriculum policy and practice. In discussing some of the current practices adopted, five issues are identified for inclusion on the policy agenda of church schools. Church schools will thus be helped to review their role in relation to a changing school population and in preparing all pupils for a differentiated society.

Eschewing ready made answers to all practical questions Sutherland points out that the changes which have occurred across the board call for flexible non-dogmatic responses. In linking the concerns of theology with the priorities of education he succeeds in awarding religion and spirituality a legitimate and vital place in the classroom. He grasps the delicate issue of nurture and faces the question 'is it possible to avoid indoctrination without crippling the capacity for belief'.

The classroom being a microcosm of society at large, for Sutherland it follows that developments there are crucial for the future of our multicultural and multifaith society.

Notes

1 ILEA (1987) *Ethnic Background and Examination Results*, London, ILEA.
2 BELLAH, R. N. (1965) *Religion and Progress in Modern Asia*, New York, Free Press of Glencoe.
3 O'KEEFFE, B. (1979) 'Hindu family life in East London', unpublished PhD thesis, University of London.
4 KAHL, J. A. (1965) *Samples from English Culture*, London, Routledge and Kegan Paul.
5 DEPARTMENT OF EDUCATION AND SCIENCE (1985) *Education for All* (The Swann Report), Cmnd 9453, London, HMSO.
6 O'KEEFFE, B. (1988) 'On the margins of education: Finding a dimension for belief in GREEN T. and BALL, S. (Eds) *Inequality and Progress in Comprehensive Education: A Reconsideration for the 1980s*, London, Croom Helm.
7 GIBSON, A. (1986) *The Unequal Struggle*, London, Caribbean Centre for Education Studies, p. 26.
8 *Faith in the City* The Report of the Archbishop of Canterbury's Commission on Urban Priority Areas (1925) chapter 13, London, Church House Publishing.
9 First Report of The Home Affairs Committee, session. 1986–1987 *Bangladeshis in Britain*, London, HMSO.
10 CRAFT, M. (1984) 'Education and diversity' in CRAFT, M. (Ed) *Education and Cultural Pluralism*, Lewes, Falmer Press.
11 ASRAF, S. I. 'Foreword' in HALSTEAD J. M. (Ed) (1986) *The Case for Muslim Voluntary-aided Schools: Some philosophical Reflections*, Cambridge, The Islamic Academy, p. V.
12 *ibid.*
13 *ibid.*
14 *ibid.*, p. V1
15 O'KEEFFE, B. (1986), *Faith, Culture and the Dual System*, Lewes, Falmer Press, chapters 5 and 6.
16 *Swann Committee Report; An Evaluation from the Muslim point of view. An Agreed Statement* (1986) Cambridge, The Islamic Academy.
17 O'KEEFFE, B. (1986) *op cit.*
18 MACINTYRE A. (1981) *After Virtue: A Study of Moral Theory*, London, Duckworth and Co. Ltd.

1 A Comprehensive School in a Pluralist World — Division and Inequalities

Stephen Ball

It seems sensible to begin by setting the church school/county school division into the wider context of comprehensive provision. O'Keeffe's (1986) study *Faith, Culture and the Dual System* adds a further dimension and further evidence to the picture of uncomprehensiveness in the supposed comprehensive education system of England and Wales. While most contemporary commentaries on educational provision and policy in this country take 1965 and the distribution of *Circular 10/65* as a major break point in the history and development of secondary education it must now be clear that in practice the so-called comprehensive reform never really happened. What has happened to secondary education is a move from one set of divisions and inequalities to another. Indeed in some senses the real change in education has been to make those divisions and inequalities more complex and less visible. The secondary system in now riven with multiple division and a set of compounding privileges and disadvantages. In particular the policies of the current Conservative government have in a whole variety of ways increased and deepened these divisions. But the vast range of policy innovations, changes in the law and financial redistributions which have affected secondary education since 1965 have all added new forms of separation, differentiation and inequality to existing ones. What we have seen from successive Secretaries of State since 1965, and particularly since 1976, has been a process of *radical tinkering*. The tinkering may have become more radical but tinkering it remains. The core of the secondary system, its basic code (its voice and modality in Bernstein's (1982) terms), remains embedded in the structure, relationships and curriculum of the grammar school (that in turn being rooted in the late nineteenth-century Arnoldian public school). The vast majority of the British public remain mesmerized by the 'hegemony of the "O" level'.

This is the dominant image, the apogee of being 'educated' in the hearts and minds of most parents, almost all politicians and the entire body of the media. The disaster of educational politics in this country lies in the failure of successive governments to recognize the atavistic and deleterious nature of this vision of education — narrowly academic, culturally elitist, anti-vocational, divisive, patriarchial and ethnocentric. Much of the dynamic of educational debate continues to be rooted in the process of individual competition for access to '"O" level success' and the social advantages and life chance opportunities it continues to offer. The divisions in secondary education can be understood primarily in these terms.

The most fundamental, although smallest, division is between the 6 per cent of secondary age children in private education and the 93 per cent in the state sector. The life chance benefits of private education remain patently evident in all spheres of social life. Now added to this wealth-based division is the recently introduced, state-financed Assisted Places Scheme. While the Scheme is small in scale its existence is a clear (and practical) indication of government support for private education and their distrust of the state school. As Tapper and Salter (1986) suggest 'it is a symbolic challenge to the maintained schools whose indirect effects may be more damaging than its direct consequences' (p. 329). Within the state sector further divisions abound. Even the nomenclature of comprehensive education remains incomplete, several education authorities have maintained selective schooling and just over 200 grammar schools remain in existence nationally. In some cases so-called comprehensives co-exist with grammars. Clear evidence of the lack of any commonly-agreed educational or political philosophy for comprehensive schooling. Elsewhere, for example, Bromley, non-selective comprehensives co-exist with selective ones — super-comprehensives as they are known. Some 'comprehensive' authorities still use part of their education budget to pay for pupils to attend selective schools in other authorities. Even when these structural divisions between schools are laid aside other economic and social divisions clearly exist within the state sector to make the idea of a comprehensive system a nonsense. One example of this was evidenced in Solihull when middle-class parents defended their comprehensives against the CEO's plans to reintroduce selection. Walford and Jones (1986) put the situation into clear perspective.

> Arguments about social and educational equality were simply out of place in a comprehensive system based on catchment

areas which served to ensure that local schools, or even 'community schools', meant schools serving a relatively homogeneous social class intake. Children from the affluent middle-class areas were well catered for. In addition to their strong parental support and stocks of cultural capital, the active parent-teacher associations had ensured that any necessary extras were provided. These schools were successful and efficient and would ensure that there was a high chance of adequate certification to legitimate social class reproduction. There was certainly no social mixing with the Birmingham overspill children living in the north of the borough. (p. 251).

Walford and Jones also indiciate here a second major basis of division between comprehensive schools, that based on the buying power and the surplus income of parents. As government cuts and rate-capping have reduced LEA education budgets the day to day material support for pupil's work has been steadily eroded. In schools in affluent communities this erosion has been halted by increased parental contributions, direct and indirect, to the running costs of their schools. Pring (1986) provides some examples.

It is estimated for example, as a result of an NUT survey, that in 1981 at least £500,000 was raised by parents teachers associations in Surrey, much of which was spent on basic resources. The local branch of CASE (Campaign for the Advancement of State Education) in Merton estimate that £2–3000 per year is raised in each secondary school to help pay for essentials such as pencils, art materials, books and paper. Weymouth Grammar School has raised, through parental covenants, £10,000 to help pay wages of laboratory assistants, and school secretaries to restore a cut in their working hours imposed by Dorset County Council. Six years of parental covenanting at Hemel Hempstead Comprehensive School, Hertfordshire, now provides half the running costs of the school, the whole of which would normally be regarded as the responsibility of the authority. (p. 70)

As Pring goes on to argue, such practices not only operate to disadvantage pupils whose parents cannot afford such subsidies but they also undermine the principle that 'all children have a right to an education according to age, aptitude and ability rather than according to parental means'. The subtle and virtually untraceable effects of this kind of division of educational experiences based on ability to pay will clearly operate in a number of ways. It will separate the suburbs from the inner city, the south from the north, areas of high unemployment from those of low unemployment. As a result the educational opportunities of different social class and ethnic groups will become more and more unequal. Harrison (1983) offers the following account of educational opportunities in Hackney.

> The school system in the inner city becomes a franking machine to stamp the words 'certified failure' on most of its output. In 1978 in Hackney, no less than 28 per cent of fifth-formers came out of school with no certificate of any kind, more than twice the national average of 13 per cent. Another 42 per cent in Hackney passed out with low grades in the Certificate of Secondary Education, or with fail grades in the General Certificate of Secondary Education 'O' level (here the national average was 35 per cent). Thus no less than seven out of ten Hackney children left school unambiguously labelled as failures — as, indeed, did 47 per cent of children nationally. Only one in twenty received the clear stamp of success of five or more good 'O' level passes or CSE grade ones — half the national and London averages. (p. 205)

Significantly like the majority of commentators Harrison measures the success of schooling exclusively in terms of the narrow criterion of examination passes. The value of school is reduced to a process of individual competition for extrinsic rewards which, in the case of 'O' levels, are specifically designed to be beyond the capability of the majority of comprehensive school pupils. The system is geared to failure and once again rooted in the replication and legitimation of existing social divisions.

In all this, philosophical or political or even educational definitions of the meaning of comprehensive education are essentially redundant. The reality of comprehensive schooling, with very few exceptions, is dominated by the 'hegemony of the "O" level'. Most parents aspire to and most teachers, like it or not, work towards this end. Other possibilities must be eked out of the narrow, and narrowing 'one of tolerance' within which schools operate. Meritocracy remains the practical ideology of comprehensive education. Selection and differentiation are the key processes of school organization.

Divisions based upon *ad hoc* notions of ability and achievement (with an implict sub-text of behavioural evaluation) naturalize and reproduce divisions of race, social class and gender. Streaming, banding and setting remain the key terms in the grouping of pupils for teaching purposes in the comprehensive school. Whatever practical or ideological defences are erected to protect forms of streaming the long and short-term effects of these separations, which rest heavily upon notions of relative worth, esteem and status, are now well documented (for example, Hargreaves, 1967; Lacey, 1970; Ball, 1981). The separation of pupils into streams does not involve only a differentiation by status and a process of institutional channelling, it also gives rise to a whole series of other qualitative differences in the pupils' experiences of school. These include curricular and syllabus differences and pedagogic and relational differences. Whatever else they may do these separations are mechanisms which produce a sense of failure and rejection and engender, as a result, alienation, dissaffection and hostility. The general effects of this manufacture of apathy and enmity both social and economic are far-reaching and fundamental. Research by Eggelston *et al* (1986) provides the latest evidence of the role of streaming systems in the maintenance and legitimation of social divisions, in this case based on ethnic differences and articulated via racism.

> Evidence has been provided to suggest that within the class-room, in allocation to sets, streams or bands and in examination entries complex processes may be involved which serve to disadvantage black young people, and in this study particularly those of Afro-Caribbean origins ... However there is a considerable reluctance to acknowledge the existence of such processes. One factor behind this reluctance is a fear of blaming teachers for their actions. (p. 238–9)

The report goes on to conclude that the racism and racial intolerance of teachers is a prime and powerful factor in the generation of racial disadvantage.

It is into this background that the county school/church school division must be set. And, as O'Keeffe's research indicates, this is not a division that is in some straightforward and abstract way based simply upon the issue of the religious affiliation of pupils (or though even that is not as simple as it seems). Indeed the county school/church school division itself articulates with and ramifies the other divisions adumbrated above. As O'Keeffe demonstrates, the attraction of the church school for many parents who choose to send their children lies in image (and the reality) of the church school as holding out the 'modalities and voice' of the lost world of the grammar school, academic reputation. What many parents seek from these schools is not, or not solely, a religiously grounded education but educational and social advantage (O'Keeffe, 1986, p. 38). As is the case in so many developing countries church schools are seen as being educational conduits to higher education and sought after occupational positions. What were once missionary outposts intended for the civilizing of the urban working-class masses are now regarded by many as bastions of middle-class values and vehicles for the social reproduction of social status divisions.

While the composition differences between the church and county schools are by no means clear cut in the O'Keeffe samples the tendencies are evident enough. Eight out of ten county secondary schools have higher percentages of children taking free school meals (p. 60). Six out of ten county schools have a marginally higher percentages of pupils from single parents families (p. 61). And 80 per cent of church schools have a higher percentage of pupils whose parents are non-manual workers (p. 63). In some cases the differences between matched church and county schools in these terms are extreme, more than 20 per cent. There is also a far higher incidence of parental unemployment among pupils in county schools, again in several cases the scale of the differences is marked. Concomitantly '70 per cent of church schools succeed in getting their full quota of pupils who are above average ability whereas for county schools the comparable figure is 30 per cent' (p. 66). As is demonstrated in so many other pieces of educational research where there is advantage in the system parents of middle-class background will seek it out and exploit it for the benefit of their offspring.

Clearly though the issues raised by such an analysis are not just ones of sociological significance. The role of church schools, as an arm of the Church of England in this case, in perpetuating inequality and disadvantage, is a moral and religious issue. But if further evidence were needed here is clear confirmation that the idea of a comprehensive education system is a nonsense and comprehensive reform a non-event.

Furthermore, O'Keeffe highlights the ways in which this social selectivity and concentration of ability has direct effects upon the county schools which in a situation of falling rolls, and particularly since the 1980 Education Act, are in competition with the church schools for pupils. Church schools are far more likely to be oversubscribed, and as indicated above they are more likely to recruit high ability pupils (82 per cent of the church schools in the sample were oversubscribed). This is damaging to county schools in several ways. As one of the O'Keeffe's county school respondents commented 'We lose some of our brightest kids in this way. Transfers never affect the troublesome ones' (p. 33). The 'attractions' of the church schools initially 'cream off' high ability children from the county schools and thus enhance the public examination performance of the church schools to the detriment of their county counterparts. The judgments of 'academic reputation' becomes self-fulfilling. This is further exacerbated by the higher proportions of pupils faced with social problems — poverty, poor housing, unemployment and single-parent status — remaining in the county schools. Of necessity the county schools must devote greater time and energy to pastoral work while the church schools can concentrate to a greater extent on 'academic' work. The nature of the school experience for teachers and pupils is different in the different kinds of schools. In addition the county schools which find themselves undersubscribed as well as grappling with the consequences of the reputational effects of this 'stigma' will inevitably search for strategies to recover their position. The sense, and the reality of competition between schools, the Thatcherite vision of the cleansing and disciplining effects of the free market, will inevitably bite. O'Keeffe found that 40 per cent of the country school heads in her sample described their relationship with local church schools as unsatisfactory or 'non-existent' (p. 32). For many of the county school heads the competition was seen to be unfair. They felt themselves to be far more constrained, as they are, than the church schools in their admission policies. In all this the viability of the county school system is continually undermined. 'In 1981 Church of England voluntary-aided secondary schools provided for 17 per cent of the pupil population and the county schools 52 per cent (in the ILEA). Unless Church of England schools share the effects of falling rolls, by 1990 the pupils in county schools would be reduced to 29 per cent while the pupils in Church of England schools would account for 22 per cent of the pupil population' (O'Keeffe, 1986, p. 31–2). Together with a whole range of political attacks on the 'comprehensive school' from politicians of all persuasions and the policy thrust for the current conservative government the ground-work is laid for the dismantling of the formally comprehensive system of state education. Ball and Troyna (1987) conclude a recent article in very straightforward terms:

> It seems to us that the maintenance of this divisive system of schooling provision and treatment, *de facto*, undermines the espoused commitment of the state of equality of educational opportunity. (p. 9)

In the discussion above there is one factor of social division

17

which I have not yet addressed directly, but which is central to O'Keeffe's study. That is the question of religion, ethnicity and cultural pluralism. In straightforward terms the issue is whether church schools, as the Runnymede Trust concludes, are 'wittingly or unwittingly propping up racism and racial disadvantage' (Dummet and McNeal, 1981, p. 17). In reviewing O'Keeffe's data there is really only one conclusion to be drawn, excepting the practice of some individual schools, this is exactly what the church school system does. It contributes to racial disadvantage and perpetuates racism. In a religiously diverse and ethnically plural society, as Britain now is, the very existence of the church school system must be questionable. (All the more so when non-religious grounds play so large a part in parents choice of these schools for their children. Following O'Keeffe's analysis the question of ethnicity can be raised in three ways; (i) recruitment; (ii) religion and culture; and (iii) multiculturalism.

As regards recruitment the basic issue would seem to be a simple one, Church of England schools are for Church of England children from Church of England families, other considerations must be irrelevant. In practice recruitment policies differ markedly from the one school to another. But perhaps one of the most startling and disturbing findings to emerge from the O'Keeffe study is the apparently cynical and clearly racist strategies employed by some church school heads in manipulating their admissions policies to suit different circumstances. Where schools are oversubscribed then strict admission policies are operated to exclude non-Christians, even non-Anglicans, if circumstances allow. If full recruitment on this basis seems in doubt then some heads at least have no qualms about changing their criteria for entry. This strategic approach is justified by a mixture of pragmatism and anticipated reactions from the Christian parents and the diocese. One head explained:

> If you have a school and it is oversubscribed by practising Christian parents and pupils, if you say 40 per cent can't come because of a deliberate policy of foundation and non-foundation places then Christian parents would be aggrieved. How can you justify turning down Christians for a few Muslims? (p. 48)

There would seem to be a whole variety of valid ways of justifying such a policy, but what the head is suggesting is that the lobby of 'aggrieved Christian parents' is more powerful than any lobby that 'a few Muslims' might mount or any matters of moral principle that might be raised. Also as the quotation indicates in a situation of undersubscription the matter would be viewed differently. Then the 'few Muslims' can be regarded as a reserve pool of potential entries who can quite properly be tempted away from the county school, by exploiting the church school reputation, to ensure the survival of the church school, until matters 'improve'. Again comprehensive principles become a matter of expediency, non-Christian pupils and the county schools can be raided for bodies and talent as the market situation changes, here again we may see the logic of capitalism in operation through the free market in school places. The appearance of choice for the consumer obscures both exploitation and inequality. Clearly not all church school heads adhere to the cynical position, the majority of O'Keeffe's respondents were attracted by the National Society Green Paper, *A Future in Partnership*, which stresses the twin aims of education in the Christian faith and service to the nation. However, in some cases this appears to have been interpreted as encouragement to proselytize the Christian faith. This itself raises difficult questions about the role of the church schools, some of which are relevant to the multicultural issue discussed below. This might be interpreted as a return to the colonial role of the churches as missions, and church schools as vehicles for achieving conversions. The relationship of Christianity to other religions becomes a key problem. This leads on to the second issue, cultural pluralism. It is possible to see the National Society initiative in relation to the recent development of expressions of what Barker (1981) calls 'new racism' or 'cultural racism', wherein values and morality are taken to transcend differences of race, class and gender, the heritage is embodied in and reproduces an inherently racist conception of the nation and the nation-state. The established church, as purveyor of morals and values has a particular role to play in this. (As James Anderton, Chief Constable of Manchester has asserted). As Barker argues, the construction of a new idea of nation — feelings of belonging, of sharing traditions, customs, beliefs, language — with its arguments that it is 'natural' for a 'nation' to wish to exclude 'outsiders' is a return to the assimilation rhetorics of the 1950s and 1960s. This kind of discourse of nation, deracializes policy-making (that is to say it disengages policy-making from the issue of racism) and places a special emphasis on education in the forging of the 'one-nation' (Reeves, 1983). It is taken for granted that racial inequalities can be remediated simply by strength of will, or perhaps do not really exist in the first place. The right-wing Conservative Monday Club in its paper on *Education and the Multi-Racial Society* (Pearce, 1985 p. 7) epitomizes this view.

To say that British history, English literature, the civilization of Western Europe should have pride of place in our schools is not to argue from a sense of superiority. It is to argue for relevance. Black and white children need to learn, and they can, of the nation in which they live and the forces that have shaped it. Britain has had a great and inspiring heritage. Our children need to be fed on it, ˜to be encouraged to make its values their own. Such an approach to education will unify, not divide; nurture shared pride and common loyalties, not cycnicism and racial hatred.

Here then cultural diversity and racial inequality are irrelevant in the drive towards a new moral and national consensus. Indeed there is no room for pluralism here. What is suggested is that pluralism, in culture, values and belief, is a problem, a source of disunity and conflict, that it undermines the shared sense of nation. It follows from this, that those who oppose the born-again moral nationalism are its enemies, in the language of Thatcherism 'the enemy within'. The structures within the society which produce and reproduce division, inequality and oppression are simply ignored, set aside. Instead there is a classic scenario for 'blaming the victim'. This is racist in at least three senses, in minimizing or treating as irrelevant existing structural racism, in excluding or demeaning other cultures and their value systems, and in scapegoating or targeting those who would hold out against the hegemony of the the British heritage.

Now all this may seem to move a long way from the issue of church schools within a comprehensive school system. And yet in fact it returns the discussion to the key theme with which we began, that of comprehensive education and social division. In one straightforward sense the church school system highlights and reproduces a central basis of cultural and political tension within a culturally plural, multifaith society. The parents reported in the O'Keeffe (1986) study certainly expected religious education within the church schools to 'strengthen Christian commitment' (p. 114). But as O'Keeffe indicates within the church (and the county schools) there is a continuing tension between the view that religious education is a matter of elucidation, teaching about religion and the view that it is a matter of advocacy, education into religion. In the majority of church schools the latter position is in the ascendent. For a significant number of teachers in the church schools other faiths are irrelevant, 'RE teachers in church schools were concerned primarily with enabling pupils to be informed about Christianity' (p. 116), although some were committed to teaching 'world religions'. But in the current political context this only serves to highlight the problematic nature of the church school concept. In effect the Anglican church is caught between a traditional, closed, subservient and legitimatory relation to the state on the one hand and on the other a position of what the British Council of Churches (1981) calls 'critical openness', an idea which 'is intended to suggest one is in a community, a learning community, in which one speaks and listens, being both critical and receptive' (p. 7). In the current ideological climate it is the former which is receiving greatest stress in public debate, the role of Christian religious values as a vehicle for re-establishing social order and the legitimacy of traditional authority. But the tensions inherent in the teaching of religion and the wider issue of the relationship of the Anglican church to 'the nation' and the state must also beg very practical questions about the values and perspectives being taught and transmitted in the church schools. In other words what sort of Christianity is being practised and taught? The issue of multiculturalism again provides a critical focus.

Mullard (1982) has provided the definitive analysis of changes in multiethnic education policy in Britain during the past twenty-five years. He suggests the following progression in policy-making and policy debate. In the early to mid-1960s education policies were based on an unproblemmatic assumption of 'assimilation', the 'problem' of immigrant children at school was regarded as transitory, it would simply go away as time passed and the immigrants adjusted to and internalized their new cultural milieu. These assumptions also led to the adoption of a policy of dispersal, as an attempt to limit the proportion of immigrant children (or in effect black children, whether or not they were recent immigrants) in any school. Concentration was regarded as detrimental to educational standards and a barrier to successful assimilation. (The Anglocentric rhetoric of assimilation is now being espoused again in documents like those of the Monday Club quoted previously and within the pages of the *Salisbury Review*). At the end of the 1960s the policies of assimilation were gradually superseded, or at least overlaid by those of 'integration', this involved a minimal recognition of cultural diversity, and an avowed concern with the 'needs of black students'. However, as most commentators argued it is difficult not to see this policy movement (rather than change) as anything else then a response to fears about the potential for social disorder posed by 'alienated black youth' (for example, Troyna and Williams, 1986). In the mid-1970s integrationism shaded over into a more forthright and coherent educational position now generally referred to as 'multiculturalism'. The rhetoric of multi-culturalism rests on two main premises; that for black children learning about their own ethnic heritage will improve self-image, motivation and thus achievement; and that for all children, black and white, the learning about other cultures will reduce prejudice and discrimination. Finally, in the 1980s the rhetoric, assumptions and policies of multiculturalism have been challenged by the development of 'anti-racist education'. In anti-racist teaching racism is addressed directly, in all its forms. However, policy support for anti-racism is limited to a relatively small number of individual schools and a handful of particular local authorities, within the DES and government circles it is regarded with suspicion or condemned as 'political'.

What is interesting about these shifts in policy and debate in relation to the O'Keeffe study (1986) is that it is possible to find examples of all four of these positions in policy and practice within the sample of church schools. At one extreme are those schools and heads who see multicultural education, in whatever form, as an irrele-vance. For the most part these are schools in all or predominantly white areas and their headteachers articulated forms of assimilationism or integrationism (these views were often shared by the matching county schools). One head explained:

> If multicultural education means Asian/West Indian awareness,
> it is a non-starter. When a person emigrates he/she should
> adopt the customs and attitudes of the host country. This is
> not an arrogant statement, it is common sense. (p. 132)

Such a statement from a comprehensive school headmaster in the mulitcultural Britain of the 1980s suggests a grimly narrow and dangerously naive version of education being enacted. The absences and silences it suggests in the curriculum indicate a process of school-ing tightly and unthinkingly reproducing a parochial and myopic local culture. Although it has to be said that there is little in the way of relevant curriculum materials and teaching concepts available to schools in the white highlands interested in multicultural or anti-racist education initiatives.

The middle ground among the Church schools is held by those pursuing or espousing some form of multicultural education, although here there were important differences in emphasis. Twelve of the headteachers in O'Keeffe's survey viewed multicultural education as primarily serving the needs of ethnic minority groups, another twelve offered a broader interpretation of preparing all pupils for a multi-cultural society. However, even here, in practice only 11 per cent of schools reported making 'good progress' in developing multicultural education. Furthermore, in many schools what is embedded in these initiatives is a problem-centred view of the ethnic minority pupils, as O'Keeffe notes. This sets multicultural education back into the logic of assimilation and integration policies, the victims are blamed, racism is ignored, control and containment are the key concerns. The definition of what is to count as education is set and fixed, the pupil's task is to come to grips with it as it stands, racism and all, and if they fail it is their fault. This is hardly a situation in which any but the most mechanical definitions of comprehensive education are tenable. The lives, cultures and social experiences of whole groups of pupils are excluded. The barriers to their achievement, the development of their talents are repudiated. The comprehensive school in these terms educates for failure, schools for alienation and recycles and compounds racism. It is unsurprisingly that many black parents look to supplementary schools to provide a 'proper and rigorous' education for their children.

Only five (13 per cent) of the church school heads saw multicultural education as incorporating or requiring a direct engagement with racial discrimination, bias and stereotyping. (A view of racism itself limited to aspects of behaviour.)

Perversely there seemed to be little evidence within the church schools of links being made between Christianity as a value system and the evils of racism within society. Heads seemed reluctant,even fearful of taking a proactive stance towards multiculturalism and racism, they remained locked into their own racist assumptions of either there being no problem in their school, or the idea that what problems did exist were generated by the ethnic-minority groups themselves. Paradoxically the 'ideologically acceptable modes of understanding educational issues' (Troyna and Williams, 1986, p. 44) related to multicultural education and anti-racism are severely constrained in these schools by the prevailing notions of 'a Christian education'. In many cases it seems Christian teaching remains dogmatic or academic and is not related to or translated into personal philosophies and views of society. Christianity may be learned and not lived, and not made reflexively applicable to life in schools, or life in a multiethnic society. Ball and Troyna (1987) suggest that 'Voluntary schools need to consider how their established policies and procedures may deny black and white students equal access to, and appropriate educational experiences in school' (p. 7).

Expressed in crude terms it seems valid to conclude from the O'Keeffe study that church schools (or the vast majority of them) are in practice a denial of comprehensive education. As with other schisms within the comprehensive system the continued existence of the church school embodies and perpetuates social divisions and inequalities. As O'Keeffe puts it: 'Every policy, every practice which excludes sections of the population informs such groups that church schools do not "belong" for them' (O'Keeffe, 1986, p. 152)

Any sensible discussion of the issue of comprehensive education in the United Kingdom must eventually attend to two key questions. First, have we ever achieved a system of comprehensive education? And, second, and perhaps most important, what does comprehensive education mean? The answer to the first question must be an unequivocal no. Leaving aside the continued existence of state subsidized private schooling, a significant number of education authorities have continued to maintain forms of selective schooling, even in a number of cases where their schools are comprehensive by name. But even the existence of comprehensive schools does not automatically provide or ensure a comprehensive education. Which leads us to the second question what do we mean by comprehensive. In practice the term is meaningless, for there is no agreement, no shared definition as to the aims and objectives of comprehensive education, and thus as to how it should be provided, and thus how it should be evaluated. The comprehensive system in this country is a clear result of halfhearted political compromise rather than the outcome of educational principles. It is a pretence. And by all accounts it is a pretence which has, in the eyes of most commentators failed. But how can failure, or success, be judged in the absence of agreed criteria, political impetus and economic support. For the representatives of the New Right the comprehensive system has failed because it does not produce enough 'O' levels; for David Young it has failed because it does not encourage industrial spirit and enterprise; for Norman Tebbit it has failed because it does not disseminate the values of conservatism; for politicians of all persuasions it has failed because it has not prevented Britain's slide into economic recession; for many parents it has failed because it does not ensure that their children get jobs when they leave school; for industrialists it has failed because it does not produce compliant workers; for Douglas Hurd it has failed because it does not prevent street riots and drug abuse; for sociologists it has failed because it has not broken the cycle of social and economic reproduction; for feminists it has failed because it contributes to the continuing oppression of women; and for members of ethnic minorities it has failed because it does little more than perpetuate the institutional racism they confront elsewhere. Teachers might say, with some justification, that a society gets the education system it deserves and that the condition of the school system does no more than reflect the condition of the society. The concept of comprehensive education is nothing more than a tattered and half deflated political football, which inside its worn patches contains no more than other footballs that are kicked around a lot, hot air. Clearly the church schools would score better by some people's criteria in all this than by others. However in terms of the analysis suggested here the failure of the church schools to 'be comprehensive' is a failure rooted in history and in politics, this is just one more source of inequality in an education system pervaded by inequalities.

From an unreserved pessimistic perspective it could be argued that our current school system is doing more harm than good; it is actually encouraging and reproducing nascent conflicts. From a cautiously optimistic perspective it would be fair to claim that many schools are doing many good things, some in the field of multicultural and anti-racist education. The problem with the latter position is that it has to be set against a total absence of coherent policies on comprehensive education from any of the major political parties. In the short term at least any serious response to the reproduction of inequalities and divisions via schooling must come from the schools themselves. Comprehensives, church and county, will continue as sites of ideological struggle in a pluralist world.

References

BALL, S. J. (1981) *Beachside Comprehensive*, Cambridge, Cambridge University Press.

BALL, W. and TROYNA, B. (1987) 'Resistance, rights and rituals: Denominational schools and multicultural education', *Journal of Education Policy*, 2, 1, pp. 1–11.

BARKER, M. (1981) *The New Racism — Conservatives and the Ideology of the Tribe*, London, Junction Books.

BRITISH COUNCIL OF CHURCHES (1981) *Understanding Christian Nurture*, London, BCC.

DUMMET, A. and McNEAL, J. (1981) *Race and Church Schools*, London, Runnymede Trust.

EGGLESTON, J. et al (1986) *The Educational and Vocational Experience of 15–18-Year-Old Young People of Ethnic Minority Groups*, Stoke, Trentham Books.

HARGREAVES, D. H. (1967) *Social Relations in a Secondary School*, London, Routledge and Kegan Paul.

HARRISON, P. (1983) *Inside the Inner City*, Harmondsworth, Penguin.

LACEY, C. (1970) *Hightown Grammar*, Manchester University Press.

MULLARD, C. (1982) 'Multiracial education in Britain: From assimilation to cultural pluralism' in TIERNEY, J. (Ed) *Race, Migration and Schooling,* London, Holt, Rinehart and Winston.

O'KEEFFE, B. (1986) *Faith, Culture and the Dual System: A Comparative Study of Church and County Schools,* Lewes, Falmer Press.

PEARCE, S. (1985) 'Education and multiracial society', *Monday Club Policy Paper* no. 1R4, London, The Monday Club.

PRING, R. (1986) 'Privatization of education', in ROGERS, R. (Ed) *Education and Social Class,* Lewes, Falmer Press.

REEVES, F. (1983) *British Racial Discourse: A Study of British Political Discourse About Race and Race-related Matters,* Cambridge, Cambridge University Press.

TAPPER, T. and SALTER, B. (1986) 'The assisted places scheme: A policy evaluation', *Journal of Education Policy,* 1, 4, pp. 315–30.

TROYNA, B. and WILLIAMS, J. (1986) *Racism, Education and the State,* Beckenham, Croom Helm.

WALFORD, G. and JONES, S. (1986) 'The Solihull adventure: An attempt to reintroduce selective schooling, *Journal of Education Policy,* 1, 3, pp. 239–54.

2 'Critical Openness' as a Platform for Diversity — Towards an Ethic of Belonging

D. N. Aspin

One word has been prominent in reports in the Western media of recent developments in the Soviet Union — 'Glasnost'. The Secretary of the Communist Party of the USSR is concerned to introduce new policies of reconstruction, acceleration and openness; for Mikhail Gorbachov the only way forward for the Soviet State is through programmes embodying these virtues. 'The choice', he is reported as saying, 'is either democracy or social conservatism and inertia'. This statement, and the new practices and policy proposals associated with it, must have been welcome news to those who have been waiting for a translation into institutional reality of the commitments entered into by the then Soviet leadership in the Helsinki *détente* of 1975 as must be increasing signs of emancipation and liberation in many aspects of Soviet life hitherto regarded as closed.

The commitments made in the Helsinki agreement were cited by many Western politicians not merely as emanating from the values characterizing our preferred form of institutionalizing our political arrangements — what we might call the four 'freedoms' of NATO — but as providing proof of the superiority of that form of polity to others that did not conform to them. Chief among those values were those emphasized by some of our politicians as being the ones marking the distinction between democratic and totalitarian forms of society — openness, dialogue, public accountability, reversability and periodic review; without these, it is widely believed, there can be no real social justice, no sense of community and no possibility of building bridges of peace and understanding, not only between different elements in a plural society such as ours but also with different systems and states in the international community.

These are values we take for granted. Yet the reality is somewhat different: we have media subject to an Official Secrets Act, Section 2 of which is regarded by many as a state licence to censor any kind of information that may be deemed by the government of the day as injurious to it; we have no Bill of Rights and apparently no power to impeach; we only have the first moves now towards the passing of a Freedom of Information Act; and we still have in many schools and LEAs restrictions on the public's right of access to records. We have in sum a society that is supposed to be 'open' and schools that are, as agents of society, also .supposed to be 'open'; as yet, however, we may see some contradictions in the ways schools are run — the power of the head often being regarded as arbitrary and autocratic — and their policies on curriculum, institutional norms, staffing, methods of instruction and materials, educational policies, and assessment and examining procedures, and those supposed community values. These apparent contradictions may be observed in operation in such tangible features of school life as the environment itself and in the dress worn by staff and students, and in such intangible ones as the 'hidden' curriculum and the ethos and atmosphere of the institution. In certain current educational understakings they get an especially sharp point of purchase — TVEI, GCSE and teacher appraisal, for example; a particular area, in which policies of openness and building bridges may be said to be at a premium and yet where such contradictions are clearly apparent, is that of multicultural education.

It might be as well as to decide at this stage what sense we can make of the notion of 'multicultural education', insofar as this relates to any descriptions that might be given of how programmes devoted to that idea in schools might look or, on the other hand, to prescriptions that might be developed and promulgated as to how such programmes ought to be framed and implemented.

Perhaps one preliminary remark ought to be made. Multicultural education is regarded by some people as belonging to the same class of activity in education as, say, health education or urban education: it is a *species* of a larger *genus* and is to be seen merely as a narrowing of the focus of overall educational undertakings so as to bring their general scope and direction on to the particular topics, issues and problems that constitute its staple. In this case these would relate to the educational challenges posed by the number of students in our educational institutions from ethnic, cultural or religious minorities that make up a plural community whole. Multicultural education seen in this light is education 'writ large', as it were. By others, however, multicultural education is seen differently. The main concern of general education is held by them to have to do with the perpetuation, transmission and promotion of the cultural beliefs and norms of the original indigenous community and the ways in which these can then function as a paradigm to which the beliefs and values of minorities should expect to be accommodated. Multicultural education is thus proposed by them as a necessary redressing of the balance to cater for the particuar needs, interests and aspirations of ethnic and religious minorities and the ways in which these can be preserved, defended and emancipated in a culturally alien — not to say hostile — environment. It represents a move away from an ethos where the dominant stress is on homogeneity and conformism towards an alternative view celebrating plurality and heterogeneity. It encapsulates, in short, concern for the addition of a further — even a competing — concept of education.

It is clear, of course, that these views both rest upon a similar, if not the same, set of theoretical preconceptions. For the idea that there can be some sort of overall concept of education, and a further competitor to it is a function of the view that has been labelled 'essentialism' — a view often associated with early analyses of 'education' and other terms in educational discourse essayed by R. S. Peters and others of the 'London' persuasion.[1] According to this account all that is involved in the attempt to produce a definition of education is the utilisation of the instruments employed by conceptual analysts — etymological derivation, dictionary definition and the collection of examples of the 'standard' uses of the term — to produce a set of necessary and sufficient conditions for the correct, standard, central or paradigm application of the term. The paradigm case then becomes normative for the coercive upon all acceptable uses of that term in educational discourse, whether these are standard too, or peripheral to or parasitic upon it. This, or at any rate something like it, is the philosophy that seems to me to lie behind many discussions centring upon the various versions or 'meanings' of multicultural education.

It is certainly a view that underlies one of the earlier versions of that idea that has been called 'assimilationism'.[2] This, by and large, is the emphasis of the first of the two approaches to it adumbrated above: the notion that there was an overall cultural identity in a host community to which newcomers so-called were expected to conform. This idea received official sanction in a report of the Commonwealth Immigrants Advisory Council in 1964, where it was stated that

> a national system of education must aim at producing citizens who can take their place in a society properly equipped to exercise rights and perform duties which are the same as other citizens' ... (it) cannot be expected to perpetuate the different values of immigrant groups.[3]

Lest anyone think that this view has now ceased to have respect in the thinking of those responsible for education in our multiethnic society of the 1980s we might do well to recall the words of one of the heads who were interviewed in the O'Keeffe study published in late 1986[4]:

> If multicultural education means Asian/West Indian awareness, it is a non-starter. When a person emigrates he/she should adopt the customs and attitudes of the host country. This is not an arrogant statement, it is common sense.

And there are other instances of views such as this in the O'Keeffe report which suggest that the 'assimilationist' approach to multicultural education is still enshrined in official thinking in schools in this country. The same might also be said of Australia, Canada and the United States, where the distinction that some have made between a 'structural' and a 'liberal' assimilationism in matters of official educational practice and public policy can be observed rather more clearly,[5]

Another version of multiculturalism is to be observed in other 'official' pronouncements that have been called 'integrationist'. In its political form this view may be said to have been given expression in a statement made in 1966 by the then Home Secretary who defined integration

> not as a flattening process of assimilation but as equal opportunity accompanied by cultural diversity in an atmosphere of mutual tolerance.[6]

Thus in 1971 a government report was able to recommend that the education service could

> help promote the acceptance of immigrants as equal members of our society ... (while also) permitting the expression of differences of attitudes, beliefs, customs, language & culture ... which may eventually enrich the main stream of our cultural and social tradition.[7]

What seems to be involved here is the notion that the cultural norms and aspirations of ethnic and religious minorities will be accepted as worthy of incorporation into the main stream community's ethos so as to enlarge and transform it — a kind of 'water and wine' immixture in which both cultures would transform and be transformed by the resulting changes in the overall emergent cultural identity, the integrity of which would nevertheless still be preserved by the ways in which differences would be accepted, tolerated and absorbed — what some have seen, to change the metaphor, as a 'cultural mosaic' version of multiculturalism in which the heterogeneity of the individual parts made up an identifiable cultural homogeneity.

For many people, however, this represents more of an ideal than a reality — rhetoric rather than an accurate portrayal of the continuing ideology of assimilation which it masks. What emerging ethnic cultural awareness and revitalization movements demand is a shift towards ethnic and cultural pluralism which accepts and actively promotes diversity so that both the white community can appreciate, understand and value the different conventions and cultural norms of other and smaller groups of fellow-citizens; and the members of racial and ethnic minority communities can perpetuate their own cultural identities and develop and enhance a positive self-image. This view was given official sanction in the 1977 Green Paper *Education in Schools: A Consultative Document*[8]:

> Our society is a multicultural and multiracial one and the curriculum should reflect a sympathetic understanding of the different cultures and races that now make up our society ... the curriculum of schools must reflect the needs of this new Britain ...

an emphasis which was reflected in the comment in the Swann Report[9] that

> multicultural education has usually tended to have two distinct themes — firstly, meeting the particular educational needs of ethnic minority children and secondly, the broader issue of preparing all pupils for life in a multi-racial society.

But the point of multicultural education was sharpened by a further recommendation of the Swann Committee: that the above two aims must be seen only in a context in which all those in the education service appreciate the importance of creating 'strategies to combat attitudes, behaviour and practices which discriminate against individuals and groups who are culturally, linguistically, religiously or racially different'. Alma Craft[10] points out the complex interrelationship between multicultural education defined as the celebration of diversity and the preservation of cultures and that version of it which sees its main thrust as being concerned to promote anti-racist policies and practices in all public institutions:

> On the one hand, the celebration of diversity is no more than patronising tokenism unless_ it is accompanied by a fundamental belief in the equality of individuals from every background: a multicultural approach must embrace an anti-racist one. On the other hand, anti-racist strategies alone are unlikely to be successful in attaining equality of outcome unless the educational system is permeated with a real and fundamental sensitivity to diversity and ensures a formal curriculum response.

This view is a necessary corrective to the emphasis that has been in some quarters recently to the need for multicultural education to be seen as a part of more widespread political and community initiatives to end discrimination in all its forms, an undertaking pointed up in the commitment of the ILEA to:

> the development of an education service from which racism, sexism and class discrimination and prejudice have been eliminated so that the Authority can respond fully to the needs of our multi-ethnic society.[11]

This note is also present in the characterization of multicultural education proffered by Philips-Bell, one of the recent writers on the philosophy of multicultural education, who sees 'education for a multicultural society' as involving not merely 'education through many cultures' or even 'education into many cultures' but is rather

> a wider conception than the previous two insofar as many more practical implications follow. It implies a determination to work towards bringing about social change both in schools and society by eliminating institutional racism and promoting equality and justice.[12]

All these recent moves seeking to promote social cohesiveness by way of the acceptance and valuing of diversity and to a positive self-image while at the same time eradicating racism and discrimination have not, of course, been without their critics. For some the search for such policies and strategies has not been radical enough; for others it has been much too liberal and seen as part of a whole movement towards the politicization of education seeking to convert schools from culturally 'open' agencies of education into 'closed' centres for indoctrination — the political view in question being that of the so-called 'hard left'.[13]

At the root of these controversies lie certain philosophical issues and problems, axiological, epistemological and metalinguistic: firstly, can there be some 'overarching' values or system of values for all cultures; secondly what account of knowledge must be presupposed in any version of multicultural education, and can there be some common policies regarding the content of a curriculum seeking to promote it; can there be some common language in which cultural differences can be intelligibly articulated, considered and concluded upon; how, if at all can we resolve the paradox of 'openness', that could lead us in one direction to the kind of libertarianism some detect in the 'Summerhill' approach to schooling or, in another, to that kind of authoritarianism some maintain is predominant in the dirigiste basis on which Muslim schools are both staffed and run? Is it even possible — never mind desirable — to build the bridges that the Swann version of an 'education for all' would require, when there exist so many walls already? And I do not mean to talk here of empirically realizable possibilities; if a commitment to current conceptions of multicultural education requires an atmosphere of toleration and openness, we must ask, not only do we in fact inhabit an 'Open Society', but rather in what sense, if any, such a society is possible. For, we may say, it is all very well making equality, justice and freedom dominant in the collection of virtues we associate with the principles, policies and practices that 'have collectively come to be known as multicultural education', but what if our elevation of these militates against other values and principles held equally dear — single-sex education, for instance, parental freedom and desire to educate the child in accordance with their own wishes, or even a determination to treat women and children in ways we may see as denying them the emancipation for which the forbears of their fellow citizens struggled so hard and so long[14]? Will it then be realistic to talk of a regard for diversity that still makes for an ethic of overall belonging? Maurice Craft points up this dilemma for educationalists well:

> (they) have to decide at what point the acculturation necessary for full participation in society becomes a repressive assimilation; and at what point the celebration of diversity ceases to enrich and becomes potentially divisive.[15]

With this we enter into some of the controversies of multicultural education — that concerning the question of values. As pointed up by Mal Philips-Bell and other authors, the chief emphasis is on the pursuit of a parity in education and equality in society, both being necessary if we are to see a community emerging from a plethora of cultural pluralisms in which a concern for social justice and individual freedom can be given expression in forms of communication and institution that all can respect and make their diverse contributions towards preserving, and in whose products all can indifferently respect every citizen's right to share. Such an emphasis might go far towards resolving some of the tensions betwen virtues of cohesiveness, stability and cooperation, on the one hand, and of diversity, separatism and a regard for recognizably different cultural and ethnic identities, on the other; for there would seem to be wide support for the view that the extremes of both sets of values — conformism and homogeneity on the one hand, divisiveness and community fragmentation on the other — are neither of them forms in which the rights and responsibilities of all parts of our multicultural community can hope to find best and surest expression and activation. That view seems to rest upon a preference for such further values as toleration, respect for other people and concern for their well-being in social surroundings in which a premium is placed on amity, peace and concord, in letting people follow their chosen path in working out patterns of life-options for themselves; and a corresponding disvaluing of disharmony, strife and conflict animates our regard for those forms of social relation in which those choices have best chance of being made. That is why one of the first things teachers in programmes devoted to these ends are encouraged to promote is the need for their students to have 'positive' attitudes to those who look, speak, or behave differently from themselves.

The difficult question for educators, however, is how far they should encourage their students to go in their pursuit of openness. We may agree that toleration should not be extended to the abuser of children or the pusher of heroin but, in these days, they might well want to ask us questions about its extension to the purveyor of pornography, to the keeping of disorderly houses, the smoking of ganja as a religious act or even to the speaking of patois to misinform, mislead or deceive those who are thought to be discriminating against one. They might find sacrificial killing of a sheep in the street or some minorities' treatment of women as unacceptable interpretations of the kind of openness and toleration multiculturalism might be thought to enjoin, to say nothing of the view they might take of the evidence of secrecy and concealment in the operating procedures of the government, the courts, the police and the business world that some recent events have suggested to be an overriding concern of such bodies or groups. Indeed at this point commitments to toleration and openness might part company: if disclosure of the actions of some city firms, police actions or ministers of the Crown had been more open than it was, we might have been inclined to tolerate them less readily. It is perhaps here where we may begin to see the beginnings of a hierarchy in the values of pluralism and multiculturalism: some would place a commitment to openness and truth-telling at the summit of their scale of values others may prefer the elevation of a necessary degree of tolerance in the promotion of the public interest and the inhibition of harm to the common weal, if necessary at the expense of openness and disclosure. Perhaps it is in defence of the latter principle that we may seek to explain the decisions to prosecute employees of government institutions who thought that they had a duty to the other one, to make available 'no platform for racists' by some student bodies, and to go through schools and their resource centres (as did some officers of some LEAs recently) rigorously removing any material having the adjective 'black' used in it or applied to it — all of which, it might be thought, could be seen as examples of a fundamentalist approach to matters of public policy and practice that ends up by engaging in activities that seem everything to the contrary of tolerant.

The justification for such activities can be found in Marcuse[16]. He contends that the commitment to tolerance and openness in debate in so-called democratic societies is vitiated by the actual conditions that so operate as to remove real openness and substitute oppression: for him

> The antagonistic structure of society rigs the rules of the game. Those who stand against the established system are *a priori* at a disadvantage, which is not removed by the toleration of their ideas, speeches and newspapers.

Active and official toleration of dissent is, for Marcuse, a specious cover for the continued pre-eminence of the establishment, which appears to be well-disposed towards the availability of alternative viewpoints but is in reality actually protecting and promoting 'the already established machinery of discrimination'. For this reason Marcuse advocates such measures as

> the withdrawal of toleration of speech and assembly from groups and movements which promote aggressive policies, armament, chauvinsim, discrimination ... or which oppose the extension of public services ... Moreover, the restoration

35

of freedom of thought may necessitate new and rigid restrictions on teachings and practices in educational institutions
which, by their very methods and concepts, serve to enclose
the mind within the established universe of discourse and
behaviour ...

This is the so-called 'paradox of freedom' with a vengeance: in order
to get our students to be truly autonomous and free-thinking we shall
have to submit them to a kind of counter-indoctrination. And this
paradox leads us in the case of multiculturalism to two further ones:
those between the intolerance characteristic of autocracy, and the
toleration of pluralism; between the need for secrecy and concealment
in matters affecting the common good (if there can be such a thing)
and the desire for disclosure and openness, that are held by some to be
amongst the most distinctive and prime virtues of that form of political arrangement that we call 'democracy' and that are bulwarks behind
our endeavours to promote pluralism and yet to secure a sense of
community belonging in it.

David Bridges considers the arguments of Marcuse seriously and
sees that, while much of the criticisms have force, they are nevertheless flawed by some difficulties and contradictions of their own. As
a rejoinder we may find his citing of the classic sources of the principle of liberty and openness in public matters useful and helpful.
Mill's essay *On Liberty* he calls 'a classic source' enshrining the crucial
importance of openness in anyone's search to acquire wisdom:

In the case of any person whose judgment is really deserving
of confidence, how has it become so?
Because he has kept his mind open to criticism of his
opinions and conduct. Because it has been his practice to listen
to all that could be said against him; to profit by as much of it
as was just, and expound to himself, and upon occasion to
others, the fallacy of what was fallacious. Because he felt that
the only way in which a human being can make some
approach to knowing the whole of a subject is by hearing what
can be said about it by persons of every variety of opinion, and
studying all modes in which it can be looked at by every
character of mind. No wise man ever acquired wisdom in any
mode but this; nor is it in the nature of human intellect to
become wise in any other.[17]

He also refers to Voltaire and Milton as bearers of the same tradition
and values. For Bridges, as for Milton, 'Truth' will provide us with

the means of refuting falsehood and subverting intolerance, in-doctrination and secrecy:

> Where there is much desire to learn there of necessity will be much arguing, much writing, many opinions; for opinion in good men is but knowledge in the making ... So Truth be in the field, we do injuriously, by licensing and prohibiting, to misdoubt her strength. Let her and falsehood grapple; who-ever knew Truth put to the worse, in a free and open encoun-ter? Her confuting is the best and surest suppressing.[18]

So in the case of multicultural education a diversity of views, opinions and life-styles is something that our commitment to openness and the liberty of the individual should welcome; for the concept of 'truth' will, so Bridges believes, give us a touchstone against which our attempts to reconcile our commitments to diversity yet cohension, harmony yet heterogeneity, equality and justice yet cultural freedom and plurality must be measured.

There are at least two problems with this position, however. We may reasonably enquire, following the line of Marcuse, how such attempts at reconciliation are to succeed, when, for one thing, some of our public institutions and policy-making procedures seem to cele-brate confrontation and denigrate consensus, down-grading equality and fairness in favour of some Platonic version of justice in society as 'knowing one's place and keeping it' — or even of some Thrasym-achean 'market-place' notion of the pre-eminence to be given to par-ticular interests and values; and when, for another, there is not even any consensus about the membership or range of the much sought-after overarching system of values to which it is supposed all elements of our multicultural society ought to subscribe — a problem both of normative and meta-ethics. For we may also reasonably enquire whether there can be such a thing in ethics as agreement about some set of 'basic' moral principles — or are differences on moral matters a function of radically different ethical preconceptions, as Phillips and Mounce[19] claim. Is culture and value merely a matter of context and convention, of — at best — form rather than specific content? Perhaps the differences between Milton, Mill and Marcuse are irresolvable, and not merely in virtue of the empirical conditions in which we are endeavouring to articulate our version of a just and equitable society for all its citizens. Perhaps the evident lack of agreement in the var-ious sectors of the education service as to what policies and practices might be thought to conduce to the achievement of justice, equality and tolerance for all is founded upon a solid point — that cultural pluralism is merely a reflection of the truth of an underlying cultural relativism. And with that, the second difficulty with Bridges' view comes to the fore: for if relativism in matters of knowledge and belief, as well as of ethics, holds, how can we make sense of his injunction to employ Truth as a criterion against which such policies and practices might properly be measured? In that case the cognitive realm becomes quite as much a set of walled-off and inward-looking ghettos as does the moral and the religious. At this point our enquiries move from the axiological to the epistemological to see whether such a criterion can in fact be found.

The 1977 *Green Paper* urged that the curriculum of schools 'should reflect a sympathetic understanding of the different cultures and races that now make up our society'. The chief aims of its version of multicultural education therefore are the moral and epistemic ones of sympathy and understanding. The task for curriculum theorists then becomes that of determining what kinds of knowledge will make for success in the promotion of these aims. If we are to follow the recommendations of the Swann Report we shall perhaps distinguish between the particular sets of knowledge and skill that will help us cater for the special needs of ethnic, racial and religious minorities *and* the larger repertoires of cognitive competence needed to promote understanding and sympathy in students' growth towards the acculturation necessary to enable all of them to respond to their social and civic responsibilities and opportunities. Among the first set of subjects we might place the provision of teaching of mother-tongue languages and a stress on bilingual competence; and attempt to develop and enhance self-image undertaken in, say, 'living and growing' courses, attention to special dietary requirements in health education or home economics courses; and a reference to religious practices in humanities or RE courses. The second aim might be thought best promoted in courses of general and social studies or personal education, as well as in such subjects as, say, geography, history, literature and the arts, languages, biology and European or world studies, which would afford teachers the opportunity of enabling students to make a *critique* of racism and ethnocentrism, to question the bases of Anglo-Saxon values attitudes and beliefs, and to highlight the unexamined bias and prejudices inherent in many of the cultural stereotypes and myths that many of us — even teachers — unconsciously hold.[20]

Teaching in these subjects will undoubtedly give students access to facts, information and knowledge; it may also introduce them to the kinds of skill that acquiring and evaluation this kind of information requires and get them started on the road towards mastery of the procedures that produce it. But we may ask whether this will be sufficient to guarantee that they will come to have the sympathy and understanding of which the *Green Paper* speaks; we can endeavour to dispel ignorance and to show the fallaciousness and incorrectness of racial myths and cultural stereotypes easily enough but may still doubt whether that will self-evidently bring about changes in underlying attitudes on the parts of all our students, much less give them the ability to see and be able to identify with the situations of ethnic minority children from the inside.

The epistemic problem is neatly encapsulated in, and presented by, the challenge of teaching RE — the one compulsory subject on the curriculum. We may think it important to give all our students exposure to the full range of facts about alien religious practices and experience but still wonder whether, and if so how, it is possible in some way to get students 'on the inside' of what it is to believe religiously, so that we can understand the core beliefs, sympathize with the values and have 'a positive attitude' to the norms and axioms of other faiths (even supposing for a moment they would be willing to want their children to do the same in reverse). Setting on one side for a moment the question of whether other faiths (such as, for instance, Islam) have an equal regard for and concern to promote openness and pluralism and think them desirable rather than decadent features of a tolerable form of society, we may ask whether understanding from the inside and empathy is in fact possible. Is there not, we might ponder, a paradox in the aim assigned to RE by Hudson[21] as being to introduce students not only to 'theology' but also to 'devotion'? How can we, in a state school at all events, seek to introduce them to the latter and then, having got them to know what it is to be devoted, expect them to be able to stand back, turn off, and go on to make an open-minded and fully informed choice between different faiths, lifestyles and cultures, now that they know what it is to be committed to just one? It is just here that the problem of objectivity and relativism raises its head, for the possibility postulated by some educationalists expecting their students to have knowledge, sympathy and understanding of other cultures rests on the tacit assumption that there are objective forms and norms of understanding that are cross-cultural or, at any rate, common to all cultures and that thus make that kind of sympathy and understanding conceivable and possible.[22] But what, we may ask, if the converse is the case and there are no over-arching forms and norms of knowledge, categories of understanding, concepts of truth or criteria of rationality itself; that knowledge and 'universes of discourse' are only intelligible from within the forms

of life that generated and articulate them; that, in short, no understanding 'from the outside', from a stance of neutrality and openmindedness, is possible; that even to discuss and appraise the values
and beliefs of the various elements that constitute our multifaith, multiethnic society requires one to have mastered the norms and forms of
rationality that are endemic to them and without commitment to
which the idea of having sympathy with or understanding of them is
not only impossible but incoherent?[23] What, in other words, if the
theses of Sapir and Whorf, Malinowski, Talcott Parsons, neo-
Wittgensteinians in language and Kuhnians in science, and the extreme ethnomethodologists is true? Then any idea of openness,
building bridges, and multicultural education as providing for all
students a way into the tolerance of diversity on a basis of informed
sympathy, much less a rejoicing at the beauty of the separation yet
conjunction of the various discrete parts of the complex creature that
is our multicultural society would be a gratuitous fiction, at best a liberal ideal or aspiration, at worst a cruel deception practised on ethnic
and cultural minorities to disguise the reality of the deep, and irre-
concilable divisions that continue to determine the structure and social
relationships of its discrete elements that would remain always part-
itioned.

As I have argued elsewhere,[24] there are good reasons for the rejection of this standpoint as unintelligible itself. Such a rejection does
not, however, necessitate our adopting the contrary position and accepting the theses of those like Chomsky who hold that all human-
beings have one and the same device for acquiring language, that all
languages are, at the deep structure level, irreducibly the same, that
particular linguistic differences are supervenient upon building-blocks
of language potentiality that function so as to make intercultural translation, and thus understanding, possible in principle. We have no need
to support the hard-line universalism of such a position when there
are ready at hand positions that go beyond this kind of objectivism and
relativism to make such an understanding a viable educational enterprise. We might make use of Quine's epistemic holism[25] to point out
that, even though there may be an indeterminacy of translatability at
the radical level between different cultures and that, following
Duhem,[26] the theories such cultures employ are under-determined by
the empirical data, there are, nevertheless, still ways and means of beginning the attempt to make sense of another person's interpretation
of those data, even if these operate at the most rudimentary level of
negative or affirmative behavioural stimulus and response and on or in
respect of such transcultural biological universals as coming-to-be and

passing-away, needing sleep and feeling hunger, attraction and re-pulsion, and even if the consequent construction and reconstruction of our own theories of reality may take an immense amount of time and energy. On this basis, we may conclude, multicultural understanding, even if of a limited kind only, is a possibility, though it is not going to occur overnight. It is the fact of the presence in all humans of the potentiality for language-and-theory that gives us the entering wedge into any sort of minimal cross-cultural communication and under-standing.[27] For the possibility of knowledge will emanate from the impossibility of our framing negative answers to questions con-cerning the possibility of language itself.

Where does this leave us? If, as I now maintain, the enterprise of multicultural education is epistemically possible, can we produce an argument to show that it is desirable? I beiieve that such an argument can be made, on various grounds: community harmony and recon-ciliation, the promotion of health, peace and justice for all members of a community, the encouragement of individual interest and talent to emerge and prosper so as to enhance the overall fabric of society, the minimization of strife and conflict, the elimination of injury and other factors that diminish self-image and a sense of human dignity and personal worth — all the things that conduce to an ethic of be-longing, both within minority groups and to the majority community that fosters and defends such ideals yet still ensures and tolerates indi-vidual and group diversity. Ideals of personal autonomy are clearly paramount here, though that might on occasion have to be tempered to the demands of justice as fairness, for few would be ready to see the extension of complete autonomy outside the confines of other constituents' interests to such iconoclastic groups as the National Front, Black Muslims, the IRA or the Red Bridgades.

This predilection for diversity in cohesion, pluralism in social coalescence that I have adumbrated here as ideals for a mulitcultural community can, I believe, serve to provide us with an overarching ethic of belonging and for overcoming or, best of all, dissolving some of the apparent paradoxes in the idea of multicultural education to which I have referred above. This is, of course, provided that we are indeed persuaded of the logical possibility and the moral desirability of such an idea in the first place. But there may still be some who might think that all these considerations amount to no more than special pleading, at best — at worst to a misconception, not merely about the concept of education but concerning the status of the meta-theory on which such a conception rests.

I have already intimated that there is controversy concerning the status of the metatheoretical underpinnings of the view that there can be any overarching norms for educational undertakings, or — come to that — any one definitive concept of education of which multi-cultural education is a particular conception or to which it may be an addition or a competitor. Such a view would itself be a function of a meta-philosophical position that some have called 'essentialism', others have seen as a desire to hypostatize mere working definitions or stipulations into some kind of ontologically distinct entity. The re-buttals of such a view, from directions as diverse as Wittgenstein and Popper,[28] have been to the effect that no such preconceptions can be plausibly entertained and that, as Rawls might put it,[29] education is only one of many 'concepts' of which we can find virtually as many conceptions as there are people to employ them. For these people, then, it would be a mistake to look for a set of necessary and sufficient conditions to define multicultural education so loose as its set of characteristic features. All education is particular, special and distinctly — related to the groups whose interests their or even anything involve-ment in it is meant to serve by those planning it for, and then offering it to, them. In this sense all education is plural and infinitely variable, such that there might well be little, if any, necessary connection between the policies and practices developed for the edification of schools in the East End of London with very large Asian popula-tions and those that might be judged appropriate for school popula-tions in, say, rural Devon or mining villages in South Yorkshire — though there may, of course, be some contingent connections due to accidents of examination requirements or economic circumstance. This consideration might cause us then to regard with some dubiety moves towards the centralization of the planning function for edu-cation or the imposition of a DES-inspired common curriculum; for, on this model, there can be no such centrality or commonality: each school's needs will determine its own preferred version of the know-ledge and skills that it regards as necessary to enable its students to structure and direct their growing consciousness, so as to enlarge their horizons and prepare them for the various types and levels of en-vironment in which they might have in future to operate.[30]

This view in turn is not without its detractors. Some hold that a world in which instant communications and the possibility of our all being affected adversely by such large-scale disasters as that which nearly took place at Chernobyl has made us all inhabitants of what is virtually a global village and in which there is for that reason a pre-mium on the development of common curricula to give us the knowledge and skills we all require to enable us to cope with the exigencies of living in such a close-knit and interdependent network of contiguity. Others have maintained that an overriding importance must attach to the idea of knowledge that transcends all adventitious considerations such as those arising from particular economic circumstancs, political ideologies or sectional interests and gives us the cognitive equipment that is the *propria* of every rational being and enables us all to achieve the autonomy required for the adjudication and comprehension of the competing claims of all such lower-level demands on our time and energy.[31] For both parties arguing along these and/or other lines the notion of an entirely pluralist approach to matters of curriculum planning based on a rejection of the logical requirements of some definitive concept of education, objectivist theory of knowledge or centrally-dictated political economy, would be anathema.

Faced with such a division of opinion those charged with the construction of curricula for multicultural education might be tempted to take the easiest way out and simply let things be, grafting a supposed 'multicultural' element on to existing curricula, much as was done with the raising of the school leaving age problem in the 1960s, or simply accept unquestioningly advice handed out to them from their nearest 'official' quarter. Worst of all would be to do the curriculum equivalent of tossing a coin and allow curriculum decisions in this case to be made on the basis of subjective preference, historical accident or chance. Yet any approach involving an unquestioning acceptance of heteronomously-dictated prescriptions or any kind of uncritical 'plumping' would be an abdication of teachers' educational responsibilities, a negation of their accountability, perhaps the highest principle incumbent on those engaged in the carrying out of public duties. Is there a way in which they can find a non-arbitrary and impersonal rule that can function as a benchmark against which all such curriculum models and theories can be measured?

I believe that there are at least two; there may be more. One way of cutting through the Gordian knot of the choice of curricula for multicultural education would be to employ the critical openness advocated by Karl Popper as a criterion of demarcation between the realms of science and of myth and metaphysics.[32] His suggested approach of treating every theory, no matter where its provenance, as a hypothesis for potential refutation can offer us a touchstone for the appraisal of any and every cultural artifact put forward in the public domain — the world of 'objective knowledge', to use his phrase — to which we are all privy and by the cultural products of which we all stand to benefit and be enriched. David Bridges lays stress on the virtues of this kind of openness and cites Charles Bailey as one who shows its educational generalizability:[23]

> That all is subject to argument, that no person counts for more than his argument counts, even the teacher, and that all statements are subject to rational criticism — all this is part of the rational commitment and is picked out in the conception of impartiality ... To be impartial is to consider views and interests in the light of all possible criticisms and counter-claim, and to ignore any kind of special pleading, whether from authority or whatever, from myself or whomsoever.

From this kind of approach Bridges extracts three principles that he sees as features of an education in the liberal-democratic tradition:

> the importance of the ready availability of the full range of opinion on an issue (a free market in ideas); an acknowledgement of the fallibility of opinion including our own: a confidence in the free competition of ideas as a condition for the emergence of a true or ... (at any rate) the best opinion available.

And it might be thought that there could be few places in education where these principles could find better expression or implementation than in that aspect of it that we call multicultural.[34]

Such ideas lie at the root of the argument presented by Bruce Ackermann for the kind of liberal education he describes as necessary to secure engagement of all citizens in the public processes of any liberal state.[35] For him complete openness of discourse, with all its moral purposes and presuppositions, is a condition of ensuring the security of the bridges we seek to build between individuals and groups to promote and maintain that toleration of diversity in opinion, and the equal worth of diverse opinions, that we see as one of the principal *desiderata* of social justice in a democratic state.

This is, of course, an ideal and perhaps an idealization of how we see our own situation; for it is a further question as to whether we in this country actually inhabit such a state. Marcuse, already referred to, would, one suspects, very much doubt it; so too do representatives of the multiethnic communities themselves. O'Keeffe cites four sources[36] in which current UK ideas of multicultural education are called into question, the author of one of them, Farrukh Dondy being especially scathing when he refers to it as

a massive public relations exercise ... that the Schools Council, the Humanities Curriculum Project and other white-haired
respectables have disseminated as an answer to the contradictions that black youth point up in the schools

— a contradiction many of their parents and others would also see in
UK society generally. For this reason, some have urged, the existing
order of that society has to be subverted and replaced with other
structures in which the balance of the social, political and economic
power relations, which are inimical to real multicultural
understanding, equality and justice, has to be redressed.

If we are inclined to assent to this view of the need for change in
the structure and composition of our social and political institutions; if
we believe that the form of society in which we currently live is as
deeply undemocratic as Hailsham's account of it as 'elective
dictatorship' suggested; if we wish to move away from the dominance
of assimilationist ideologies towards an acceptance of diversity and
pluralism, then it may seem as if there are only two ways in which we
could effect such changes — radical revolution, or gradualism — what
some people would call piecemeal social change.

Revolution seems to me to be no kind of answer; past experiences
of such alterations of the *status quo* have not been invariably felicitous.
My Popperian proclivities make me want to opt for the latter — an
approach that also derives its strength from the power of the ethic
underlying and embodied in any attempt at interpersonal communication — an ethic that sees interlocutors in any occasion of
conversation bound by the same rules of equality, mutual regard, a
minimal (at least) willingness to listen to and tolerate the other point
of view, as well as the implicit agreement to eschew the discussion
and settlement of issues and difficulties by any other than rational
means that Bailey highlights as being the guarantee of the impartiality
between opinions that it thus allows to be tolerated in such
discussions, though not necessarily to win in them. And in those
conversations we hold with our fellow-citizens what is important is
not so much our background, colour, class or creed, but our joint
treatment of a problem to which we can all agree it to be crucial for a
solution to be found, whether this be a search for policies to end the
dysfunctionalities of racism or other forms of discrimination or for a
cure of AIDS. In our community attack on such problems all elements
are involved — and that means that we have, as a minimum, to talk to
each other.

Some may very well aver that those conversations cannot be in any absolute sense 'open': none of our talks can be free from subjectivity or slanting on account of the preconceptions in which the contributions of parties to them are inevitably framed. This in turn will make for the bias that Habermas's criticism of repressive tolerance[37] implies in the dialogue between defenders and objectors to any *status quo*. Yet this very possibility is conceded and then proposed as a solid basis for progress in the effort to achieve an informed understanding of the values, beliefs and attitudes of all other persons and groups by Hans-Georg Gadamer.[38] The hermeneutic perspective in and from which he claims we all have to work accepts the critical importance — though not the pejorative overtones — of the idea of 'prejudice' that we both bring to and face in our efforts to comprehend and participate in the various 'traditions' of which different cultural standpoints are constituted. This means self-consciously opening up and accepting one's own prejudices and then seeking to highlight, refine and enlarge them by engaging with them in the processes of a critical reading of the 'texts' of various human communications, part of which also involves us in endeavouring to make sense of the contexts within which they are articulated and must be understood.

In our attempt to elucidate both our own and other's prejudices in this way — and even the attempt to understand is obviously, as well as an attempt to deal with one's own puzzlements, part of a moral enterprise — we can only start from where we are and seek gradually to expand, criticize, analyze, and refine the existing sets of observations, judgments and perceptions that structure and define our endeavours to render intelligible and thus tractable the problems and predicaments that constantly beset us in our struggle to come to grips with and control the world we share with other people, maybe from other traditions and with other sets of prejudices, but equally struggling with similar predicaments. In these struggles to achieve mastery and find solutions individual effort, though important, will either fail or be slower to succeed than cooperative enterprise and the bringing to bear of wide-ranging sources of wisdom. Thus sharing will be all-important, and readiness to admit to the critical part played by tradition and the need for openness in the effort to understand the contributions that can be made by other traditions to shared problems paramount. For if we do not try to practise and display it, we are likely to remain forever locked within an inward-looking solipsistic world, looking, like the prisoners in Plato's Cave, at what can only be dimly-lit shadows of the real world outside ourselves, in all its richness, complexity and diversity.

In the last analysis multicultural education might be seen as an instance of what John Passmore apotheosized as the aim of education for a community of creatures uniquely social and solitary, solitary yet social — the realization of the importance of learning to participate in what he calls 'the great human traditions of critico-creative thought'.[39] That participation will give us the means of appreciating heterogeneity and diversity from the inside and so enable us to enter into the conversation of mankind. That is why a predilection for communication, conversation and discourse, combined and focused on problems of theory and practice in an approach of critical openness, helps us build a platform of diversity, on which we can nevertheless all stand as equals in an ethic of community belonging.

This resolution of the paradox of the 'One and the Many' is hardly new. Heraclitus, though concerned to find some underlying unity to integrate the multiplicity of phenomena in the natural world, could still see a resolution of an apparent paradox when he wrote:[40]

> Things taken together are whole and not whole, something which is being brought together and brought apart, which is in tune and out of tune; out of all things there comes a unity and out of a unity all things. (Fragment 10)

In his attempt to reconcile the apparent plurality of physical phenomena with the unity of nature Heraclitus was not, of course, alone, as reports of the thoughts of other presocratic philosophers by both Plato and Aristotle make clear.[41] Xenophanes, Parmenides and Melissus are cited as among those who have postulated some underlying unity to provide such a common ground for all things. What was different about Heraclitus, however, was his fixing upon *Logos* as the formula of the arrangement of orderliness in things that enables us to discern their fundamental unity and coherence: ουκ εμου αλλα του λόγου ακούσαντας ομολογειν σοφόν εστιν εν πάντα ειναc. ('Listening not to me but to the Logos it is wise to agree that all things are one' (Fragment 50))

Logos is, as generations of would-be translators of Greek from presocratic times to those of the Gospel of St. John will testify, one of the most difficult and arcane concepts to construe, yet there can be little doubt that it has to do with the idea of 'Word, speech, discourse, conversation' (as well as 'study, science, account' and so on). In this context it is not without interest for our present purposes to point to the elevation of such an idea as the ground of coherence in the relationships of all things. At one point Heraclitus expresses this principle as God.[42] Of Fragment 67 Kirk remarks:[43]

47

God cannot here be essentially different from Logos; and the Logos is the constituent of things which makes them opposed; and which ensures that change between opposites will be proportional and balanced overall ... Thus the total plurality of things forms a single coherent, determinable complex — what Heraclitus called 'unity'.

It is noteworthy that that unity consists finally in what can be *said* — a metaphor and a motto, perhaps, for multiculturalism and for the enterprise of multicultural education. For all there is, finally, is people talking to each other; insofar as we fail to help young people and children learn to be able to engage in conversation with the widest range of people, we fail to prepare them for the complexities of the world and the problems of all its denizens.

Notes

1 See PETERS, R. S. (1965) 'Education as initiation' in ARCHAMBAULT R. D. (Ed) *Philosophical Analysis and Education*, London, Routledge and Kegan Paul, pp. 88–9.
2 See LYNCH, J. (1986) *Multicultural Education, Principles and Practice*, London, Routledge and Kegan Paul, p. 5ff citing GORDON, M. (1964) *Assimilation in American Life*, New York, Oxford University Press. See also BANKS, J. A. (1986) 'Multicultural education: Development, paradigms and goals' in BANKS, J. A. and LYNCH, J. (Eds). *Multicultural Education in Western Societies*, Eastbourne, Holt, Rinehart and Winston, chapter 1, pp. 2–3, and 21.
3 HOME OFFICE (1964) *Second Report of the Commonwealth Immigrants Advisory Council*, London HMSO, para 10.
4 O'KEEFFE, B. (1986) *Faith, Culture and the Dual System*, Lewes, Falmer Press.
5 Of articles on policies and practices in the United States, Canada, Australia and Western Europe by J. A. Banks, K. A. Moodley, B. M. Bullivant and J. Lynch respectively see BANKS, J. A. and LYNCH, J. (1986) (Eds) *op cit*.
6 In a speech on 23 May 1966 at a meeting in London, cited by O'KEEFFE, B. (1986) *op cit*. p 128; and CRAFT, M. (1986) 'Multicultural education in the United Kingdom' in BANKS, J. A. and LYNCH, J. (Eds) *ibid*, p. 80.
7 DEPARTMENT OF EDUCATION AND SCIENCE (1971) *The Education of Immigrants*, London, HMSO, p. 120 cited in CRAFT, M. (1986) *ibid*.
8 DEPARTMENT OF EDUCATION AND SCIENCE (1977) *Education in Schools: A Consultative Document*, Cmnd 6869, London, HMSO.
9 DEPARTMENT OF EDUCATION AND SCIENCE (1985) *Education for All* (The Swann Report), London, HMSO.
10 CRAFT, A. (1986) 'Multicultural teaching' in WELLINGTON, J. J. (Ed)

Controversial Issues in the Curriculum, Oxford, Basil Blackwell, chapter 5, pp. 75–6.

11 ILEA (1983) *Race, Sex and Class: 2: Multiethnic Education in Schools*, London, ILEA, p. 23.

12 PHILIPS-BELL, M. (1981) 'Multicultural education: What is it?', *Multicultural Education*, Journal of the National Association for Multicultural Education (NAME), 10, 1, autumn, p. 21. Cf also PHILIPS-BELL, M. (1981) 'Multicultural education: A critique of Walkling and Zec', *Journal of Philosophy of Education*, 15, 1, pp. 97–105; WALKING, P. H. (1980) 'The idea of a multicultural curriculum', *Journal of Philosophy of Education*, 14, 1, pp. 87–95; and ZEC, P. (1980) 'Multicultural education: What kind of relativism is possible', *Journal of Philosophy of Education*, 14, 1, pp. 77–86 reprinted in JAMES, A. and JEFFCOATE, R. (Eds) (1981) *The School in the Multicultural Scoiety*, London, Harper and Row, pp. 29–44.

13 Cf CRAFT, A. (1986) *loc cit*, p. 77 and notes 6 and 7. See also JAMES, A. AND JEFFCOATE, R. (Eds) (1981) *ibid*, section 1 'Critical perspectives', articles by Jeffcoate, James, Stone and Hall. See also GUNDARA, J. JONES, C. AND KIMBERLEY, K. (1986) *Racism, Diversity and Education*, London, Hodder and Stoughton, chapters 1 and 2.

14 See HARRIS, J. (1982) 'A paradox of multicultural societies', *Journal of Philosophy of Education*, 16, 2, pp. 223–33.

15 CRAFT, M. (1984) *Education and Cultural Pluralism*, Lewes, Falmer Press.

16 MARCUSE, H. (1976) 'Repressive tolereance' in CONNERTON, P. (Ed) *Critical Sociology*, Harmondsworth, Penguin cited in BRIDGES *q.v. inf.*, p. 34 ff.

17 MILL, J. S. (1971) 'On liberty' in *Three Essays by John Stuart Mill*, London, Oxford University Press.

18 MILTON, J. (1985) 'Areopagitica' in *Prose Writings*, London, Dent. Both these last two are cited in BRIDGES, D. (1986) 'Dealing with controversy in the curriculum: A philosophical perspective' in WELLINGTON, J. J. (Ed) *op cit*, chapter 2, pp. 19–38.

19 PHILLIPS, D. Z. and MOUNCE, H. O. (1970) *Moral Practices*, London, Routledge and Kegan Paul.

20 See JONES, M. (1987) 'Prejudice' in HAYDON, G. *et al* (Eds) *Education for a Pluralist Society: Philosophical Perspectives on the Swann Report*, London, Institute of Education, Bedford Way Papers no 30.

21 HUDSON, W. D. (1973) 'Is religious education possible?' in LANGFORD, G. and O'CONNOR, D. J. (Eds) *New Essays in Philosophy of Education*, London, Routledge and Kegan Paul.

22 TRIGG, R. (1973) *Reason and Commitment*, Cambridge, Cambridge University Press. So also WATT A. J. (1974) 'Forms and knowledge and norms of rationality', *Educational Philosophy and Theory*, 6, 1, March, pp. 1–11.

23 See WINCH, P. (1972) 'Understanding a primitive society' in WINCH, P. (Ed) *Ethics and Action*, London, Routledge and Kegan Paul.

24 Cf ASPIN, D. N. (1983) 'Church schools, religious education and the multiethnic community', *Journal of Philosophy of Education*, 17., 2,

pp. 229–40. See also a special number of *The Monist*, 67, 3, July 1984, articles by McCULLAGH, B. 'The intelligibility of cognitive relativism', pp. 327–40, BRANDT, R. B. 'Relativism refuted', pp. 297–307, DEVINE, P. E. 'Relativism', pp. 405–418, QUINE, W. V. O. 'Relativism and absolutism', pp. 293–5, and VALLICELLA, W. F. 'Relativism, truth and the symmetry thesis', pp. 452–8.

25   For this theory see QUINE, W. V. O. (1961) 'Two dogmas of empiricism', *Philosophical Review*, 60, pp. 20–43, reprinted in his *From a Logical Point of View*, Cambridge, MA, Harvard University Press. Also, for a summary of Quine's view on these matters see his 'The nature of natural knowledge' in GUTTENPLAN, S. (Ed) (1975) *Mind and Language*, London, Oxford University Press, pp. 67–81. See also QUINE, W. V. O. and ULLIAN, J. S. (1978) *The Web of Belief*, New York, Random House. For the educational import of all this see EVERS, C. W. 'Epistemology and justification: From classical foundationalism to Quinean coherentism and materialist pragmatism' in WALKER, J. C. and EVERS, C. W. (Eds) *Epistemology, Semantics and Educational Theory*, Sydney, University of Sydney Department of Education, Occasional papers no 16, pp. 1–29.

26   DUHEM, P. (1906) *The Aim and Structure of Physical Theory* (translated by WEINER, P. P. 1954), Princeton, NJ, Princeton University Press, 2nd edn (1914), p. 11, reprinted in HARDING, S. G. (1976) *Can Theories Be Refuted?*, Dordrecht, Reidel.

27   I owe this phrase to Colin Evers; see EVERS, C. W. (1983) 'Logical structure and justification in educational theory', unpublished PhD thesis, University of Sydney.

28   See WITTGENSTEIN, L. (1953) *Philosophical Investigations* (translated by ANSCOMBE, G. E. N.), Oxford, Basil Blackwell, paras 19–23; also POPPER, K. R. (1972) *Objective Knowledge*, London, Oxford University Press, pp. 123–4, and 194–7.

29   RAWLS, J. (1973) *A Theory of Justice*, Cambridge, MA, Harvard University Press.

30   See the argument for that put forward by HARRIS, K. (1979) *Education and Knowledge*, London, Routledge and Kegan Paul.

31   For a clear persentation and discussion of these points of view see CRITTENDEN, B. (1982) *Cultural Pluralism and the Common Curriculum*, Melbourne, Melbourne University Press, chapters 1 and 5. Also see SMOLICZ, J. J. (1979) *Culture and Education in a Plural Society*, Canberra, The Curriculum Development Centre, chapter 10.

32   POPPER, K. R. (1959) *The Logic of Scientific Discovery*, London, Hutchinson. For a criticism of this view see O'HEAR, A. (1980) *Karl Popper*, London, Routledge and Kegan Paul, chapter 6.

33   BAILEY, C. H. (1975) 'Neutrality and rationality in teaching' in BRIDGES, D. and SCRIMSHAW, P. (Eds) *Values and Authority in Schools*, London, Hodder and Stoughton.

34   BRIDGES, D. (1986) in WELLINGTON, J. J. *op cit*, p 34. See also WALKLING, P. H. (1980) *loc cit* (*vid* n 12 *sup*).

35   ACKERMANN, B. (1980) *Social Principles and the Liberal State*, New Haven, Yale University Press, especially chapter 7 on 'liberal education'.

36 See O'KEEFFE, B. (1986) *op cit*, p 149, note 9; DHONDY, F. (1982) *The Black Explosion in Schools*, London, Race Today Publications; Mullard, C. (1981) *Racism in Society and Schools: History, Policy and Practice*, London, University of London Institute of Education, Centre for Multicultural Education; and STONE, M. (1981) *The Education of the Black Child in Britain*, London, Fontana. See also HALL, S. (1980) 'Teaching race', *Multiracial Education*, 9, 1, pp. 3–12, reprinted in JAMES, A. and JEFFCOATE, R. (Eds) (1981) *op cit*, pp. 58–69. One of the most sophisticated analyses of this area is to be found in BULLIVANT, B. M. (1981) *Race, Ethnicity and Curriculum*, Melbourne, Macmillan. See also his *Pluralism: Cultural Maintenance and Evolution* (1984) Clevedon, Multilingual Matters.

37 HABERMAS, J. (1973) *Legitimation Crisis*, Boston, MA, Beacon Press, also published in 1976 by Heinemann, London; and HABERMAS, J. (1979) *Communication and the Evolution of a Society*, London, Heinemann. A debt to Habermas is acknowledged by LYNCH, J. (1986) *op cit*, pp. 11ff.

38 GADAMER, H-G (1975) *Truth and Method* (translated by Glen-Doepel, W.), London, Sheed and Ward, part II, part 2, chapter 1, pp. 235–74.

39 PASSMORE, J. (1967) 'On teaching to be critical' in PETERS, R. S. (Ed) *The Concept of Education*, London, Routledge and Kegan Paul, p. 200.

40 Heraclitus in Diels-Kranz (1958) *Fragmente der Vorsokratiker* (DK), Berlin, 31, B10. This translation is by G. S. Kirk in KIRK G. S. and RAVEN, J. E. (1957) *The Presocratic Philosophers*, Cambridge, Cambridge University Press, p. 191.

41 See Plato SOPHIST 242 D (DK 21 A 29) and Aristotle *Metaphysics* A 5 986 b 18, both cited by KIRK, G. S. and RAVEN, J. E. (1957) *ibid*, p. 165.

42 DK 31 B 67: 'God is day night, winter summer, war peace, satiety hunger (all the opposite, this is the meaning); he undergoes alteration in the way that fire, when it is mixed with species, is named according to the scent of each of them' (translation by Kirk).

43 KIRK, G. S. and RAVEN, J. E. (1957) *op cit*, p. 192. A similar strain may be observed in the Epistles of St Paul: *Romans*, chapter 12, verses 4–6 and 10; I *Corinthians*, chapter 12, verses 12–14 and 20–26; and *Ephesians*, chapter 4, verses 1–12.

3   Believing in Multicultural Education

Maurce Hobbs

If truth were told, not many people in Britain really believe in multicultural education!

Some do, of course, and are truly enthusiastic about 'the richness of cultural diversity' and its contribution to national life. Many more, I suspect, are bewildered by the variety of definitions of what multicultural education might be. Others would question the necessity for change to accommodate, as they see it, a few 'immigrants'. Some more conservative Christians are opposed to what they regard as official sponsorship of heathen religions and withdraw their children to private 'Christian' schools. Black parents may be critical, not only of traditional schools and curriculum, but also of the time and effort expended on new items which, however interesting, have not produced marketable qualifications in terms of examination results. They believe multicultural education to be diversionary and palliative when the real need is for justice and enabling to compete in a society in which the odds are stacked against their children.[2]

Over the years, attitudes, even among teachers, have not changed much. In 1973, 561 schools in Britain were invited to reply to three questions:

1   Do you consider that your syllabuses should have as one of their aims the preparation of pupils for life in a multiracial society?
2   Do the syllabuses at present ... include any items intended to prepare pupils for the multiracial aspect of society?
3   Do you foresee any changes in your syllabuses in order to make them more applicable to pupils in (such) a society?

The answers are summarised in Schools Council Working Paper No. 50, *Multiracial Education — Need and Innovation*, and show that while many teachers believed that they should prepare pupils for life in a multiracial society, fewer had included in their syllabuses any items specifically designed to carry out such an intention. Fewer still were able to claim that they proposed to do anything more about it.[2]

In 1986, Bernardette O'Keeffe has reported on a survery of '103 schools involving sixteen local education authorities and nine dioceses' of the Church of England as far apart as Canterbury and Blackburn. Her research instrument was sharper, her questions more detailed, but the answers detailed in chapters 6 and 7 of *Faith, Culture and the Dual System* are virtually the same as those recorded thirteen years earlier by Townsend and Brittan.

For example, almost word for word the same are:

1973:   'We have so few immigrants (who) present no insurmountable problems ... I cannot see a necessity for any particular structured 'preparation for a multiracial society'. (Head of a primary school)

1986:   We haven't really got any (problems) because we have so few children from ethnic minority groups. Not having many of them, it (multicultural education) is not really so relevant. (Head of primary school)

1973:   I do not consider it the responsibility of an English state school to cater for the development of cultures and customs of a foreign nature. I believe it is our duty to prepare children for citizenship in a free Christian democratic society, according to British standards and customs. (Head of primary school)

1986:   We don't have any of this multicultural nonsense because we are a Christian culture.

And so we could go on!

Bernardette O'Keeffe summarizes her conclusions as follows:

It is quite clear that both church and county schools are at variance with the the ideal of multicultural education set out in the Swann Report (which) advocates that a broadly multi-cultural approach to curriculum should be implemented in all schools regardless of the pupils' backgrounds ... it has failed to impinge on practice for the majority of schools in our study.[3]

There is little room for doubt that this is true for the majority of schools nationwide.

Yet during the thirteen intervening years a number of things have happened that might have been expected to bring about changes in attitude and practice, and so, in the outcomes of education for the successive generations of 'infants' who have turned into adults with votes at 18 years of age in the same period.

First and most vivid, though local and short-lived, is the series of disturbances on the streets of Southall (1976 and 1979) Bristol (1980), Brixton, Southall and Toxteth (1981) and Tottenham and Handsworth (1985). The police call them 'riots', black people call them 'rebellions'.[4]

Though schools in rural areas and towns with few 'immigrants' may understandably, though wrongly, have taken little notice of these events, they have in fact had an important impact. Lord Scarman, reporting on *The Brixton Disorders, 10–12 April 1981*,[5] identified education as one of 'three areas of disadvantage which emerge ... as particularly important', and his assessment of the situation quite obviously weighed heavily with the Committee of Inquiry into the Education of Children from Ethnic Minority Groups (1985) in preparing their final report, *Education for All* (The Swann Report)[6]. This large and wide-ranging document called upon 'all LEAs (to) expect their schools to produce clear policy statements on "Education for All" and (to) monitor their practical implementation'. Unless this was done, says the Report, 'there is real risk of the fragmentation of our society along ethnic lines, which would seriously threaten the stability and cohesion of society as a whole'.

Unfortunately, there is reason to doubt whether many LEAs or schools have moved with urgency to comply with the recommendation; and whether the existence of a 'policy statement' which is not owned or believed in by teachers or administrators will issue any better institutional response to the dangers highlighted by the Swann committee, or in changed professional practice on the part of many teachers, however detailed the machinery for monitoring. Furthermore, central government response to the Report has been muted, in spite of the appeal for a positive statement of support, 'as a matter of urgency' (p. 363). No wonder that 'multiculturalism' has not been high on the agenda of many schools, particularly as they have faced falling rolls, reorganization and reduced resources, as well as industrial action about pay and conditions.

On the other hand, that Department of State which is responsible for law and order, for nationality and immigration, the Home Office, rather than the Department of Education and Science, has made available considerable funds to LEAs in certain areas, 'in consequence of the presence within their areas of substantial numbers of immigrants from the New Commonwealth'. These funds have supported the appointment of large numbers of specialist teachers and advisers to address the educational needs of 'all immigrants ... whether born in this country or elsewhere, aged 20 or less', particularly 'those whose language and customs differ from the rest of the community'. This targeting of resources has been patchy, has focused upon 'language', upon culture maintenance and 'pluralism'. Since Afro-Caribbean people have been deemed to be Christian, speaking English, albeit with a difference, and more anglicized than Indians or Pakistanis, they have profited less from 'section 11'.[7]

As a result of their separate funding and their particular brief, the section 11 teachers, operating largely outside the mainstream educational provision, have been the foremost pioneers and advocates of sometimes quite local versions of 'multicultural education'. Something approaching a common mind has, however, been developing through their conferences and journals.[8] Yet their perceptions and prescriptions have not penetrated the schools in the 'white highlands' nor very far into the suburban schools with a majority white pupil body, who do not feel the pressure of black parents or councillors, nor engage in immediate relationships with black pupils. Even in the 'inner-city' schools to which they may be attached to help develop 'appropriate curricula', individual 'section 11' missionaries have not always been able to secure agreement or cooperation from the regular staff — at worst, their presence has produced acrimony and counter-charges of racism.

However, it has to be recognized that without this Home Office concern, and without the skill and devotion of the 'section 11' teachers, in developing and disseminating good practice, and their persistence in raising awareness, the situation might have been very much worse.

Another large and influential group of opinion-formers over the period has been the academic researchers; psychologists interested in comparative studies of 'educability' and 'learning difficulties; sociologists examining the impact of 'institutional racism' and the differential outcomes of education for various ethnic groups; ethnomethodologists making detailed examination of what goes on in classrooms. Their number and the variety of their interests reflects the salience of 'race' and related issues in British life and politics, and the function of compulsory schooling as an instrument of social control in a plural society.[9] Without in any way calling into question their integrity as individual investigators, it seems unlikely that so much detailed work could have been supported unless politicians and administrators were convinced that the presence of black children in school and society constitutes a 'problem', not merely complex but also dangerous.

In view of the number and variety of theoreticians and practitioners, the majority of them white, it is understandable, though unfortunate, that the language in which these issues is discussed is so frequently fuzzy and imprecise. Words like 'race' and 'culture' are often used interchangeably, so that the genetic determinism of the first moves imperceptibly over to the other, while the newer and more academic word 'ethnicity' does little to clarify matters for the lay-man. When 'multicultural' and 'multiracial' are applied to education, they often seem to imply a new academic discipline, a new and specific kind of curriculum, composed of 'add-on' items to treat a large number of different people-groups more or less equally — which many teachers rightly protest is impossibly demanding, even if desirable.

The cluster of words 'plural', 'pluralism' and 'pluralistic' are often used carelessly. It may well be that Britain is culturally 'plural', rather than homogeneous, in spite of compulsory schooling. However, in the absence of a consciously developed doctrine to explain, justify and advocate the virtues of 'plurality' within a common polity, it cannot properly be described as a 'pluralist' society; certainly not a 'pluralistic' one, since that would imply that the doctrine had been accepted and embodied, not only in law, but also in the popular will.[10] The utterances, not only of the National Front but of MPs, like Enoch Powell and Harvey Proctor, as well as the writings of Roger Scruton and Ray Honeyford, fully demonstrate that this is not the case.[11]

They are no more happy with 'multicultural education' than with 'education for a multicultural society', a formula adopted in teacher training institutions as 'assimilation' was gradually seen to have failed, and 'integration' was espoused in its place.[12] This more purposeful formula, however, still focuses upon 'cultures' as 'givens' (in sociological terms, 'ascribed') rather than 'emergent', as people of all ethnicities engage with each other in communal life in the cities and in competition for jobs, housing and life-chances.

'Multicultural education', in whatever its precise formulation, has been based on the conviction that out of increased knowledge of different cultures will grow mutual acceptance and toleration. That this idealism has not been fulfilled to any great degree has been shown by increasing racial violence on the streets, attacks on mosques and fire-bombing in homes,[13] often carried out by young folk not long out of school. Racist abuse has also been directed at black footballers from the terraces by young white men who have grown up during the period in which 'multiculturalists' have been developing their programmes. It cannot be claimed that all — or even most of them — have come from schools which have made no attempt to address the issues, or which have not had a mixed school population.

Not only so, but 'multiculturalism' cannot be shown to have greatly improved the outcomes of schooling for black people, though as long ago as 1971 Bernard Coard wrote *How the West Indian Child is made Educationally Sub-normal in the British School System*,[14] a book which marks the beginning of black awareness and dissatisfaction with education and its outcomes. The point is made directly and strongly in *A Different Reality — An Account of Black People's Experiences of their Grievances before and after the Handsworth Rebellions of September 1985*.[15]

> It was felt that the education system promoted perceptions about black people's cultural inferiority, whether through food, dress, language or religion. Multicultural philosophy as currently practised is not tackling 'respect' for other's cultures, it continues to reinforce the hierarchy of cultures created by the State ... in which black cultures somehow 'fail' to live up to the high regard given to white middle-class English culture.

The comment refers to Birmingham, a city which has made considerable investment, at least through 'section 11', in developing a policy of *Education for Our Multicultural Socity*.[16] There is no reason to suppose that black people elsewhere are much less critical.

As a result of black dissatisfaction with educational achievement on the one hand, and political fears of unrest in the cities on the other, combined with sound evidence of discrimination in jobs and housing, 'racism awareness training' (RAT) and/or 'anti-racism training' (ART) have replaced 'multiculturalism' as the course to be followed, not only in schools but also in other places where adminstrators are trained and decisions are made. American experience has been very influential in this development, notably through the work of Judy Katz, explained in her book, *White Awareness*.[17]

Criticism of RAT has come from all sides: the Bristol teacher, Jonathan Savory, achieved some notoriety when he described anti-racism as 'the witch-craft of the Left', in a controversial article in the right-wing *Salisbury Review*. Ray Honeyford, former Head of Drummond Middle School, Bradford, more recently has discussed it in an article in the *Daily Mail* of 20 October 1986, as 'This most evil force in Britain'.[18] On the other hand, A. Sivanandan, Director of the Institute of Race Relations, has criticized RAT as follows:

> The fight against racism is a fight against the state which sanctions and authorizes it ... in the institutions and structures of society, and in the behaviour of its public officials ... RAT, however, professes to change attitudes and behaviour, and thereby power relations — not in reality, but in sleight of definition; by defining power relations as personal relations ... (it) is a betrayal of political black struggle against racism.[19]

The conclusion so far would seem to be that multicultural education as well as RAT, whatever it might or might not do for personal relations, is incapable of tackling the real issues because they lie in the realm of power and institutions. Faced with such a welter of conflicting perceptions and policies, disappointed hopes and the prospect of continuing social unrest, the questions arise: 'What is the way forward?', 'How may we, teachers, governors and administrators, address the very real and urgent situation?', 'How may we "believe in multicultural education"?'

However much it has been criticized and ignored, the Swann Report is surely right in insisting upon *Education for All*. This is a matter for all LEAs and all schools, whether 'maintained', 'aided' or 'controlled'. Institutions in the 'private sector' should not opt out, nor should they be allowed to do so, as long as they continue to educate people who are privileged to enter the decision-making professions, with power over others of whom they may know very little.

Clearly, perceptions of what is needed by way of curriculum content or administrative change will vary from place to place, with the presence or not of black pupils, and with the political or religious affiliation of teachers: unless, of course, a more directive and centralized system is imposed upon schools. As things are, teachers who are daily meeting black children from homes in the immediate neighbourhood will be impelled, as professionals, to 'being where they (the children) are', and make appropriate changes more or less willingly. Yet their colleagues in rural schools may be less informed but more apprehensive of rising tension, without appreciating the reality of their common responsibility for the well-being of our whole society. They may be inclined to prescribe the curriculum 'mixture as before', though the votes of their pupils will in due course help to determine the policies that affect the destinies and citizenship of their black peers.

The 'voluntary agency' schools may also be expected to have a particular perspective on *Education for All*, but Bernardette O'Keeffe has demonstrated (for Church of England schools at least) the dilemmas they face and the differing views of their teachers about their role within a plural society.[20] As a result of 'white flight' from the inner cities, some schools have found themselves admitting a large proportion of Sikh or Muslim children, in order to stay in being at a time of falling rolls. Not all teachers, even in such circumstances are happy to follow the recommendations of the National Society (Church of England) for Promoting Religious Education, that

> If the Church is serious about the educational contribution it can bring to schools, and committed to its mission . . . then it may have to be far more deliberate in opening its service to the nation and forming, through its schools, communities of many faiths which in their life begin the slow and painful process towards unity and diversity.[21]

Other schools have drawn upon themselves accusations of 'racism' and 'racial discrimination' by admissions policies based upon family church adherence, certified by the clergy, which appear to favour white Christians. Relatively few blacks seem to be admitted, which is only partly explained by the withdrawal of black Christians to separated churches. In these circumstances and in areas where few black people are settled, it is obviously easier for 'the Christian ethos to manifest itself in all aspects of the school's life', and to be epitomized and sanctified in an assembly for 'collective worship' as required by law. On the basis of her study, O' Keeffe concludes that 'Church schools continue to hold assemblies that are mostly Christian . . . and the percentage of children belonging to faiths other than Christian does not affect the content to any great extent' — this in great contrast to the county schools, in the London area, at least.

Beyond the narrower questions of admissions policies and curriculum content in church schools, but brought into focus by them, lie much bigger issues: about the place of Christianity as defining and sanctifying white British ethnicity; about the subordination of a universal Gospel of a loving God and Saviour to the demands of a national or 'folk' religion; about power and equality in a plural society, in which compulsory schooling functions to induct the young into norms of thought and behaviour, as well as allocating them to 'bands' or 'modules' and so to HE, FE, or to 'life', to careers and 'life-chances' generally.

Years ago, it was assumed that the addition to the religious education syllabus of some information about other faiths in their classical forms was all that was needed by way of multicultural education, together with some help in learning English for those children who were said to 'have no language'. It will no longer do for a single subject, accorded minority time and status in the curriculum to carry the weight of a schools adjustment to the realities of the modern situation. Such limited provision was (and is) incapable of addressing conflict with racial overtones in some schools, the disproportional 'suspension' of black children from others,[22] or their general underachievement according to the usual measures of success in education — to say nothing of racism in society.[23]

The problem is to formulate a philosophy and a programme in which we may believe, sufficiently broad to command support from teachers, parents and pupils in all kinds of schools in all parts of the country; sufficiently flexible to avoid the charge of indoctrination on the one hand and to promote individual fulfilment on the other, yet at the same time to embody a set of organizing norms and values for a society which desires unity combined with freedom; yet sufficiently professional to stimulate a reorientation of the curriculum towards a coherent response to the challenge of big issues, like justice, harmony and the completest possible human well-being, both individual and corporate. We are, of course, talking about the 'kingdom of God', which according to St. Paul, 'is justice, peace and joy, inspired by the Holy Spirit' (Romans 14.17, NEB).

A formula which I believe has, at least, some validity in attempting to meet these exacting criteria was worked out with the experienced teacher-students on the in-service BEd (Multicultural Studies) course at Birmingham Polytechnic (1978–81). It was decided that

> We teachers are in the business of the formation of the citizens
> of just, harmonious, plural democracy.

This brief, almost corny, statement obviously invites the question 'What's new?'. There must be few British teachers who would not agree with it. Nearly all will maintain that they are 'preparing children for life', which usually implies the development of individual human potential. Some have gone further in 'preparing for life in a multicultural society', which might, however, mean little more than preparing for the place in the existing social order to which the teacher has consciously or unconsciously assigned the child, adding some items of exotic information about other cultures.

The 'Birmingham formulation' goes further. It replaces the

omnibus and imprecise word 'society' by 'democracy', which is at once dynamic and demanding, since all citizens are to be equipped to participate to the fullest of their powers in pursuit of justice, harmony and the common good, through institutions which have been developed over the centuries, often at considerable personal cost. Such instruments need to be understood and improved, used and defended.

This formulation is more demanding — yet we believed it to be more satisfying both to teachers and pupils — because it relates the present work of school of future engagement with opportunities and constraints in decision-making, not merely in occasional elections, but also expressing and defending their opinions in the day-to-day business of communal living. As things are at present, all school-leavers will be able to vote in political elections at 18 years of age, whatever their religion or racial origin. For their own good and that of the groups to which they belong, to say nothing of the well-being of society at large, it is essential that they are well-equipped to participate in the processes that govern our lives and to do so with integrity and respect for the persons and the rights of their fellow-citizens.

'Citizens', in this formulation, are not simply individuals who 'look after number 1'; nor in the circumstances of our life together in this island can they be 'tribal' in outlook and behaviour. Therefore schools which are the institutions through which citizens are compulsorily inducted into life in society cannot but ask themselves the following questions:

1 What should a citizen know on leaving school, to enable him/her at least to vote intelligently, and to engage with understanding, as fully as he/she may wish, in the continuing democratic processes?

2 What should a citizen be able to do in these respects? For example, to keep himself well-informed; to formulate appropriate questions for candidates for election; to join a party as a matter of considered and principled decision; to engage in pressure-group activity, if so desired; to negotiate and persuade.

3 What qualities of character should such a citizen possess? Honesty, commitment to justice, and what else?

Obviously the word 'citizen' means both men and women of all the distinct ethnic groups now living in Britain. Democratic processes' include, not only the business of voting, canvassing or candidating in local or parliamentary elections, but also engagement in the other institutions of society, in which individual or group rights have to be maintained and responsibilities assumed.

It goes without saying that this particular emphasis need not and should not imply a narrowing of educational aims about personal development and qualifications leading to careers but rather to an enlargement of vision and abilities generally, for the fully equipped citizen will be someone who is well-informed, and capable of finding out what he/she does know; will be able to make comparisons and judgments on the basis of knowledge and not prejudice; will be aware of the rights of others and their mutual responsibilities.

School staffs will thus require to ask themselves the further questions:

4 What kind of curriculum is calculated to produce the wise adults who can engage as citizens with the issues of racial discrimination in employment, for example, and in the activities necessary to solve them, with courage, integrity and clear judgment, wherever they occur?

5 What kind of staff, with what community of purpose, can address this complex and enormous task with the urgency that the situation demands? How are they to understand, and then to work out the strategies and the tactics — the professional practice and the institutional embodiment of the principles required for the 'formation of the citizens of a just, harmonious, plural democracy'?

Obviously, it will be a curriculum in which accurate information is made available to all future citizens, not simply because it is interesting and might make class-control easier, but because justice cannot be done without it, whether in individual attitudes and behaviour, or in the courts and administrative offices. Similarly, the curriculum will enable the future citizens to combat racism in school or society, personal or institutional, in the media or in the queue at the Post Office.

Though it may well include elements of the multicultural thinking which has already been described, and teaching materials already developed, a curriculum designed for the 'formation of citizens' would require a conscious 'whole-school' purpose, not merely the individual *ad hoc* response of 'teacher-missionaries', nor merely that of inner city schools impelled by force of circumstances to 'do something'. The Swann Report calls for the curriculum of all 'schools to be permeated with a genuinely pluralist perspective', though the word 'reorientation' would be stronger and more thorough-going, applied not only to separate subjects but to the total school experience of the future citizens. Whether the school has a predominantly white or a predominantly black pupil body, the general orientation of its curriculum will be the same, towards participation in a just, harmonious, plural democracy.

The fact that ours is a small island — a fact which is often used to discourage further immigration — with a Parliamentary democratic constitution, requires and at the same time facilitates the development of aims, understanding and skills to be held in common by all its citizens. The particular 'problems' of schools in the white highlands — distance from and infrequency of encounters with black people — should not be exaggerated, but overcome. The fact that the barriers are not primarily those of distance, but of will, is demonstrated by the city schools which are white enclaves, in but not of, their particular neighbourhoods. Bernadette O'Keeffe has shown how this comes about, when the 'message is Christian education for Christian children ... they (some schools) become denominational because service to the nation is no longer a priority (but) ... to the worshipping community'. However, even if admission policies cannot be changed overnight, there can be no reason why schools in such a situation should not undertake the reorientation of their curriculum in the ways now being advocated. In this they might be exemplars for others at a greater distance!

Of course, it cannot be denied that some curriculum changes in this direction have taken place, and probably few schools nowadays treat 'citizenship' as arcane knowledge about Black Rod or Mr. Speaker's reluctance to be seated as President of the House of Commons. However, not many schools have introduced 'political education' as recommended by the Swann Committee, 'the essential aim (of which) should be to open pupils' minds to a full appreciation of the role which they as adults can and should play in shaping their futures'. 'Effective political education', says the Report, 'should also leads youngsters to consider fundamental issues such as social justice and equality', and it 'can also provide ethnic minority youngsters with the skills necessary to participate in political activities, thus helping to channel their energies into positive rather than negative forms of expression' — and lead them to challenge the negative assumptions about them which are implicit even in that sentence!

The Swann Committee was aware of the possibility that 'this one particular area of the curriculum' might be 'regarded ... simply as a form of indoctrination ... with clearly defined "party political" beliefs', though they took the view that 'encouraging pupils to consider how power is exercised, how resources are allocated, how policies are determined ... how conflicts are resolved (should be) no more likely to lead them to question and to challenge the *status quo* other than where this is justified, than to defend and seek to retain it'.[24] However, there is danger that political education might be resisted as another intrusive 'add-on' subject, for which, like multicultural education, there is no room on an already over-full timetable. All subjects have their political aspects, often unrecognized because they lie within the 'hidden curriculum', even when historians, for example, seek to avoid bias.

Neutrality is itself a political position, capable of unintended but dangerous outcomes when pupils are left to make sense for themselves of the disparate topics to which they are introduced at various stages of schooling, specially if they are given no real opportunity to try out accepted principles and practices against the realities of modern life. Clearly education for participation in democracy cannot be so prescriptive as to rule out the possibility of conflict between differing points of view and interest; on the other hand, it cannot be indifferent about the underlying principles of democracy, justice and equality under law, freedom of thought and speech, participation in decision-making and the two-way responsibilities between citizen and authority.

Of immense, if not paramount, importance is the defence of minorities, specially those who are marked out by factors such as skin-colour over which they have no control. About that there can be surely no place for 'the teacher (to) act as Chairman aspiring to procedural neutrality' as was the case in the controversial research programme conducted by Lawrence Stenhouse and his team in the Humanities Curriculum Project.[25] Even if 'the teacher adopts a procedural neutrality to avoid asserting his views with the authority of his position behind him', all the 'opposing sides in pupil discussion' must be brought under obedience to the vision of a 'just, harmonious, plural democracy'. Freedom of speech has already been restricted by legislation against 'incitement to racial hatred'.[26] Young citizens, both black and white, must learn to think and behave in ways that ensure that justice is done, conflict is managed and 'shalom' established by democratic means, by people who understand and appreciate each other in a common belonging to this country. This cannot be achieved unless all teachers really do see themselves as in the 'business of the formation of the citizens of a just ... democracy', and direct their professional activities to this end.

To say this is to exalt the role of teachers in the belief that schools can do more than merely reflect society. It is to give them a common purpose greater than the transmission of disparate, received and often inert facts and opinion. It is to offer them at a time of confusion and conflict a unifying vision of society of which they, in common with their pupils, are citizens. The alternative is a continuation and extension of social control by force, and increasing resistance by those who see themselves as unjustly 'oppressed' in a democracy, falsely so-called.

All this may sound high-falutin, vague and impractical, and it is necessary to flesh it out with something less visionary! And to face some possible objections.

Purposeful direction of in-school activities towards the 'formation of citizens' presents a challenge to concepts of education based upon 'maturation', 'waiting for readiness' and 'discovery methods', which depend upon children's curiosity as the strongest of motivations. That is to say that this kind of 'citizenship' is not something of which only sixth formers doing general studies courses are thought to be capable. That, in any case, would mean that pupils who do not 'stay on' would be deprived of the kind of initiation that is envisaged, even though they would encounter the workaday world out of school earlier. But even primary school pupils — certainly those in the older classes — are aware of the long-term unemployment of parents or older brothers, and of discrimination in housing, as well as of graffiti and name-calling in school and playground. Some of the pupils are very young, who are currently engaged in the struggle against 'apartheid' in South Africa. The system, itself, has politicized them, though African culture does not unduly prolong childhood, but imposes adult awareness and responsibilities earlier than is common in more 'developed' countries. The same is true of the children of the ethnic minorities in Britain today. Of course, very young children cannot be required too soon to bear the world's sorrows; neither should they be protected too long, nor fed with 'fairy tales' which have to be corrected later.

Reorientation towards 'the business of the formation of the citizens of a just, harmonious, plural democracy' will involve much discussion and examination of syllabuses, the 'school rules' and the pastoral/disciplinary arrangements in order to arrive, not only at an agreed 'policy statement', but also change in course content and fresh awareness and procedures for the management of conflict, in school but also capable of being used outside. There would seem to be no good reason why older pupils, at least, should not take a real share in such developmental activities. After all it can only be to their long-term advantage, though teachers too might benefit from the engagement of their pupils as allies rather than the opposite. Obviously, the circumstances of schools at a distance from the areas where black people are settled will demand special efforts and methods to respond to the concept of a 'plural democracy', accepted as natural, right, and a positive resource — but the goals will be the same for schools everywhere.

Such a wide-ranging programme can hardly be called 'multicultural education' in the senses from which we started, but it is one in which I, at least, feel it possible to believe.

Notes

1 See, for example, STONE M. (1981) *The Education of the Black Child in Britain: The Myth of Multiracial Education*, London, Fontana.
2 TOWNSEND, H. E. R. and BRITTAN, E. (1973) *Multiracial Education — Need and Innovation*, Schools Council Working Paper 50, London, Evans/Methuen.
3 O'KEEFFE B. (1986) *Faith, Culture and the Dual System*, Lewes, Falmer press.
4 See, for example, the Report of the Chief Constable of the West Midlands on *Handsworth/Lozells, September 1985*, the Report of Julius Siverman of his *Independent Enquiry into the Handsworth Disturbances, September 1985* and *A Different Reality: An Account of Black People's Experience and Their Grievances Before and After the Handsworth Rebellions of September 1985*, West Midlands County Council.
5 SCARMAN, Lord (1981) *The Brixton Disorders, 10–12 April 1981*, London, HMSO.
6 DEPARTMENT OF EDUCATION AND SCIENCE (1985) *Education for All* (The Swann Report), London, HMSO.
7 *Section 11 of the Local Government Act, 1986*, Home Office Circular, No. 97/1982.
8 For example conferences organized by NAME (formerly the National Association for Multiracial Education, now the National Anti-racist Movement in Education) and journals such as *Multicultural Teaching to Combat Racism in School and Community*, published by Trentham Books.
9 The number of researchers and reports is enormous and to list them all would be impossible. Early in the field were the psychologists, BAGLEY, C. and VERMA G., with titles such as *Race and Education Across Cultures, Self-concept, Achievement and Multicultural Education* and, more recently, (1986) *Ethnicity and Educational Achievement in British Schools*, Macmillan. Classroom practice is discussed in STENHOUSE, L. *et al* (1982) *Teaching about Race Relations*, London, Routledge. Professor John Egleston and his team examined the *Educational and Vocational Experiences of 15–18 Year Old Young People of Minority Ethnic Groups*, (University of Warwick,

1984), having already reported on in-service courses for teachers in the field of multicultural education in 1981.

10   This point is developed in rather more detail in my article, 'Teacher education for a pluralist society, the British case', *European Journal of Teacher Education*, 5, 1–2, 1982.

11   See LEVITAS, R. (1986) *The Ideology of the New Right*, Cambridge, Polity Press, especially chapter 4, 'Culture, nation and "race" in the British and French new right', by Gill Seidel. See also, PALMER F. (Eds) (1986) *Anti-Racism: An Assault Upon Education Value*, London, Sherwood Press.

12   In a rough and ready way it can be said that 'assimilation' was the aim of schooling for 'immigrants' in the 1950s and 1960s, followed by 'integration' and 'cultural pluralism' in the 1970s. 'Race awareness' and 'anti-racist education' are increasingly demanded in the 1980s. Bernardette O'Keeffe has helpfully described this process of ideological change in (1986) *Fiath, Culture and The Dual System*, Lewes, Falmer Press, p. 127–30.

13   *Race and Immigration*, the monthly bulletin of the Runnymede Trust, provides a sickening catalogue of such attacks. Available from the Trust, 178 Gower St., London, NW1 2NB.

14   COARD, B. (1971) *How the West Indian Child is made Educationally Sub-normal in the British School System*, London, New Beacon Books.

15   ⸱ ʋblished by the West Midlands County Council (since abolished) *A Different Reality* is the Report of a Review Panel, chaired by Herman Ouseley, Asst. Chief Executive of the Borough of Lambeth, and including Professor Stuart Hall of the Open University and others.

16   The title of a document intended to explain, and assist the delivery of, the City of Birmingham's policy on equal opportunities.

17   KATZ, J. (1978) *White Awareness — A Handbook of Anti-racism Training*, Oklahoma, Universities of Oklahoma Press.

18   Quoted in *Race and Immigration*, 198, December 1986.

19   SIVANANDAN, A. (1985) 'RAT and the degradation of the black struggle'; *Race and Class*, spring, XXV1, 4. Published by the Institute of Race Relations.

20   O'KEEFFE, B. (1986) *op cit*.

21   *A Future in Partnership*, a Green Paper published by the National Society (Church of England) for the Promotion of Religious Education, London, 1984.

22   An examination of the Birmingham LEA's suspensions policy, by the Commission for Racial Equality, revealed that, in 1984/85 black students were four times more likely than whites to be suspended, at a young age, and after shorter periods of reported 'bad' behaviour.

23   In an article in *New Society*, 17 May 1984, entitled 'I'm not National Front myself, but …', BILLING, M. and COCHRANE, R. of the University of Birmingham, reported that over half their sample of pupils in West Midlands secondary schools had views which 'coincide with those of extreme right-wing groups'.

24   The Swann Report quotes with approval from CRICK, B. and PORTER, A. (Eds) (1987) *Political Education and Political Literacy*, London,

Longmans, which reports on the Hansard Society's major programme on political education.

25 STENHOUSE, L. *et al* (1982) *Teaching about Race Relations*, London, Routledge.

26 Race Relations Act 1976.

4   A View of Education —
an Islamic Perspective

Syed Ali Ashraf

Great Britain became a multi-denominational country long ago. With the advent of the new waves of Jewish community in the twentieth century its multifaith character became a bit pronounced. It was only in the post-Second World War period that the immigration of non-white Asians and African and West Indian people brought into the limelight its mulitracial, multicultural and multifaith character.[1] The all-white authority who had Christianity at the roots of their culture but who had been following a primarily secularist policy in education tried to assimilate these new immigrants and later on to integrate them into their own cultural fold. Because of the strong and almost indissoluble links between the cultures of these immigrants and their religions and also because of linguistic varieties and difficulties the assimilationist and integrationist methods failed and the theory of pluralism and multiculturalism was enunciated.[2]

British educationists and authorities must, therefore, be credited with genuine attempts to be open-minded and sincere in so far as learning from experience and acting accordingly is concerned. They have realized the terrible danger of racism which is present in this country and which gets open support from 'Powellists' and 'National Front' activists.[3] They also realize that the newcomers have settled down in this country; they are making or marring their fortune in the open field and their children are growing up in British surroundings. That is why the Swann Report has devoted a major section to the methods of uprooting racism through a newly devised 'Education for all' policy[4]. They would like the white majority to realize and accept this multicultural character of the society. They feel that only when this initial 'purification of the soul' is effected, it will be possible for different cultural groups to share their values and thereby get integrated into a comprehensive cultural entity in which each cultural group will retain and maintain their separate identity but at the same time become united into a humanistic democratic, pluralistic culture-sharing-and-caring-whole. 'Unity in diversity' will emerge.

With this intention the Schools Council planned a transformation of the 'religious instruction' clause of the 1944 Education Act (1967) and by 1975 the Birmingham Agreed Syllabus gave a major lead in this direction. Instead of being 'nurtured' in their respective faiths, pupils were expected to be aware of different faiths, different faith-communities and develop a kind of understanding and openmindedness. 'Religious education' has thus become, the authorities and the Swann Committee think, a very useful, convenient and major method of cultivating a 'multicultural outlook' in pupils and a 'tolerant attitude' to all faiths.

From a pragmatic point of view the whole approach seems to be highly plausible and desirable. There are, however, serious shortcomings both theoretical and practical.

The first shortcoming is in the attitude of the authorities in their assessment of minority cultures. By minority cultures they mean the cultures of 'ethnic minorities' and they divide them into 'Asian' and 'West Indian' groups. So far as the Muslims are concerned, this division is incorrect and misleading. Muslims of this country are themselves multiethnic in character. The Semitic Arabs, the Indo-Aryan Iranians, the Panjabis, the Bangladeshis, the Gujaraties, the Turks — all these different ethnic groups together form the Muslim community. The Sikhs and the Hindus have distinctive cultural identities and in spite of some similarities with Indo-Pakistani-Bangladeshi Muslims in so far as some customs are concerned, there are basic cultural differences. The authorities ought to be scientifically accurate and not be governed by preconceived notions about culture derived from sociologists who want to dissociate religion from culture. Culture is integrally related to values and values are derived from religion. This is true of all traditional societies including the British society. And this is specially true of the Muslim community. Islam is such a complete code of life, the Qur'an is so explicit in rules and regulations regarding character and conduct, and the sayings and practices of Prophet Muhammad, peace be upon him, are so detailed and historically accessible and emotionally moving that whatever be the superficial trappings of distinctive cultures, Muslims all over the world have been following a common cultural pattern, a common way of life. Islam is that comprehensive all embracing way of life. Unless the Muslims are treated as a unit, it will not be possible for authorities (LEAs) or headteachers or teachers to understand, appreciate and hence meet the needs and requirements of Muslim children.

Authorities are trying to avoid using the religious criterion because they think that that will help the maintenance and perpetuation of separation and of division in the society and prevent the growth of unity and understanding. People in authority consider the secularization of society more conducive to cultural tolerance than the religious approach.[5] They give examples of past religious intolerance even among the Christians, not to speak of the intolerance and bloodshed in India. But the authorities forget that their secularist policy is regarded by the Muslim community as an attempt to brainwash Muslim children, uproot them from their cultural moorings, create tension between the house and the school, the parents and the children and, what is most dangerous for the upcoming generation, does not provide children with certainty and a reliable, sustaining and accepted and acceptable norm to fall back upon. If the curriculum, the methods of teaching and the school ethos are based on the philosophy of changing values that are dependent on external social change and not on the philosophy of the absolutes in human nature which provide the unchanging universal norms of truth, justice, righteousness, freedom, pity, mercy, honesty, compassion and charity, Muslim children will suffer from the conflict that people suffered in England in the nineteenth century and the sense of loss, uncertainty and insecurity that is prevalent in the twentieth century. The result will be not unification of society or 'unity in diversity' but more stress on diversity without any roots in unity. Whereas religions provide a norm and a sense of accountability to God in the 'other world' and hence a check on selfishness, racial or colour-pride, secularism will lead to power-struggle between the races without any check. The failure of the 'assimilationist' and 'integrationist' policy should have taught a salutory lesson to the authorities and they should have searched the nature of fundamental values and tried to find the Common Frame of Reference and draw inspiration from that ideal. Even though a section of the British society would be unwilling to subscribe openly and overtly to that Common Frame it is a well-known fact that that section of the society even now accepts and upholds it in the name of humanism, democracy universality and rationalism.

The source of that Frame of Reference is in the common spiritual attitude to life that is bred by the Judaeo-Christian-Islamic beliefs in God, man's accountability to God and afterlife. Though Islam rejects the concept of incarnation, it accepts all Judaic prophets as their own and accepts Christ as the 'word' of God and a perfectly valid source of spiritual inspiration and self–purification. Islam wants mankind to go back to the original code of life which embraces the Ten Commandments revealed to Moses and all the fundamental values that Jesus Christ enunciated[6]. The source of all these commandments and values are in the Absolute Names and Attributes of God which provide mankind with that eternal and Absolute Frame of Reference which is continuously realized in contingent circumstances.[7] In different periods of history and in different areas of existence different emphasis became necessary, but the basic reference did not change.[8] Through the example of Prophet Muhammad, peace be on him, Islam gives a balanced and comprehensive human expression of those Absolutes and provides the believers with a complete code of life. The Jews, the Christians and the Muslims thus share a common frame of reference in these Absolutes whatever be the difference in their theories regarding the manifestation of these values.

The acceptance of this Frame of Reference for education has to be seen from the religious-cum-social point of view. From the religious point of view this is acceptable to Jews, Christians and the Muslims and also to the Hindus, the Sikhs and Buddhists. As regards these three religions, especially Hinduism and Buddhism, the method of presentation may differ. But the roots are the same. And in each case the invocation of the Absolutes is based on the realisation of certainty by certain individuals whose spiritual impact on the society and faith in whom by the believers become the source of stability and permanence of these Absolutes in the hearts of the followers. Faith in Abraham, Moses and other Prophets are at the roots of the acceptance of the Absolutes as the ethical frame by the Jews. Faith in Christ incarnating them is what the Christians believe. Faith in all the Prophets, known and unknown, and lastly in Prophet Muhammad as the supreme exemplar of these Absolutes is the source and foundation of the ethical code for the Muslims. Thus the Muslim community affirms that truth was revealed through all the Jewish prophets and Christ.[9] Islam broadens the base further by asserting that Truth was revealed through other Prophets who came to each human habitation in the world and received messages in the language of the people to whom they preached.[10] Becuase of this statement in the Qur'ān, the Muslim community is ready to believe that the Hindus, the Buddhists and other religious groups have also the same Absolutes at the basis of their values. There is no reason therefore why this common Frame of Reference should not be the basis of educational planning for the faith-communities living in this country and should not be the source of unity in diversity. We shall then accept the difference not only in customs, conventions and rituals but also in the nature and method of the manifestation and expression of those Absolutes in different societies. At the same time we shall make everyone aware of the source of their own values and hence of their commitments. Thus the source of 'certainty' will not be challenged unnecessarily and at the same time opportunity to accept or modify and control changes will remain open.[11] Instead of teaching children to adjust to changing circumstances we can then teach them how to control and guide the circumstances. External changes are brought about by changes in the mind of Man, and not vice versa. Man must retain the controlling authority and not become a passively controlled unit.[12]

The question then arises: How far and in what manner is this concept of God and His Attributes necessary for the education of the children? This concept may be necessary for the maintenance and transmission of values in a particular community, or, in a broader sense, in the faith communities of this country. It may bring the communities together in that they would realize that the roots of most of those which are regarded as fundamental values are the same. But in what sense is it necessary for the education of children to have this spiritual basis in so far as the acquisition of knowledge in subjects such as natural sciences or social studies is concerned? Is this concept of Man-God relationship necessary for any subject other than religious studies? Are we not thereby destroying the 'autonomy' of individual subjects, restricting man's freedom of judgment, choice and use of the rational faculty, imposing an ethical code from without rather than allowing the morality to grow within, and, worst of all, allowing different religious authorities to exercise their power and thereby ultimately leading the society to rigidity, conflict, and even bloodshed? In other words, are we not then ultimately, even unknowingly, allowing 'walls' rather than 'bridges' to be built? A clear understanding of the Islamic point of view will indicate that if education, including teaching in all branches of knowledge, is guided by the religious approach to life, the true nature of man is nourished and developed, the interrelationship among all branches of knowledge understood and appreciated and all faculties of a human being grow in such a way that the autonomy of each branch of knowledge is seen in the context of Unified Truth and not in segregation, the hierarchy of knowledge is realized and established and all branches of knowledge are seen in their proper perspective within the orbit of the supreme knowledge that man can attain, that of Man's relation with God. In order to appreciate this concept of education, it is necessary to give a brief description of this theory and the method of realizing it in curriculum and teaching of methodology. For the sake of brevity and a clear-cut picture, it will not be possible for us to enter into a discussion of its justifiability except from the point of view of the faith, history, culture and tradition of the Muslim community and its relevance in the context of other faith communities, especially the Christians and the Jews. We cannot discuss philosophically the truth and otherwise of all basic assumptions because not only is that itself a topic deserving a new detailed study, but it is also unnessary for an analysis of the educational aims, objectives and philosophy of a convictional community.

In Islam the purpose of education is to enable man to fulfil the purpose of his creation, of his coming to this world. The purpose of the creation is to become a wholehearted servant of God.[13] This servitude is not forced but freely, willingly and completely given so that such a person says to God, 'O my Lord, my prayers, my sacrifice, my life and my death are for Allah, the Lord of the Worlds Who hath no peer'.[14] This a person can say only when his love for God is greater than his love for this world and all that is available here.[15] Love for God is manifested through that person's love for the Prophet because the Prophet personally exemplified in this world all that God is known by. Man can know God by His Attributes such as truth, freedom, knowledge, goodness, justice, mercy, freedom, charity, love and beauty. Prophet Muhammad, peace be upon him, is the personal, human example of those norms in their spirit and application. Love of God and the Prophet therefore guides man and is expressed in man's love for those qualities. Education must therefore make man aware of those attributes and the life and character of the Prophet so that love is generated by that knowledge.

This knowledge is not therefore just an intellectual acquisition but an assimilation of those truths into oneself. Unless man acquires 'certainty' (*yaqın*) about them this assimilation is not possible. This certainty is acquired through faith. Knowledge must increase the range and depth of that faith and not destroy it.[16] That which destroys faith is not really knowledge but a form of ignorance (*jehl*). Faith and knowledge must go hand in hand.[17] Faith is a spiritual gift and knowledge is an intellectual acquisition through the use of man's intellect (*āql*). Faith is inherent in man's nature but it remains as a potential force that requires cultivation and growth only because God has given man freedom and a will to turn the potential energy into kinetic reality. That potentiality is evident in childhood through the inherent sense of justice, truth and charity and inherent love of goodness and love of knowledge. Cultivation of faith in God and the Prophet leads to the efflorenscence and fructification of those potential qualities. The primary job of educationists therefore is to lay down a process that would not create doubts but help pupils in removing doubts and acquire certainty and apply that knowledge in real life.

This implies that man's nature demands such cultivation. Through this inherent sense of justice, love of truth, urge for charity, hankering after knowledge, craving for love and sense of beauty it becomes evident that these qualities which are God's own are inherent in humanity. That is what is meant by the Qur'ānic statement that God taught Adam the names of everything.[18] As a thing's essence is implied implicity by the name of the thing, and as the essence of every single created object has been brought into existence by God by His use of some specific power (or quality) by the 'names' of things the Qur'ān is informing us of the Attributes of God that God implanted within the spirit of man. Potentially therefore man can know the essence of every single object in this universe and thereby expand his 'self' and see reflection of God's attributes within his own self. Thus his love of God goes on increasing till he forgets himself and his will is turned into God's will and God works through him.[19] He also realizes that nothing ultimately belongs to him. Everything is a gift which he can lose at any moment. This creates in him a sense of humility. And 'humility is endless'. The purpose of seeking knowledge is not just to become a good citizen of a state but to become a complete human being who reflects God's Attributes in his character and conduct and fulfils God's will through the exercise of his will and through action (*amal*) in this world. In other words, the system of education must be so designed that it reflects not just any man but the Universal of Perfect Man (*al-insān al-Kāmil*). As the Prophet, peace be upon him, is the person in whom that Perfect Man is realized, and as the concept of education in Islam pertains to man alone, the system of education conceived in Islam has always been a system that describes the model of man as perfected in the sacred person of the Holy Prophet. The function of that system is to produce men and women resembling the Prophet as far as possible, each, of course, according to his or her inherent capacities and potentials.

What the Prophet represents is known as *Sharia* (divine law). Spiritual growth through *tariqa* (spiritual path) is attained within the orbit of *Sharia*. Sharia is also a public matter. It integrates the political social and economic life of the community and the individuals and thereby compels a Muslim to grow within the sanctioned orbit. Only then can he ultimately succeed in becoming the vicegerent of God on the earth. Whereas the secularist or rationalist concepts demand an understanding through reason before acceptance and obedience, Islam demands an acceptance by *qalb* (heart) and obedience first and then seek assistance from *'aql* (intellect). If a person's *qalb* is full of doubts and he approaches truth with that attitude, he can never attain to that truth because his *'aql* is already vitiated by preconceived notions and doubts and his Will is tortured or twisted and is not fit to appreciate truth untramelled by worldly suppositions.

That is why a Muslim considers the secularist education policy that aims at producing scepticism and at proceeding through doubts (*shakk*) as destructive of the balanced growth of the individual. Faith and not doubts should be cultivated from childhood. At the same time, the intellect has the freedom to explore experiences and judge with reference to the norm of culture and behaviour of the Prophet and the conduct and sayings of the Companions. Faith is a precondition of the realization of truth. And as the dimension of that truth is infinity and eternity, there is no limit to that realization and hence to the expansion and growth of the human being. Whereas the secularist and scientific truths are based on hypotheses and have no norm that touches the heart (*qalb*) the spiritual organ, the realization through *qalb* according to Islam, is constantly assessed by the intellect (*'aql*) with reference to the norm exhibited and established by the Prophet both in the spiritual and in the intellectual, rational, and physical realms of existence. Thus Faith, Heart, Intellect and Body work together in unison.

In view of the fact that Islam does not allow the Muslims to dichotomize life and divide it into that which belongs to God (Divine) and that which belongs to Caesar (Secular).[20] Islam wants education to be a process in which the curriculum and teaching methods help each individual child to unfold its own unique potentiality as a representative of God on the earth. Each subject taught must contribute its quota to the realization of this overall aim. The Muslim community therefore assumes that religious and moral teaching should be incorporated in the curriculum not as much as a separate item but mainly as a governing and guiding principle. That is why the community demands that the teachers should be religious and hence, moral. Morality is an integral part of Islam. *Iman* (faith) must be manifested through *'amal* (deeds). Such a criterion is not applied in order to appoint teachers in maintained schools. Nor is it possible for the Muslim community to realize its educational aspirations in such schools. Even the approach to education, morality, religion and culture in maintained schools is dominated by concepts which stress rationality and ignore faith, doubts and not spiritual certainty, changing values and not essential unchanging norms, worldly life and this worldly culture and not life in the other world and culture governed by spiritual certainties about which the Muslim community has unquestioned conviction. After examining all counter-arguments against Muslim voluntary-aided schools, Halstead rightly concludes that the only alternative is to allow Muslims to have their own voluntary-aided schools so that they may be permitted, like the Jews, Roman Catholics and Church of England people to join the group that supports the religious criterion.[21] Because of the long standing Muslim tradition in the advancement of knowledge and also because of the inherent competition in performance and achievement, there is no justification to assume that such schools will be backward and will turn schools into ghettoes.

Logistics of course tells us that even if such voluntary-aided schools are permitted, probably a majority of Muslim children will have to go to maintained schools. Simply for financial reasons such voluntary-aided schools cannot but be a very few. From the point of view of Islam to which the Muslim commitment is uncompromising, it is necessary to have single-sex schools, to appoint senior Muslim teachers in schools where Muslim children are in a majority, so that there is someone who can understand the problems of Muslim children and take pastoral care, to provide facilities for 'halal' (permitted by religion) food in schools, to permit grown up Muslim girls to wear long dresses and cover their heads, to allow parents to withdraw their children from worship and assemblies and religious education classes, to provide facilities for religious instruction classes in schools, and for single-sex swimming and biology classes, and also separate changing rooms.[22]

More important than all these is the need for a complete amendment of religious education classes.[23] If the intention of having religious education courses is to make different people of different countries understand each other, then is it not better to say that we should have cultural heritage classes based on religion? It will then give a worthwhile motivation to children to attend such classes. The Qur'ān tells us clearly that this difference of colours and races has been created by God so that we may know each other. This is acceptable and highly justifiable but the idea of critical openness which demands an 'evaluation' even of the values and assumptions of a religion is repugnant to Islam and the Muslims in so far as 'religious education' classes are concerned.

The Muslim community has started realizing that even if these are accepted and done, the secular denudiation of fundamental values demands that through home and mosque teachings we should build within the hearts of all Muslin children forces of resistence to counteract these forces of evil. Such work has already started all over the West and England is not an exception. Along with this it is necessary to remove from the hearts of white British children the shadow of the Crusades generated by thousands of years of propaganda, false presentation of Islam and the Prophet and sterotypes and myths in history and religious education texts. It is also necessary to make British children aware of the positive side of the impact of Islamic civilization on the West through diverse cultural, scholarly and scientific modes. This will bring flexibility in the minds of the younger generation, and a broadening of their vision. What is needed is a drastic change of the curriculum and the syllabuses and production of good books in all these fields in which Muslim scholars and British experts may cooperate. Only through these changes will there be some hope of building bridges and breaking down walls.

Notes

1 For details see TAYLOR, MONICA J. with HEGARTY, SEAMUS (1985) *The Best of Both Worlds?*, London, NEFR-Nelson, section 5; and BROWN, COLIN (1985) *Black and White Britain: The Third PSI Survey* London, Gower pp. 23–33.

2 See DEPARTMENT OF EDUCATION AND SCIENCE (1985) *Education for All* (The Swann Report) chapter 4 for a summary of these policies, London, HMSO, pp. 191–203. For details see DEPARTMENT OF EDUCATION and SCIENCE (1965) *The Education of Immigrants*, Circular 7/65, London, HMSO; (1971) *The Education of Immigrants*, London, HMSO; DEPARTMENT OF EDUCATION AND SCIENCE (1974a) *Education Disadvantages and the Needs of Immigrants, London, HMSO*; Department of Education and Science (1974b) *Education in Schools — A Consultative Document*, London, HMSO

3 See DES (1985) *op cit*, chapter 2.

4 *ibid*, chapter 6.

5 *ibid*.

6 *al-Qur'ān*, 42, 13; 46, 9.

7 *al-Qur'ān*, 10, 37.

8 *al-Qur'ān*, 10, 47.

9 *al-Qur'ān*,46, 9; 46, 12; 42, 13.

10 *al-Qur'ān*, 14,4.

11 I am using the word 'certainty' in the sense of the realization of truth. Revelation is possible because of that realization. Without faith one cannot reach 'certainty' though faith may be explained as commitment both public and individual and 'certainty' as something personal and

private based on individual spiritual insight. But there are different stages of certainty that the Qur'ān itself refers to and Muslim scholars have categorized as *'ilm al-yaqīn* (based on logical thinking) *'ain al-yaqīn* (based on observation and experiment or on primary historical sources) and *haqq al-yaqīn* (based on the direct experience of the soul). The Qur'ān says: And serve your Lord until certainty comes to you.' (15, 99).

12 Islam believes in man's responsibility to assert the authority of the norm revealed in the Qur'ān. That is why the Muslims believe in the Reformers and in going back to the norm revealed through the Prophet.

13 'I did not create jinns and Man except to worship Me (or serve Me)' *al-Qur'ān*, 51, 56.

14 *al-Qur'ān*, 6, 162.

15 *al-Qur'ān*, 9, 24.

16 As Franz Rosenthal has shown in his book *Knowledge Triumphant* (Brill, 1970) 'In Islam the concept of Knowledge enjoyed an importance unparalleled in other civilizations'. It dominated 'all aspect of Muslim intellectual, spiritual and social life.' (p. 334)

17 At the very outset it is stated that the Qur'ān is a guide only for those who believe. (2, 2).

18 *al-Qur'ān*, 2, 31.

19 This is the stage of *rādiyatam mardiyyah al-Qur'ān*, 89, 27–28.

20 As is done by Christian Theologians

21 See HALSTEAD J. M. (1986) *The Case for Muslim Voluntary-Aided Schools: some Philosophical Reflections*, Cambridge, The Islamic Academy.

22 See the minimal of concessions granted by LEAs. Jørgen S. N. (1986) *A Survey of British Local Authority Response to Muslim Needs*, Birmingham, Selly Oak Colleges.

23 See JØRGEN S. N. (Ed) (1987) *Muslims in Europe*, no. 33 which contains an essay by J. J. Shepherd 'Islam and religious education in England'. This essay clearly reveals the intention and goal of this type of religious education classes. See also Swann Report and its stress on phenomenological approach (chapter 8). See also the criticism of this approach in *Swann Committee Report: An Evaluation from the Muslim Point of View: An Agreed Statement* (1985) Cambridge Islamic Academy and a philosophical criticism of this approach by FARUQI I. R. (1986) 'Meta-religion: Towards a critical world theology', *American Journal of Islamic Social Sciences*. 3, 1.

5   Muslims Community and the Issues in Education

Mahammad Anwar

Introduction

Britain is now a multiracial and multicultural society. It includes several racial, national, religious and ethnic groups; commonly known as 'ethnic minorities'. Among these groups are Muslims, an estimated number of about one million. The estimated population of ethnic minnority groups is 2.4 million which is 5 per cent of the total population of this country. Almost 50 per cent of these are now British born. This means that significant demographic changes have taken place. Many ethnic minority parents have school-age children who have been born here and are not 'immigrants'. Are the needs of these children being properly identified and met by schools and relevant authorities? In this chapter an attempt is made to look at the British education system, its relevance to Muslims settled in this country and the issues involved in this context.

The Muslim Community

Muslims are the largest 'minority religious group' in Britain.[1] Many of them came from the New Commonwealth (including Pakistan)[2] countries, mainly in the last four decades. The largest number originated from Pakistan (about 380,000). There are sizeable groups from Bangladesh, India, Cyprus, Malaysia, Arab countries and from some parts of Africa. There is an increasing number of British-born Muslims. There are also small numbers of indigenous Muslims, mainly those converted to Islam in recent years.

Most of the first generation Muslims, particularly from South Asia, are economic migrants. Muslims are mostly to be found in the

South-East, especially in the Greater London conurbation, the West Midlands, West Yorkshire and the South Lancashire conurbations. There is also a concentrated Muslim community in the Central Clydeside conurbation, mainly in Glasgow. This tendency of concentration among Muslims is found because like other recent immigrants from the Third World countries, they were attracted to these areas in search of employment when they first arrived in Britain. At the same time, the active kinship and friendship networks and the process of chain migration have contributed to these concentrations of Muslims.[3] They are mostly owner-occupiers and live in inner city areas. Therefore, they encounter the inner city problems of high unemployment, bad housing, poor schooling, lack of proper community facilities etc., like other residents of those areas. On top of that, Muslims face racial disadvantage and prejudice and discrimination like the other ethnic minority groups in Britain.[4]

Muslims are mainly employed in manufacturing industry, in particular textiles and the metal industry. There are growing numbers of Muslim businessmen. There is also a significant number of Muslim doctors, working in the British National Health Service, teachers, engineers and other scientists.[5]

The community facilities include some 350 mosques throughout Britain. Apart from places of worship, mosques are also used as supplementary schools for teaching the Quran and mother tongues, as cultural centres and for social and welfare work. The first mosque was established at Woking in Surrey in 1980. Mosques now include both converted houses and other old buildings in the inner city areas and newly purpose built mosques in London, Birmingham, Bradford, Manchester and Glasgow to mention only a few. The number of new purpose built mosques is likely to increase in the future. For example thirty new mosques were registered in 1985.

It is clear from the evidence available that the organized religious activities which take place in the mosques and are run by Muslim organizations locally and nationally, provide an opportunity for the development of religious awareness of their members and bring the Muslims together as a community. The efforts made by Muslim religious leaders and organizations generally seem to stress the values of Islam to Muslims and to emphasize the importance of its practice, continuance and transmission to the next generation of Muslims as it regulates the whole way of life. My research shows that the majority of the first generation Muslims seem to be more committed to religious allegiance and observance and are orthodox in their response to 'Western' values.[6] Whether second generation Muslims will continue to behave in this way depends on how they are brought up, what information and facilities they get at school, through the media, and in the community, to facilitate this process.

The Education System

The education system in Britain is based on various Educatin Acts since 1944.[7] The 1944 Act makes parents responsible for the education of their children. The Act in particular states that children get a suitable education between the ages of 5 and 16.[8] How that legal duty is carried out is left to the individual. It can be done by employing private tutors, sending children to private schools or making use of the education facilities provided by the state.[9] But failure to provide adequate education for their children may result in parents being fined or imprisoned and in some cases, in having the children taken away by the local authority, as being in need of care and protection.

The state education system is organized in three main stages: primary, secondary and tertiary (further education and higher education). The primary stage includes the first period of legally required children's schooling, between the ages of 5 and 11, but it also embraces the pre-schooling period of children who go to 'nursery schools' before the age of 5. Children between the ages of 5 and 7 may be educated in separate infant schools which will cater for boys and girls together. Such children will then go, at the age of 7 to 11, to junior schools which may be co-educational or, rarely, single sex schools. The primary school which caters for the whole range from 5 to 11 is usually co-educational and normally the work of the early years is organized as a separate department within the same building (also, is some areas a system of 'first schools' 'middle schools' and 'high schools' is now developed).

Transfer to secondary school generally takes place in the September after a child reaches the age of 11. Secondary education is administered either through secondary modern schools, grammar or various forms of comprehensive schools, whose number is increasing and an over-whelming majority of children now go to these schools. It is on the results of GCE 'A' level that selection for entry to universities, polytechnics and colleges of education is normally made. In theory tertiary education begins when secondary education is concluded.

Now let us look at some other characteristics of British education, those particularly relevant to this chapter. First, there is a 'dual system' of schools, 'church schools' and county schools' both included in the state-financed system. The church schools are mainly run by the Church of England and the Roman Catholic Church and the state schools are controlled by local education authorities (LEAs). Under the 1944 Act non-provided schools could opt for a voluntary 'aided' or 'controlled' status. Secondly, unlike many countries of the world, the administration of the educational system is also characterized by another form of dualism — between the central government and the local authorities, 'A national system locally administered'[10]. The administration and conduct of schools is supervised by civil servants at the national and local level, aided by Her Majesty's Inspectors (HMI) and by local inspectors, advisers and organizers.

The schools have a tradition of academic freedom. Each school is free to plan its own curriculum and syllabuses (with the exception of religious education)[11] and to choose its own textbooks. Teachers play the key role in British education system. Especially, the headmaster or head-mistress in the British educational system has an importance and a responsibility rarely found in other countries.

British schools are regarded as 'communities' where total responsibility and the development of individual personality are as important as academic achievement. Therefore, the role of schools, teachers, etc. is crucial in a multicultural society, and consequently for multicultural education. Because all aspects and elements of British education should be subject to change, no system and practice, however good, can be expected to stand unchanged for long. The question arises how far the needs of Muslims in Britain, in this context, have been realized and are being met.

Plural Society

The fact that Britain is a multiracial and multicultural society is recognized in the government's 1977 Green Paper, *Education in Schools: A Consultative Document*. It states 'our society is a multicultural and multiracial one and the curriculum should reflect a sympathetic understanding of the different cultures and races that now make up our society ... the curriculum of schools ... must reflect the needs of this new Britain.'[12] In addition, the *Green Paper* emphasized 'we also live in a complex interdependent world, and many of our problems in Britain require international solutions. The curriculum should therefore reflect our need to know about and understand other countries'.[1]

The Rampton Committee Report also stressed:

> A 'good' education should enable a child to understand his own society, and to know enough about other societies to enhance that understanding ... A 'good' education cannot be based on one culture only, and in Britain where ethnic minorities form a permanent and integral part of the population, we do not believe that education should seek to iron out differences between cultures, nor attempt to draw everyone into the dominant culture. On the contrary, it will draw upon the experiences of the many cultures that make up our society and thus broaden the cultural horizons of every child. That is what we mean by 'multicultural' education.[14]

The question arises, what steps are being taken in Britain to make the education 'multicultural'? A document published in March 1981 *The School Curriculum*[15] also referred to the need for the work of schools to reflect the fact that 'our society has become multicultural by encouraging children to develop an understanding and tolerance of cultural and religious diversity'. The Home Affairs Committee also noted that a curriculum suitable for ethnic minorities will have as many hours of mathematics or modern languages as any other curriculum, but it will be flexible enough to allow the continuing English language support teaching and wide enough to ensure that modern languages should not be restricted to European languages, nor religious education to Christianity, nor history to British history, nor music to Western music, nor literature to British literature.[16]

The Swann Report *Education For All* has also stressed the racial and cultural diversity of British society.[17] It points out that an individual's ethnic identity is an important and influential aspect of our society. It rejects 'assimilation' and 'separatism' as unacceptable conceptions and advances an ideal of a pluralist society in which cultural diversity is seen as a source of unity not as a 'problem'. It warns, however, of the 'fragmentation of our society along ethnic lines' unless major efforts are made to reinforce the vision of a pluralist community. The Report makes several recommendations in the education field to make Britain a proper pluralist society.

In a pluralist society ethnic minority groups desire and need to keep their cultural identity (religious practices, distinguishing patterns of family relationships, mother-tongue and other aspects) while adapting to various modes of the dominant culure such as language, educational system, employment patterns and civic life. For them, integration means acceptance by the majority of their separate ethnic and cultural identity.

However, in a dominant group approach, the concepts of 'assimilation', 'absorption' or 'integration' reflect the ideology of the dominant group. Any group which remains unabsorbed, or unassimilated, is usually considered as upsetting the equalisation of social relations in the society. This relates to Muslims in Britain.

What Are the Issues?

Some of the religious activities and demands of Muslims in the field of education are seen by the indigenous community as alien, upsetting the status quo, due to perhaps lack of understanding of Islam as a religion and differences in outlook and behaviour. Some think this behaviour appears as the cause of conflict with indigenous people. Problems relating to Muslims have arisen in terms of worship and burial facilities, in employment, education and habits of hygiene and eating.[18] But here I would like to concentrate on educational issues.

Education can be contrasted with informal aspects of socialization. For example, if family and friends emphasize values that are different from those a child is learning at school, then the child may experience special problems in adapting to life both in school and at home — this is the problem which Muslim children in Britain face at the moment, because they are living between two cultures.[19] Therefore, education should not be isolated from its religious and social settings since it is one of the important influences that determine what a child learns in the schools. Because of this, as we have discovered in one of our studies, greater importance is attached to religious education in schools by the respondents.[20]

In our study over half of the respondents[21] spontaneously mentioned that young Muslims face difficulties because of their religion. Respondents commented on difficulties with food, dietary restrictions, the question of dress, the problems of finding good religious education for children in schools, school curriculum, and the special problems of Muslim girls in the religious context (single sex schools, physical education, sex education, etc.).

When respondents were asked about some of these issues one by one, the picture became clearer. For instance, over two thirds of the respondents thought that it was difficult to find good religious teaching. The difficulty of finding suitably trained religious teachers was also mentioned by a significant majority. These findings are also confirmed by a recent study on this subject.[22]

One place where Islam as a subject could be taught is in state schools. Roughly 80 per cent of both parents and young people agreed that there is not sufficient formal teaching of Islam in English schools. Many Muslims feel that there should be facilities within the school system of religious instruction as a fact that we live in a multi-religious society.[23] One of the worries in this context they seem to have is that if they are not taught Islam in school, children may be influenced by Christianity.

Almost half of the Muslim parents (47 per cent) and 41 per cent of young Muslims in our survey felt that the 'children are influenced by Christianity because they attend assemblies at school with a Christian service'. However, 41 per cent parents and 50 per cent young people disagreed with the statement.

Interestingly, those who felt strongly about this issue said that because of the influences to which Muslim children are exposed (through media, at school etc.) they tend to think more about Christianity than their own religion. Some religious leaders and Muslim parents generally take this issue very seriously and would no doubt like to see facilities for teaching Islam provided in schools. It was also pointed out by some respondents that some schools do teach comparative religions, including Islam. However, it was widely felt that there should be separate teaching for Islam in schools. This clearly raises the question of school policies in this regard and curriculum changes to meet the changing needs of our society.

In the meantime, outside the state education system Islam is being taught after school hours or at weekends by local mosques and Muslim organizations through supplementary schools. The National Muslim Education Council of the United Kingdom (formally set up in 1978 by the Union of Muslim Organization in the UK and Eire (UMO) the Islamic Cultural Centre (London), the Islamic Education and Research Centre, the Muslim Education Trust (founded in 1964), the UK Islamic Mission, the Islamic Foundation in Leicester and other organizations encourage and help local Muslim organizations to set up Muslim supplementary schools teaching Islamic religion, culture, civilisation and in some cases mother tongues.

The National Muslim Education Council was trying to coordinate all Islamic educational activities in Britain and in particular to set up Muslim single-sex schools in areas with large Muslim communities. In 1976 the UMO published a guide to Muslim education, *Guidelines and Syllabus on Islamic Education*[24] which discusses the teaching of

Islam to children at primary, secondary and advanced level. Some books for children are also being published. The Muslim Education Trust produces books for teaching purposes and supplies teachers who take classes about Islam in state schools, mosques and other premises outside schools hours.

The UK Islamic Mission, with its branches throughout the country, is also concerned with teaching Islam to both children and adults. It also deals with other religious, welfare and cultural activities. The Islamic Foundation produces publications for school children and adults and undertakes general educational work to spread Islam. A complete and comprehensive list of activities of Muslim organizations up and down Britain or for that matter, of their educational activities, would be an impossible job. While community initiatives in this regard are important to fill the gap, what I would like to come back to is what action is being taken by the education authorities regarding religious education and other related cultural aspects.

It appears that some education authorities now recognize the special needs that arise from different cultural and religious backgrounds of Muslims and other religious and ethnic groups in these areas. A survey by the Schools Council of local education authorities (seventy responded by questionnaire, seventeen by letter and seven by personal interviews) and 188 headteachers and a few hundred heads of departments from 'high' and 'medium' concentration of pupils from ethnic minority groups confirmed that: 'Aspects of special arrangements which are causing some difficulties when Townsend and Britten reported — such as those for religious education and school worship, school meals, school dress, physical education — are not now generally seen as problem areas.'[25] Local education authorities reported that they had given formal or informal advice to schools which were now well aware of the issues, and replies from headteachers largely confirmed this. But what action is being taken by schools remains to be seen, particularly about the issue of religious education. Since we know that not many schools have made any basic changes in their curriculum, school timetables or taken action for the recruitment of such teachers, or, in-service training of existing teachers to materialize such an awareness.

It is worth mentioning here that the National Association for Multi-Racial Education (NAME) whose aims include the encouragement of the efforts of members working in multiracial schools and the development of the curriculum to reflect the multiracial character of society, has been pressing for such a change.

No doubt, the content of religious education and religious

education syllabuses have been revised in some areas after discussions between local authorities, schools and representatives of Muslims. But a lot more needs to be done in this area of concern to meet Muslim parents' wishes.

The Swann Committee identified three approaches to religious education:

1 The confessional ie the traditional notion of 'religious instruction' into a particular faith to the exclusion of other faiths which are often presumed to be inferior.
2 The anti-dogmatic ie the comparative and 'objective' study of world religions usually within an historical or social science framework.
3 The phenomenological ie the understanding of religious faith and experience. Though it does not attempt to promote any particular faith, it does aim to go beyond mere description and engage the subjective elements of religion.

The Committee found the phenomenological, multifaith approach as the one which conforms to the philosophy of 'Education for All'. However, the Committee recognizes that this approach would not be acceptable to those sections of the community who see religious education in schools as more confessional or instructional. In its comments on the Committee Report the Commission for Racial Equality (CRE) said, that it is disappointing that, in the preparation of agreed syllabuses, LEAs have not used their powers under Schedule 5 of the 1944 Act to involve minority faith communities of 'such religious denominations as in the opinion of the authority ought, having agreed to the circumstances of the area, to be presented'. The Commission agreed with the Committee's concern about the complexities and confusions surrounding the religious clauses of the 1944 Act and that some of its provisions would appear to be redundant in a multicultural society.[26]

In addition to the evidence which was submitted to the Swann Committee by the Muslim community, various responses have been made to the Committee's Report.[27] Muslims generally feel that facilities for religious education should be provided and need to become part of an agreed syllabus. This is an area in which a lot of Muslim parents remain worried and dissatisfied as shown in the survey findings referred to above.

Under the Education Act 1980, the government attached great importance to meeting parents' wishes about the way they want their children to be educated.[28] For instance, many Muslim parents wish their children to go to single-sex schools at the secondary stage as the mixing of boys and girls in adolescence does not accord with Islamic beliefs.[29] The Act provides a basis for Muslim parents seeking admission for their children to a single-sex school and we hope it will make it easier for parents, where there are no such schools, to apply to schools in neighbouring authority areas. But we also know that such schools are disappearing fast. So what are the alternatives in this connection? It is worth mentioning here that apart from Muslim parents, many indigenous parents and parents from other ethnic minority groups would like to send their children to single-sex schools as well.

The Swann Committee recommended, 'where there is parental concern about the education of girls, existing co-educational schools with multiracial pupil populations could do more to ensure that in certain specific areas separate provision is offered on a single sex basis as appropriate in the schools activities' (p. 773). It added, 'we hope that LEAs with multiracial pupil populations will consider carefully the value of retaining an option of single sex education as part of their secondary school provision and that the Secretary of State will also be sensitive to the wider ramifications of any decisions he may make on proposals which lead to loss of single sex provision in multi-racial areas. In cases where an LEA either no longer provides for single sex education at all, or make only limited provision, we hope that the possibility of establishing or re-establishing single sex schools will be given serious consideration' (p. 773). This recommendation is in line with the demands of the Muslim community.

A Muslim Charter of Demands issued by several national and regional Muslim organizations at the time of the recent General Election also included, continuance of single-sex schools for both boys and girls as part of the state school system'.[30]

One other relevant area is the teaching of mother tongue and of culture of the country of origin to ethnic minority children, including Muslims. An EEC Directive on the Education of the Children of Migrant Workers was adopted in July 1977. It came into force on 25 July 1981.[31] Before this, the Bullock Report recommended that positive action shound be taken regarding bilingualism.[32] In spite of this Directive and these recommendations, and pressure from the CRE, Coordinating Committee on Mother Tongue Teaching, and ethnic minority groups, not enough progress is made on this front. However, it would be relevant to divide this issue into three:

(a) the teaching of ethnic minority group's first language in the State schools;

(b) support for such languages outside the state schools; and

(c) teaching other subjects in these languages.

Teaching of other subjects in ethnic minority groups' mother tongues is clearly a controversial area and the Schools Council survey (mentioned above) shows little support among the majority of authorities. 'There is considered to be no real educational need and no apparent demand from ethnic minority communities and because there are other more pressing priorities.'

As far as teaching of the languages of ethnic minority groups in schools is concerned, there seems to be little progress. The Schools Council survey showed that there were only fourteen authorities who expressed support for teaching these languages, but also pointed out the practical difficulties which usually limit the number of schools involved and the languages which can be offered. The Commission for Racial Equality's national survey of local authorities on this subject showed a qualified support for mother tongue teaching generally, but there seemed to be reluctance to provide this facility in schools.[33]

However, it appears that a significant number of authorities support mother tongue teaching organized out of schools by the ethnic minority groups. In the Schools Council's survey, forty authorities reported a wide variety of languages being taught out of school, organized by the ethnic minorities. Twenty-eight of these authorities said that they gave support usually in the form of providing free accommodation. A small number of authorities reported giving other forms of financial assistance for part-time instructors, coordinators, and small grants for equipment, tools and materials[34] Is this enough?

Similarly, other evidence shows that the voluntary provision, mostly unaided from the State, is playing a crucial role as far as the issue of mother tongue teaching is concerned. The Home Affairs Committee Report also acknowledged this fact. In this regard, the Committee indicated that the work of the voluntary classes should be integrated into the normal school curriculum. This suggestion is worth welcoming. But it seems that there will always be a role for voluntary self-help in this field. In particular, for Muslims, as they would possibly like to keep the Quranic teaching in the community as part of mosques and religious organizations' activities. Moreover, until the state system can begin to make adequate provisions acceptable to the community, the role of voluntary sectors is crucial to fill the gap.

The NAME statement points out that 'practical measures to enable these languages to take their rightful place in the British education system have been quite inadequate'.[35] The Association makes eleven suggestions which it considers should be taken up without delay throughout the state education system. The CRE made several recommendations to the DES, to local authorities, to examination and validating boards, to teaching unions and to the TUC and CBI in its policy statement on the subject. In general, it recommends that in the interest of good race relations and equality of opportunity in education, all languages, whether mother tongue or languages of the ethnic minorities, should be taught in response to demand, through a planned programme of development.[36]

In this context the principle of funding mother tongue teaching should not be discretionary but obligatory, otherwise just goodwill of LEAs might result in little progress in this field. Also appropriate teacher training and recruitment for both religious teaching and mother tongue teaching are prerequisites in achieving these goals. The possibility of using section 11 of the Local Government Act 1966 to appoint religious and mother tongue teachers, should be explored. The question is usually realized, where do we get such teachers? In Britain there are already a large number of teachers working in schools from the same religious and language groups as the ethnic minority communities. There are other overseas trained teachers who can be recruited and trained to meet the demand. In this connection, the DES will need to look at its qualification demands. Because I feel that the fundamental task of public services, such as education, is to meet the needs of its population and as Muslims and other ethnic minorities are part and parcel of this population, then their needs should be met. To plead poverty is to say that past practices and expenditure take precedence over current needs.

The national debate on school curriculum is relevant here. In January 1980 a consultative document issued from the DES and Welsh office *A Framework for the School Curriculum* called for special consideration to be given to the curricular needs of ethnic minorities, but without outlining those needs and ways and means of meeting those needs.[37] However, the Schools Council's survey shows that considerable work on the appropriate nature of curriculum development in multiracial schools has taken place. 'Emphasis has also shifted from the insertion of additions, such as 'black studies' into an established curriculum, to the notion that an awareness of Britain's multiethnic society should permeate the curriculum as a whole, and that this will to a greater or lesser extent have relevance to most subjects taught at secondary level'.[38] The obvious need is to consider primary level education in this light as well.

To make the curriculum realistic, to reflect the multiracial, multicultural and multireligious society, certain support for teachers, support for work to develop new materials and teaching approaches in the various subject areas, specialist advice, in-service training and training of new teachers would be required. I feel that the Muslim community in Britain could play an important role at all levels in terms of providing help and giving advice. In this connection, contacts with and involvement of Muslim organizations need to be developed on a more formal and informal basis rather than on an *ad hoc* basis as it is at present.

The role of organization of multiethnic or multiracial education services within local education authorities is also important. It is not only based on language teams seconded to secondary schools but also they are taking additional responsibilities. Similarly, the role of advisers for multiethic education appointed by LEAs is changing. But there are authorities without such advisers which means that there is inadequate emphasis for developing policies and provision regarding multiethnic education, in those areas. Not to appoint such advisers in relevant LEAs is not justified anymore.

At the same time some authorities at least recognize this critical period of change and development of education for a multicultural society, In its report *Multi-Ethnic Education — Progress Report*, the ILEA stated four objectives:

(a) to prepare all pupils and students to live and work harmoniously and with equality of opportunity in that society;

(b) to build upon the strengths of cultural diversity in that society;

(c) to define and control racism and the discriminatory practices to which it gives rise; and

(d) to meet appropriately and effectively the particular needs of all people, having regard to their ethnic, cultural, linguistic or historical attachment.[39]

The last objective among others raises the question of books and teaching materials used in the school. What is being taught in schools is important. Concern is often expressed by the Muslim community in Britain (and others) about the presentation of a negative picture of their religion, culture and history. This does have a damaging effect on a Muslim child in the school and inaccurate information about Islamic beliefs, values and culture is provided. Such an approach without doubt, reinforces myths, helps prejudice and could lead often to misunderstandings and sometimes to discrimination. Therefore, some offensive books to Muslims (and other ethnic minority groups) need to be replaced immediately and teachers also need to review the books and materials they use, to take account of their appropriateness to Britain today.

In this connection, a number of organizations are helping teachers to detect any cultural bias in the materials they use, The Muslim community also does this on an *ad hoc* basis which requires much more effort and organisation. But the NUT's guidelines *In Black and White — Guidelines for Teachers on racial stereotyping in Texbooks and learning Materials* are worth following.[40]

I feel that in spite of these guidelines and efforts by many in the field of education, Muslims in Britain themselves have to be vigilant and examine critically the textbooks and teaching materials used in British schools. They should point out to LEAs, advisory services, headteachers, etc. books which display any negative religious and cultural bias. In addition they need to cooperate with those who are looking at stereotyping in textbooks and learning materials.

There is also a general shortage of teaching materials which reflect the diversity of religions and cultures present in our society today. Some effort is being made by the Muslim organizations to provide material about Islam, but a lot more needs to be done in this field.[41]

Other educational issues such as 'examinations' and career advice are also equally relevant to the Muslim community in Britain, like other ethnic minority groups. But the links between schools and the community are crucial. Because the education of children is a partnership between parents and teachers. The home-school link is particularly important when some Muslim parents are new in this country and probably not very familar with the education system.

The language barrier may discourage many Muslim parents from making contact with their children's teachers or their night-shift work or need to work long hours for relatively low levels of pay many restrict them from attending parent-teachers associations (PTAs) or parents' evenings generally. It is worth stressing here that in the British education system parents and teachers are supposed to work together. Many Muslim parents, it appears, have yet to realize this. And many schools have yet to make efforts to this end.

It is equally important that, as the Home Affairs Committee stated the formal structures associated with schools and particularly the governing body, should reflect the community it srves'.[42] If this suggestion is accepted, many members of the Muslim community should be present on school governing bodies. This is in line with the Taylor Report *A New Partnership for our Schools* on the need for parental and community representation on governing bodies.[43] More representation of Muslims at schools and other educational institutions' overall policies, including its curriculum, and to reflect the presence of Muslims and other religio-cultural groups in our society.

Generally, schools need to foster links between the school and the community they serve. Education Act 1980 deals with parents' choice in their children's education. These links surely would help this process. The appointment of home-school liaison officers might help to strengthen this process of greater involvement of parents or as the Rampton Committee recommended: 'All schools, but particularly multiracial schools, should designate a senior member of staff to be responsible for the coordination of links between the school and the community it serves.'[44] At the same time, schools should make contact with supplementary schools being run by Muslims and other ethnic minority groups in their areas, because links between these schools and teachers is important to understand and perhaps appreciate what children learn outside mainstream school.

There is also the overall question of support for supplementary schools, be they mother tongue schools or religious teaching schools. As these provisions are not yet properly provided within the school system, the LEAs should look at application for assistance for accommodation and/or finance to appoint teachers favourably because they are providing a service which the education system ought to be providing. It is for this and other reasons that Muslims are trying to establish their own schools. There are now eleven Muslim schools.

The role of teachers in British schools is very important. Therefore, the way teachers are trained to meet the needs of ethnic minority pupils and in developing a multicultural approach to their work is crucial too. In this regard, initial induction training and in-service training are all relevant. For instance, those already in-service need to learn to cope with their Muslim and other ethnic minority children. They also need to prepare other children to live in a multi-ethnic society. This raises the question of the overall revision of teacher education, probably on the lines as NATFHE's evidence to the Rampton Committee:

> Teacher education, embracing as it does initial training, induction and later in-service studies, is an indivisible process. All colleges, no matter where they may be situated, can play their full part with teachers, professional tutors, advisers and institutes of education to develop a wide range of multicultual studies, both full-time and part-time. Unless studies are updated to meet the emergence of a society which contains not only the seeds of racial disharmony but also the potential for immense cultural and human enrichment they will become increasingly irrelevant and anachronistic. Far too many teachers and lecturers are under-prepared to cope with the changes needed.[45]

I fully agree with this statement and feel that all teachers should have some experience in a multiethnic classroom as part of their initial and in-service training.

We need to seek support for such an approach. Because in this context the teachers' attitudes both to develop positive policies to cultural diversity and to consider the implications of a multiethnic society for their teaching, are important to bring about required changes.

We have established so far that Muslims have different and special needs related to education, for example, teaching of mother tongue, religion, history and culture, aimed at maintaining or providing religious and ethnic identity and culture. They have roughly the same education objective — basic skills and knowledge with the appropriate formal qualifications — as that for all children in Britain.

But to assess the educational needs and achievements of Muslim children a system of monitoring would be essential and helpful. Such a system would also be helpful for LEAs in allocating resources and planning to meet special needs of schools with Muslim children, because, this is the only way to help assess the special needs and to do something about them. Absolute accuracy is not necessary since such monitoring should be concerned with groups of pupils to look at patterns rather than the situation of individual pupils.

The Rampton Committee recommended that ethnically based statistics should be kept. It states:

> Ethnically based statistics can, we believe, be of value at all levels and to all parties within education, to central

government, in determining policy, to LEAs in quantifying and locating particular needs, to schools so that they can take full account of the cultural and linguistic background of pupils and see whether any groups are under-achieving or are disproportionately represented in any subject or class and to make an appropriate response, and to parents so that they can assess their child's performance in relation to his/her peers. We are therefore wholly in favour of the collection of educational statistics on an ethnic basis where they are to be used in establishing facts about how members of the ethnic minorities are faring in the educational system.[46]

The Committee goes on to outline the different types of information which should be collected.

The Secretary of State for Education and Science set up the Working Group on the Collection of Educational Statistics in October 1983 which reported to him in April 1986. The Group recommended that 'the Secretary of State take steps to encourage all LEAs to institute schemes for the local collection of ethnically based statistics as soon as possible'. This recommendation was accepted by the Secretary of State and steps are being taken to implement it.[47]

Among other categories the group recommended that LEAs be advised to collect data on pupil's religious affiliations. This information should help LEAs in planning the school meals service and among others in considering the balance between single sex and mixed schools.

Conclusions

The shift from assumptions of assimilation to acceptance of cultural diversity in Britain has developed slowly in the recognition of the presence of ethnic minorities and an awareness of its implications for the education system as a whole. The 1977 *Green Paper* (referred to above) emphasized the importance of all schools giving their pupils an understanding both of the multiethnic nature of British society and of Britain's place in an interdependent world. There seems to be widespread acceptance in multiracial areas of the need to meet the special needs of minority groups but not enough action is being taken across the board. However, in terms of actual provision regarding special needs this still is, in practice, largely restricted to meeting the basic language requirements of English as a second language. There has been little allocation or redirection of resources to identify and meet special educational needs of ethnic minority children, including Muslims.

In other areas, where there are fewer or no ethnic minorities generally, no plans have come to light to prepare all children to live in a multiethnic society. At the same time, teachers are not being fully equipped to perform effectively in a multicultural society.

Generally the involvement of Muslims and other ethnic minorities in the political process, recently, has helped to highlight the relevant issues in education.[48] *The Muslims Charter of Demands* referred to above is one such example. However, 'the evidence of marginalisation, of educational and social disaster gives substance to demands that the processes and structures of educational institutions should be opened as a matter of urgency. The reality of differentiation, evident on a local level as well as on a wider community level, demands an educational response on the structural level'.[49]

The genuine demands of the Muslim community in this context have not been taken on board by the relevant authorities in education. For example, the curriculum and examinations system have not taken into account sufficiently the nature of British society today. Certainly, the educational needs of the Muslim community and Muslim children have not yet been recognized in an acceptable manner.

Religious education and mother tongues are an integral part of both religion and culture. For the education system to carry out its responsibility in what is now recognized as a plural society, the religion and the languages of Muslims (and other ethnic minority groups) should not be left to an inadequate recognition and support as is the case at present. For example, their languages should be included as part of the 'modern languages' in the school curriculum.

Finally, the politicians both national and local, the DES, HM Inspectorate, LEAs, the Schools Council, teachers' unions, examination boards, teacher training institutions, school governors, headteachers and teachers generally, all need to realize and recognize that Muslims in Britain are now an integral part of the society and, therefore, their educational needs can no longer be ignored. All these relevant bodies need to face this reality of multiracial and multicultural society. The involvement of Muslims at all levels to bring about change and modifications in the educational system to accommodate the genuine wishes of the Muslim community, therefore, should be a top priority of all concerned now and in the future.

Notes

1 Muslims are also the largest minority religious group in the whole of Western Europe as their number is estimated to be over 5 million for this region.
2 Pakistan left the Commonwealth in 1973 but figures about Pakistanis are always added to the New Commonwealth category.
3 For further details of these processes see ANWAR M. (1979) *The Myth of Return: Pakistanis in Britain*, London, Heinemann, chapters 2.4 and 5.
4 Several research reports, government White Paper and Commission for Racial Equality's annual reports and Select Committee reports have highlighted the racial disadvantage and racial discrimination faced by ethnic minorities. One such report is: (1981) *Racial Disadvantage*, VOP1 HC 424–1, HMSO, London.
5 For estimates see COI fact sheet *Some Aspects of Islam in Britain*(1981).
6 See ANWAR, M. (1981) *Between Two Cultures*, (3rd end) London, Commission for Racial Equality.
7 See *Education Act 1944*: there are other Education Acts, namely 1946, 1948 1952, 1962, 1964, 1967, 1980.
8 As from 1972–73.
9 At present 94 per cent of parents send their children to state schools.
10 Through the Department of Education and Science (DES). The DES is concerned with basic educational standards, but does not exercise control over the content of education or over teaching methods.
11 Religious education and collective worship is compulsory in all schools, although no teacher is compelled to give religious instruction. Similarly parents can withdraw their children from religious education and school worship, of they so wish.
12 DEPARTMENT OF EDUCATION AND SCIENCE (1977) *Education is Schools: A consultative Document*, Cmnd 6869, London, HMSO, para 10, 11.
13 *ibid.*
14 DEPARTMENT OF EDUCATION AND SCIENCE (1981) *West Indian Children in Our Schools, (The Rampton Report)* Cmnd 8273, London HMSO, pp. 26–7.
15 DEPARTMENT OF EDUCATION AND SCIENCE (1981) *The School Curriculum*, London, HMSO, paras 21, 27, 36, Q625–6.
16 *Racial Disadvantage*, fifth report from the Home Affairs Committee, 1. HC 424–1, London, HMSO, 1981, para 155.
17 DEPARTMENT OF EDUCATION AND SCIENCE (1985) *Education For All* (The Swann Report) London, HMSO.
18 Muslims also face disadvantage in the job market, housing, and good facilities fields like the other ethnic minority groups.
19 For details see ANWAR, M. (1981) *op cit.*
20 *ibid.*
21 There were 784 respondents in all — 358 parents and 426 young people (19–21) in a nationwide sample of Muslims.
22 Survey of young people to be published by the CRE later in the year.
23 It is worth mentioning here that religious education is the only compulsory subject in schools under the Education Act 1944.

24 UMO (1976) *Guidelines and Syllabus on Islamic Education*, London, UMO.

25 See LITTLE, A. WILLEY, R. (1981) *Multi-Ethnic Education: The Way Forward*, Schools Council Pamphlet 18, London, Evans/Methuen, p. 25. For TOWNSEND and BRITTON reports see *Immigrant Pupils in England: The LEA Response*, NFER, and *Organisation in multi-Racial Schools*, NFER, (1972).

26 Commission for RACIAL EQUALITY (1985) *SWANN: A Response from the Commission for Racial Equality*, London, CRE.

27 For example, see THE COUNCIL OF MOSQUES OF UK AND EIRE (1986) *The Muslims and Swann*, London; and ISLAMIC ACADEMY (1985) *The Swann Committee Report: An Evaluation from the Muslim Point of View*, Cambridge, Islamic Academy.

28 *Education Act, 1980, 1981*.

29 IQBAL, M. (1976) *Islamic Education and Single-Sex Schools*, London, UMO.

30 'Muslims charter of demands', *Impact International*, 22 May–11 June 1987.

31 Council of the European Community Directive, 25 July 1977 *(77/486/ EEC)*.

32 DEPARTMENT OF EDUCATION AND SCIENCE (1975), *A Language for Life*, (The Bullock Report) London, HMSO, para 20–17.

33 See CRE *National Survey of LEAs on Mother Tongue Teaching*, final report.

34 LITTLE, A. and WILLEY, R. (1981) *op cit* p. 19.

35 NAME (1981) *Mother Tongue and Minority Community Languages in Education*, London, NAME. Also see Centre for Information on Language Teaching (CILT) reports.

36 See CRE *Mother Tongue Issue in Britain: A Policy Statement*.

37 DEPARTMENT OF EDUCATION AND SCIENCE (1981), *A Framework for the School Curriculum*, London, HMSO.

38 LITTLE, A. and Willey, R. (1981) op cit.

39 *ILEA, Multi-Ethnic Education — Progress Report*, June 1979.

40 NVT *In Black and White — Guidelines for Teachers on Racial Stereotyping in Text Books and Learning Materials*.

41 For example, the aims and objectives of the Islamic Education and Research Centre include 'to prepare syllabi, courses and textbooks and to publish textbooks, children's literature...'. The National Muslim Education Council also aims to commission learned Muslim educationists to write books about Islam. A series has already started which includes: ASHRAF, S. A. (1980) *The Prophets*, London, Hodder and Stoughton and UMO;. and IQBAL, M. (1980) *Call from Minaret* London, Hodder and Stoughton and UMO.

42 *Racial Disadvantage*, para 148.

43 DEPARTMENT OF EDUCATION AND SCIENCE (1977), *A new Partnership for our Schools*, (The Taylor Report) London, HMSO.

44 DES (1981) *op cit,* p. 45.

45 *ibid*, p. 60.

46 *ibid*.

47 DEPARTMENT OF EDUCATION AND SCIENCE (1986) *Working Group on the Collection of Educational Statistics on An Ethnic Basis: Report*, London, HMSO.

48 ANWAR M (1986) *Race and Politics*, London, Tavistock.

49 O'KEEFFE B, (1988) 'On the margins of education: Finding a dimension for belief' in GREEN, T. and BALL, J. (Eds.) *Inequality and Progress in Comprehensive Education; A Reconsideration for the 1980s*, London, Croom Helm.

6 Children at School: A Worshipping Community?

Brenda Watson

Many people today may regard even asking such a question as indicative of an obsolete approach to schooling. Bernadette O'Keeffe's research revealed that

> in the majority of county schools collective worship is seen as an inappropriate activity because both pupils and staff encompass a wide range of religious beliefs and secular views.[1]

The situation is different with regard to church schools, the majority of which, both primary and secondary, regard school worship

> as a collective act of worship and central feature in the life of the school ... The majority of schools teach distinctive beliefs and practices and they are frequently involved in liturgical activity as a worshipping community.

A number of church schools are however, aware that some serious problems are posed. One headteacher with a very high percentage of Muslim and Hindu pupils was reported as saying

> We are floundering. We find ourselves in a new situation and do not know how to react. In the meantime the school continues to hold collective worship with all pupils participating.[2]

To these quotations I would like to add one more addressed by an 'anxious parent' to the editor of the *Times Educational Supplement*

> At my five-year-old daughter's maintained primary school, they hold daily assemblies in which it is assumed, without argument, that God exists and that He is benevolent (my daughter sings 'I'm very glad of God. His love takes care of me').
>   ... These assemblies take place every day. Can you advise me what to do about this indoctrination ...?[3]

The question of school worship is clearly a highly controversial matter. Can even church schools be said to exist for the purpose of worship, so that they are an extension of the activity of the religious community which founded them? Was the 1944 Education Act totally misplaced in its vision of all schools, church and county, being in some sense worshipping communities? It is the purpose of this chapter to offer some guidelines for constructing a thoroughly educational rationale for the possibility of worship happening in all schools.[4]

Discussion needs to begin, I believe, not with reference to the historical background, nor with general principles, but by considering the needs of the actual pupils for whom the school exists. This is a far wider issue than that posed by the diversity of home-backgrounds represented in a school. It relates to the educational task *per se* of helping *every* child in the school, whatever his or her parents' religious or non-religious commitment, to gain sufficient understanding of religion to be able eventually to make his or her own personal authentic response.

In this respect the distinction between church and county school is strictly irrelevant because there are two requirements which apply to all children. Firstly, children in both types of schools should be introduced to the dimension of worship or meditation which in all the major religions is central to faith. Secondly, children attending both church and county schools constitute a captive audience and this has important implications for what is done and how it is done.

The Need to Educate the Child into Awareness of Nature of Worship

Pupils may be regarded as educationally deprived who are not given the chance of a significant encounter with worship. This cannot be done in any meaningful way without the opportunity to participate in it. Classroom descriptions of what goes on in worship, the occasional visit to a place of worship, and culturally-based or historically-based studies of how people believe and behave within different religious groupings are no substitute for the opportunity actually to experience worship in a way which personally makes sense. Pupils need to be given the chance to take part in such worship.

The fundamental reason for insisting on this lies in the nature of worship itself which eludes plain description. External rituals and symbols can indeed be successfully described, but this may serve to obscure rather than aid understanding of what is at the heart of worship. Knowledge of outward forms may promote only a very superficial encounter. See below for further discussion of what worship involves.

The Need to Respect the Integrity of the Child

The opportunity for a significant participatory encounter with worship must be given in such a way that it respects the integrity of the child. It is an easily-forgotten truism that children are obliged to attend school: no-one asks them whether they wish to go to school or not. This fact implies the need for a certain reticence with regard to the school's promulgation of any dogmatic stance whatever, whether religious or secular. It *is* inadmissible to assume that all pupils do agree or should agree with belief-positions which are controversial.

To hold collective worship in order to offer the day to God is appropriate on behalf of those who believe there is a God, but is an act of hypocrisy or is meaningless to those who lack such a genuine conviction. The fact that a child's parents may have such faith-commitment does not alter the fact that the child may not have, and perhaps is increasingly likely not to have, as the child approaches adolescence, because of a desire to rethink or even rebel against parental attitudes.

The school, therefore, should not aspire to being a mini-church, synagogue, mosque, gurdwara or temple. Historically the missionary or confessional impulse was effective in the setting-up of schools and the way they were run; many church schools still do regard themselves as expected to do the work of the church in either its evangelical or its witnessing capacities. Yet this emphasis is mistaken in that it takes advantage of the immaturity of children in order to impress particular ideas upon them. The autonomy of the child needs to be protected.

Some readers may be inclined however to argue that the autonomy of the child is a mistaken concept and does not contain any relevant insight. I will therefore discuss some possible objections.

The View that Nurture is what Matters

One line of reasoning may focus on the way that children are part of society: the individual as such does not, and cannot, exist, and religion in particular is concerned with nurturing children into their roles within the community. Children must not be given freedom but direction; it is not for them to learn to choose and be self-reflecting, but to play the part which society expects of them. If they are given freedom they may opt out of their responsibilities to society.

It must be conceded that such a view may be opposed at a fundamental level to the concept of education as it has developed in this country over recent decades. In the spirit however of this book which seeks to build bridges rather than walls, let us see whether there is not a way of stating belief in the autonomy of the child which is complementary to the insight contained in the 'nurture' approach.[5]

Looked at from the point of view of the educationalist the autonomy of the child ought not to be put forward as the only or as even the main purpose of educating; it must be balanced at least with that of responsibility. Society can only remain civilized if certain elementary levels of courtesy and consideration for others are observed by all. If the autonomous child or adult chooses to adhere to these necessary norms, all is well, but if not, society has to intervene, and with regard to the young it can only at its peril neglect the task of helping to pass on to the younger generations respect for such norms. The search for shared values, which is currently becoming more marked in schools, acknowledges the importance of this task.

Looked at from the point of view of parents and teachers who are sincerely religious, nurture is properly important in sharing with the child what is most meaningful to them, and what they consider to be the source of the values upon which civilized life is in any case based. Such nurture is not only unavoidable but also desirable.

Nurture must however be broadened out into education which acknowledges the uniqueness and autonomy of the child. This is not just because it may harm the child's development as a person if it does not. It is also, for the genuine religious person, because real faith cannot be simply handed on to another 'on a plate' as it were: there must be a personal, willed, free response for the tradition to be handed on in a living form.

This, however, may raise another question.

Is not Worship a Communal Activity not an Individual One?

To this one may reply that religion delights in the paradoxical; it is both communal and individual. A. N. Whitehead once remarked that religion is what a man does with his solitude, whilst John Wesley could say that there is no such thing as solitary religion. May it not be the case that both are correct? A true intention of the heart is an individual's responsibility, but the individual can be encouraged or discouraged from reaching that level of maturity by the community of which he or she is a member. Furthermore, such an intention, if genuine, is directed to the one who is responsible for and contains all. The true worshipping community consists not of those who have not psychologically nor spiritually risen to the level of being individualized persons but of those who, by accepting responsibility as individuals, have chosen to relate to God and to all others in and through God and no longer remain solitary.

Such a view of worship may raise yet another difficulty with regard to stressing the integrity of the child.

Are Children Capable of Independent Reflectiveness?

Most children are, so it may be said, incapable of such reflectiveness and self-responsibility consitituting a true intention of heart. Often it is urged that many or most adults are too, for they are not sufficiently well endowed intellectually or psychologically to be able to do other than what the majority in their particular circles do.

There is much evidence to suggest that children's capacities for worship and understanding have been seriously underrated. The greater simplicity of young children means that they are often more open to experiences of awe and wonder than adults, as the examples recorded in the Religious Experience Research Unit suggest.[6] Furthermore, the view that children's cognitive development takes place at a necessarily slow pace severely restricting any theological understanding and making apparent worship just an emotional matter has recently been challenged by educational psychologists themselves.[7]

It is indeed much to be regretted that so little education in religious concepts is attempted with young children, thus retarding their development religiously as well as intellectually. Genuine worship requires that people understand what they are doing.

The absence of the necessary degree of cognitive maturity for worship in the young may reflect not so much individual incapacity as the failure of society, of parents and of schools, precisely to educate. Have young children been helped forward in their thinking? Have their comments and their questions been taken seriously by the adults in their environment? Have avenues been opened up for them to explore? Have they been given sufficient space to reflect, and taught

Brenda Watson

sufficient skills to help them to do so wisely? Before we assume that children are incapable of genuine worship such questions need to be pondered over long and carefully.

Omission May Be Indoctrinatory in its Effect

This brings us back to the first need of the child which must be considered, namely, the importance of education into awareness of what worship is, so that the child may be able to make an authentic response on the basis not of ignorance or naivety, but of some knowledge and understanding. It is pertinent to note that failure to introduce pupils to regular opportunities for worship may in our society constitute a serious form of indoctrination in itself. This is because education takes place in the wide contact of prevalent beliefs and attitudes and in the West these tend to be those of a materialistic, consumerist society. Underlying such a society are attitudes which tend to mistrust religious commitment of any kind as not being scientifically provable; religion is therefore frequently dismissed as far as possible to the periphery of life as a purely personal or private matter. Such dogmatic secularism is so widespread that children growing up in the West are in danger of being conditioned into it. The disquiet which many immigrant families feel at the way in which education is conducted, including religious education, reflects their appreciation of this threat. For many of them, this is far greater a menace than the possibility of Christian indoctrination.

The abandonment of school worship in many county schools or by staff who hold agnostic or atheist beliefs is not therefore the straightforward solution which it appears to be. It may be a case of jumping from the frying pan of attempted religious indoctrination into the fire of actual secularist conditioning. Mr. Ghulam Sarmwar, Director of the Muslim Education Trust, for example, noted that the BBC's recent 'squeezing out' of worship from the forty-year-old weekly Thursday tradition of relaying a Christian service to primary schools is 'disturbing'. He added:

> Teachers try more and more to please minority faiths by diluting the subject of religion. It never works, you end up with a subject that has no religious element at all and the children are led nowhere.[8]

Perhaps, therefore, the concept of the school as a worshipping community should be reconsidered to see if there is a sense in which it can be educationally meaningful and desirable.

Redefinition of Worship?

It is interesting to reflect that one possibility frequently discussed in connection with school worship is virtually pre-empted by the phrase 'worshipping community'. This is the idea of redefining worship to mean acknowledging or celebrating something of worth or value, on the grounds that this interpretation is wide enough to embrace people of almost every shade of belief, religious or not. According to this need, the school assembly can accomplish what was the real purpose behind the provision for it in the 1944 Education Act, namely, to help to create a community mindful of those fundamental values upon which the school is based. As a means of giving flexibility to respond to change this re-definition of 'worship', drawing upon the ancient derivative of the word,[9] has played a valuable role.

One can in ironic mood, observe that in this sense schools are already 'worshipping communities'. They honour and do obeisance at a number of shrines, some erected to materialism, competitiveness, individualism and so forth, and others, at least in theory if not in practice, to such values as justice, tolerance, openness, celebration of diversity, kindliness and good neighbourliness.

Yet this is metaphorical language derived from the primary meaning of 'worship' which is to do with acknowledging deity in an appropriate manner. The worshipper takes for granted that there is some spiritual reality to be accorded honour or with whom to seek communion in humility and awe. The phrase 'worshipping community' needs to be understood in this sense to do justice to how the word is properly used by religious people, and renounced by those who do not wish to be associated with religion. It is hardly helping children to understand religion to confuse them by such radical redefinition.

Voluntary Assemblies

Another way needs to be found. Is it possible to speak of the school as a worshipping community if it provides a timetabled structure for voluntary assemblies according to the different faith commitments from which children come? This, however, has a number of difficulties.

(i) Even if the assemblies take place concurrently, this approach to the worship question tends to fragment 'community'. Worship is usually regarded by religious people as the highest development of community spirit. Yet separate assemblies can easily reinforce divisions and an absence of community. There need also to be occasions when all come together not just to celebrate basic human values, but also to express in some form the impulse to worship which is at the heart of the religious activities which distinguish religious people from each other.

(ii) More serious perhaps is the likelihood of imprisoning or stereotyping individuals in the belief pattern of their home backgrounds. This offends the educational concern to develop the potential of each person releasing people from forms of conditioning and indoctrination of whatever source. Even when a child does not come from a definite faith background and therefore is able to make a choice for him or herself he or she is unlikely to be really free to choose to attend a worship assembly because of pressures of peers and society and the fear of being dubbed, for example, as belonging to the 'God-squad'.

(iii) The holding of voluntary or separate assemblies tends to reinforce in a subtle and unacknowledged way a relativist assumption about religion, namely that religion is to do with culture and how different people happen to think. The content of faith does not need to be considered by anyone else because it is assumed that 'no one can know anyway about such matters, it is simply this opinion against that opinion'. Unless such separate assemblies are balanced by other assemblies which permit children of whatever background to take part in worship in order to try to find out about the truth or otherwise of religion Bernadette O'Keeffe's observation stands:

By their omission, school assemblies which can find no time for ritual or give expression to the sacred or transcendent manifest an ethic which places a low value on the collective spiritual or religious dimension to life.[10]

The voluntary opportunity approach is educationally insufficient and therefore we have to come back to the question again: in what sense can or should a school be a worshipping community?

The Worship-enabling Assembly

I want to argue that what is required is that every school be not so much a worshipping community as a worship-enabling community. Such a community would need to have five characteristics: firstly, it would give equal and genuine opportunity to all to worship; secondly, it would do this in a manner appropriate to a school setting concerned especially to protect the integrity of staff and pupils; thirdly, it would try hard to create an atmosphere conducive to worship; fourthly, it would draw attention to the diversity of beliefs; and fifthly, it would promote a positive and creative attitude towards the relationship between different religions.

Equal Opportunity for All

With regard to the first characteristic, it is important that the opportunity for worship be thoroughly integrated within the life of the school and that *everyone* has this opportunity without any external pressure of any kind being exerted on a particular child. In other words, such opportunities for worship need to take place in assemblies, small or large, in which the school community is expressed in a variety of ways, that is, in which everyone in the school, or everyone in a group of classes, comes together physically to acknowledge that they are part of a wider whole.

This does not mean that *every* assembly need have explicit opportunity for worship given, but that on a regular and fairly frequent basis, for example, at least once a week, the possibility of worship should be specifically referred to.

Protecting Integrity of Participants

With regard to the second characteristic of a worship-enabling community, opportunities for worship given in assemblies only constitute indoctrination if assumptions are made concerning what are or what ought to be pupils' responses. Such assumptions would imprison pupils within one's own expectations and this applies to church schools as much as to county schools. Worship must be a free response, and this must be made clear to children: that is, that each one is free to respond in his or her own way without any public declaration of the choice made.

The choice available may be thought of in this way. Where hymns are sung or prayers are said, one or more of three levels of involvement are possible for the pupils and teachers present.

(i)   Firstly, the response of genuine worship is possible if the individual happens to have some religious conviction.

(ii)   Secondly, it can be taken as an opportunity for educational enlightenment, of learning through empathy and the conscious use of the imagination, what it is like to worship.

(iii)   Thirdly, it can be an experience in which insight of a not necessarily religious nature is received.

An example might be the well-known prayer of Dr. Reinhold Niebuhr:

> God, grant me the serenity to accept the things I cannot change, the courage to change the things I can, and the wisdom to know the difference. Amen.

This can be said as a prayer by someone who believes both in God and in the sentiments expressed in the petition. By someone, however, who does not believe in God, or know whether he or she does, it can with integrity be said at one or both of the alternative levels of involvement. It can be a conscious attempt to try to understand what is at the heart of religion. It is also possible that the words 'God grant' and 'Amen' may be reinterpreted as a personal resolve to try to order one's life in accordance with the insight which the rest of the prayer embodies.

If it be objected that such different-level participation requires a degree of sophistication which is beyond most children, I would draw attention to the need constantly to help children forward towards their own self-education.

The educational reasons for trying to get on the wavelength of worship need to be shared with pupils, together with why it is important actually to take part in it in order to find out. This is not so formidable a task as it may appear. It can be explained to even quite young children in this kind of way. 'Anyone can find out about worship much more easily by doing it than by just reading about it, or talking about it, or watching other people. The quickest way of finding out about music for example, is to listen to it. This needs to be not just on the odd occasion, but many times because it is often difficult to get the idea of what is strange or new, and we can be easily distracted. It is the same with worship.[19]

Another way of looking at the question is to consider the function of play in helping a young child find out what it is like to be a nurse, a policeman, a mother or father. It is often not appreciated how much this 'play method' has to be used by all of us all our lives, adults as well, if we want to try to extend the range of our experience and understanding. There are many things we can never know if we sit on the sidelines and refuse to get involved. We must not be afraid of this kind of educational play for it is the opposite of hypocrisy or of deluding oneself and other people. It is a demonstration of our willingness to learn, to want to understand what it is like to be someone else, and to think in new ways. It is making ourselves available for the possibility of fresh experiences.

Making clear the educational purpose of such assemblies giving opportunity for worship involves care in refraining from phrases such as 'Let us pray' or 'Let us sing this hymn' which do not articulate the possibility that for some this is not worship. Some suggestions for assemblies given at the end of this chapter offer examples of appropriate ways of introducing a religious element.[11]

Appropriate Atmosphere

For the school to be a worship-enabling community, it is essential that it tries to provide an atmosphere conducive to worship. Elements of regularity, order, quietness, attentiveness, beauty need to be present. This is not because worship cannot happen haphazardly, amid noise and confusion and distractedness and in ugly surroundings; indeed sometimes profound worship takes place under such conditions perhaps by virtue of the very constraints which the environment provides. Rather it is the case that novices to worship need the help of an appropriate setting in order to glimpse what it is about.

Even however, if a school, whether church or county, pays a great deal of attention to this, many religious people may still have misgivings that what is happening in the school is not really worship. Does this not need a special place with relevant religious symbols and ritual?

This raises the fundamental question: what is worship? On page 107 above worship was referred to as concerned with acknowledging deity in an appropriate manner. What however constitutes 'appropriate acknowledgement of deity? I think it true that the saints of all the great world religions would unite in underlining the inportance of utter sincerity and inner conviction. External performance of rites and rituals is contrasted with the devout awareness of the true worshipper. Superstition, idolatory, formalism, and hypocrisy are in fact the enemies of worship and should never be confused with worship. The concept of *niyyah* in Islam, for example, is most significant: turning East to face Mecca is only proper worship of Allah if the intention of the heart is right. The words of Jesus to the Samaritan woman sum up a central emphasis in holiness: 'God is spirit and they who worship Him must worship Him in spirit and in truth.'[12] Religion is empty without this dimension and can become 'the drunken blurring of the distance between God and man' as Karl Barth put it.[13]

It is easy to assume that what goes on in a church, synagogue, mosque, gurdwara or temple is automatically worship. Yet this may be far from the case. The important point to notice, however, is that God, if he exists, and God alone, knows. Human assessment is apt to be misplaced. It is difficult enough, as psychologists have emphasized many times, to read even one's own heart and mind correctly; how much more difficult to presume to evaluate the degree of worship in spirit and in truth which someone else offers.

This caveat against an easy line of demarcation between a worship-enabling community in a religiously-orientated building or culture and what can happen in a school is crucial to my argument. If the school can be a worship-enabling community it can be not because it has the external trappings of religion but because there is an element present in it of worship in spirit and in truth. Whether that element is great or small, whether it includes everyone or perhaps only a very few, are questions which only God can answer even with regard to those structures set aside for explicit religious ceremonial. But just as the heart of any overtly religious worshipping community is the element of holiness in its midst, so is that true of a school or any other organization.

In brief, I want to draw attention to the continuum which can exist between what goes on in religious buildings under religious auspices, and what *can* go on in a school.

Acknowledging Diversity of Views

The school as a worship-enabling community should take seriously the question of different forms of worship and belief. Most schools reflect enormous diversity in belief, not only in the faith, religious or otherwise, of the staff and parents, but also in the level of reflectiveness and acceptance of a religious way of life which is present or not present in each individual child.

Acknowledgement of diversity is often made difficult by the

assumption that consensus is important, and that without it there can be no community. I have argued, however, that consensus, whether external or internalized, is not a measure of the degree of worship; indeed, the crucial role of the individual as such in worship means that diversity is what one would expect, because all are unique; even if brought up in the same family, each child is a person in his or her own right with distinctive characteristics and views. What a community needs in order to be a worship-enabling one is to give space for the individual to worship if he or she chooses. The community cannot dictate worship, not monitor it, but only help or hinder its participants from making their own unique response.

The presence of many faith commitments within our society, and the differences which cannot be avoided may therefore be welcomed in drawing attention to the individual's responsibility and in helping to educate that responsibility. Diversity may be seen as friend not foe in that it is so easy, if only one viewpoint is consistently put forward, for youngsters to equate this one viewpoint with authority which they either acquiesce in or rebel against. Either reaction is unhelpful with regard to worship.

A school, if it is to be a worship-enabling community, must therefore reflect diversity of belief even if it is within one external system or religion.

Inter-faith Understanding

Bernadette O'Keeffe drew attention to the importance of authentic dialogue in a community of mixed beliefs. She expressed the hope that this could take place in a way which respects the integrity of every conscience whilst introducing children to the fundamentals of worship.[14]

There is a need here for creative thinking and courageous pioneer work. Schools ought to prepare people for a new kind of conscience society, working towards real harmony of all people of goodwill. There is a marvellous chance to demonstrate this within a school setting where, in classroom study and discussions and in assembly, knowledge and understanding, reflection and inspiration can help people to push back frontiers and extend insights to include those of other as well as one's own.

A striking example of the way in which at a religious level this operates occurs in a recent article on the Jewish Day of Atonement written by Rabbi Daniel Cohn-Sherbok: here an astute individual reflects one the spiritual journey of the community to which he belongs towards a more comprehensive communal awareness.

As members of this global community, the collective 'we' of the High Holy Day prayers has a new meaning and significance. The past communal consciousness of the Jews as a small inter linked people has been superseded by a new sense of belonging to a world society in which everyone feels responsible for everyone else. Jews are no longer able to say 'we' and mean 'we Jews'. Today we means all, Jews and Gentiles, black and white, rich and poor. In our global village, all human beings are brothers, and we are all our brothers' keepers.

In this light it is not simply individual sinfulness or even the sins of the Jewish community that require atonement. It is rather wrongdoing wherever it appears.

The sound of the ram's horn beckons Jews to a recognition of his new vision of the human family and to a universal concern for all people. Their prayers for forgiveness during these holy days are not for themselves alone, but for the whole world. On behalf of all mankind they pray:

> Our Father, Our King, we have sinned before Thee.
> Our Father, Our King, we have no King beside Thee.
> Our Father, Our King, deal with us according to Thy Name.
> Our Father, Our King, renew unto us a happy year.[15]

Here, so it seems to me, is the authentic spirit of living tradition, firm in its loyalty to the insights handed down through the centuries and able to fuse them at a deep level with the insights emerging in our modern world.

Assemblies which give opportunity for worship have a very special role to play in promoting such convergence and search for greater comprehensiveness.

It is important that difficulties are not avoided but faced and creative solutions worked out. Muslim children, for example, may be introduced to singing in specifically Christian, Jewish or Sikh assemblies, whilst they share with others their own music-less assemblies, and the question of whether singing may or may not be helpful for worship should be openly debated.

This kind of wider thinking is possible. In an interview with a 13 year-old Muslim girl which was recorded in *RE Today* she noted

'Sometimes we sing hymns, but I have been brought up to sing them in my primary school so it does not worry me at all. I like music and I enjoy singing and I think of them as being part of living in England rather than as religious songs. They are usually about a relationship with God, so I see no problems about singing them'

Summary of Argument

Before concluding this chapter on a practical note, it may be helpful to summarize the main theme. No-one *can* compel worship, and it is certainly infringing responsibility to attempt to do so. True worship is in spirit and in truth which is the opposite alike of hypocrisy and of loss of freedom. The school cannot assume that all its members believe in God or share the same faith and therefore the opportunities for worship which it gives to all should invite participation at a possible level other than that of worship. For this reason it is preferable to call the school a worship-enabling community rather than a worshipping community. Such a community would positively foster integrity and autonomy based on awareness and understanding.

What constitutes such a worshipping-enabling community is not consensus or equal attainment of worship by all members of it, but of its giving a fair opportunity to people to take part at their own level. Even in specifically religious buildings attended by adults, what takes place there may not for many or most rise to the level of worship. In schools the spread is likely to be greater still, but provided the atmosphere for possible worship is attended to, the school has fulfilled its responsibility.

This opportunity for worship must, however, be given. Many schools today are not giving it in any form, and many others are offering a substitute which is so culturally and phenomenologically orientated as to undermine the seriousness of the possibility of worship. This is because however valuable educationally, for other reasons such assemblies often underline elements of external practice which are irrelevant to or distracting from the inner state of worship.

There is indeed, an urgent need to communicate firstly, to parents and staff who are agnostic or atheist the value of religious education; secondly, to parents and staff who are consciously Christian the importance of a deepening understanding of Christian commitment and witness which can include a very positive attitude to both education and to the multi-faith environment; and thirdly, to parents and staff who belong to other faith commitments, the educational philosophy centred on that respect for the child which can enable him or her to come to a genuine first-hand commitment.

Practical Questions

In order to create the right atmosphere for the possibility of worship many practical, often minute, details must be attended to. These include the setting, what focal point it provides, numbers of children, seating arrangements; the right kind of music to create atmosphere; efficient running of recordplayer, projector and any other equipment used; audibility of speakers; length of assemblies and time of day. Carelessness over such questions can make assemblies a travesty of what both education and worship ought to be about.

Timing, for example, can make or mar the impact of an assembly. One infant school in Yorkshire experimented with seven possibilities.[17] They found that first thing either in the morning or the afternoon does not allow for latecomers. It also produces, for some children, the attitude of 'school has not started yet, it is only assembly', and in other children, especially very young children, this sort of deadline creates stress. After morning play the children tend to be too excitable and assembly is subject to delays over shoes and coats, particularly in cold weather. Before lunch has the problem of the hall being used for dinners. The end of the afternoon mean that there is little flexibility for an assembly being longer or shorter than usual. Two times remain: before morning play, and before afternoon break. The school eventually favoured the latter because there was a natural break when the classes had been tidied up for the end of the day, story time following playtime. It also gave the class preparing assembly time during the day for work to be done or completed and last-minute adjustments to be made. This may not be the right time for all infant schools, and the situation will almost certainly be different in most other schools, but it serves to show what care is needed in deciding such questions.

Content of assemblies is obviously important. Some examples of different kinds of approach follow which seek to incorporate in an educationally acceptable manner opportunities for the development of skills and attitudes appropriate to worship.

A Dialogue-style Assembly

This makes a feature of conversation and children's comments within a specifically teaching framework. It should, however, also allow time for silent response which both gives the child opportunity for worship and guarantees freedom from pressures of any kind.

Such an assembly is an integral part of religious education and non-indoctrinatory. It is capable of answering the criticism voiced by an anxious parent' quoted at the beginning of this chapter who complained of children being forcibly fed with a diet of 'God loves me', and it does so without evading the educational responsibility of helping people to be religiously literate.

This particular theme explores something fundamental to most religions, and therefore bypasses the problems of the multi-faith classroom by concentrating on what is deeper than most religious differences, being basic to religion *per se*.

Overall theme: Science and Religion: Age-group: Infant/Younger Junior

Immediate purpose: to show the difference between two kinds of questions people can ask about things:
HOW was this made? and WHY? Science may be able to answer HOW? but not WHY?

1   Play the game of 'How is it that ...?' by showing the children man-made objects such as a musical instrument, a radio, or an alarm-clock.

Holding the object out to them ask each time 'How is it that there is such a thing?' or 'How does *this* come to be?' Try to establish the two kinds of answers possible:

(i)   because this and this and this were put together;

(ii) because someone made it
and that both of these answers can be taken back and back:

(i)   where did this come from? and that? and that?

(ii) why did he or she make it? and why? and why?
and that they are very different kinds of answers

(i)   refers to objects or things which a scientist can perhaps tell us about;

(ii) refers to people, ideas, purpose, liking etc., which we cannot see with our eyes and touch with our hands.

Then show the children natural objects such as a toadstool an apple, or a pebble.

Ask each time 'How is it that there is such a thing? or 'How does *this* come to be?'.

Can they give the same kind of answers?

Try to establish: that for the first type of question we can, but for the second question it is not so clear.

Explain that some people do give an answer: they say that God made it because He wanted to and because He has a purpose for it.

2 Introduce the singing of a hymn in some such way as this: Not everyone thinks that there is a God who made the world. You must try to think about this question for yourself. Let us do that by singing this song, and thinking about the words, whether you like them and whether you agree with them or not. The person who wrote it believed that the whole of nature, including people, is here because God loves it, and us

God who made the earth
The air, the sky, the sea
Who gave the light its birth
Ca — reth for me ...[18]

3 Finish the assembly by putting on some quiet music and asking the children to picture something they like very much, and think why it is there at all.

A Meditation-style Assembly

The example given uses a technique practised in Hinduism which I heard in a Christian ashram in India to which a number of Hindus go and take part in the worship as Hindus.[19] It offers a very easy and adaptable structure and can be very effective indeed. It also suggests a way forward into mutual affirmation of insights found in different religions. Introduce the assembly in some such words as these:

When religious people meet together for worship they try to remember that they are in the presence of God. But it is easy for people's minds to be distracted. To help them to concentrate they sometimes repeat the name of God, or a thought about God, over and over again.

Today we are going to do this using two names for God; one is Christian and one is Hindu. Christians worship Jesus as God and Hindus think about the power behind the universe pronouncing the word Om, (long O, letting them resonate as long as possible). These two words, 'Jesus (pronounced Yesu — with the s missed off) Om' are sung by Christians who believe that there is one God worshipped by Hindus too, and by Hindus who believe that Christians worship God as they do.

Let us sit very quielty. What we are going to do is try to imagine what it is like to be one of these Christians or Hindus.

$\frac{3}{4}$ s₁ — t₁ | ∂ — ∂ | t₁ ∂ r | ∂ — — :‖
Je — su Je — su Je — su Om — — —

$\frac{3}{4}$ ∂ — ∂ | m — f | m — f | s — — :‖
Je — su Je — su Je — su Om — — —

$\frac{3}{4}$ f — f | f s law | s — s | s — — :‖
Je — su Je — su Je — su Om — — —

$\frac{3}{4}$ f — s | maw — r | ∂ — t₁ | ∂ — — :‖
Je — su Je — su Je — su Om — — —

One person sings a line.
This is repeated by everyone.
It begins slowly and quietly.
It can be repeated any number of times getting faster and louder, then
    slower and quieter again.
It finishes almost as a whisper and is followed by silence.
It could take ten minutes.[20]

A Formal-style Assembly

This example giving suggestions possibly for three assemblies reflects a multi-faith perspective. Readers will be able to think of a great variety of ways in which this kind of material could be developed, using examples from different religious traditions. This example relates specifically at one point to the question of the use of music in worship.

Let us begin with a prayer of William Penn, one of the founders of Quakerism. If you do not believe in God you may perhaps see that it contains an important idea

'O God, help us not to despise or oppose what we do not understand'.

Religion deals with very controversial questions. In order to decide what we think about them, it is important for all of us, whatever faith we have, to try to get on the wavelength of religious language and religious ideas. Today we are going to look a little bit at the way in which the idea of God's creating the world is expressed by religious people.

The book of Genesis begins with the words 'In the beginning, God created the heavens and the earth ... Here is a Muslim prayer expressing the same idea:

> 'We worship Thee O Lord. Thou hast created us and those before us.
> Thou hast appointed the earth a resting place for us, the sky a canopy, causing water to pour down from the heavens, thereby producing fruits as food for us.
> There is no God but Thee.[21]

When people speak of what is at the heart of religion they find themselves using picture-language, because God is greater than anything that can be understood or spoken about. And so when people express what they believe about God being responsible for the world and being involved with it, they speak of God 'creating or making it' like someone 'making' pottery or 'making' a cake or 'making' a model aeroplane.

The book of Genesis uses another picture, that of God 'speaking' and telling the world to come into existence. The beginning of St John's gospel expresses the Christian belief that Jesus Christ is the Word.

> In the beginning was the Word, and the Word was with God, and the Word was God ...

The idea of the word of creation is found in the writings of a Hindu poet, named Dadu, who lived 400 years ago,

> God created the universe like a musical instrument and filled it with His word as its sound. God created the eternal OM out of Himself.'[22]

This picture of God 'composing' the world or 'playing the world like a musical instrument powerfully affected Guru Nanak, the founder of Sikhism. This is how a Sikh writing in 1969 put it:

> Wherever Guru Nanak went, large crowds used to assemble to hear them singing hymns, composed by the Guru. Always moving in natural surroundings, he sang of the marvels of mountains, rivers, woods and flowers as God's manifestations.

For Nanak, there was divine music everywhere and in everything ... 'On hearing celestial music', said Guru Nanak 'My soul becomes absorbed in God ...[23]

This is why music plays an important part in Sikh worship. Listen to this hymn of a fifteenth-century Indian saint, Kabir, who greatly influenced Guru Nanak:

Give me O God, ears to hear that the flute of the universe is played without ceasing, and its sound is love.[24]

This kind of understanding can be found in the Canticle of Brother Sun written by the Christian Saint Francis of Assisi. Let us sing three verses of a modern version of it as a hymn as a song depending on whether or not we feel we agree with its ideas.

All creatures of our God and King ...[25]

But some religious people see music as a distraction. Amongst Christians, Quakers prefer the absolute simplicity of silence. Muslims see how very easily music and singing can take over people's attention to such an extent that they forget the meaning of the words and just enjoy a nice tune. When this happens music blocks the way to worship instead of being a means or vehicle of worship.

Guru Nanak was aware of the dangers of this happening. When someone asked him about it he said

Musical sound. 'Anhada', originated from God. It is holy in its very inception. The best way of worship is to blend the divine Word with Holy Music. The music for worship is designed for spiritual realisation, and not for aesthetic pleasure.[26]

Guru Nanak wanted the music to be simple so that it would not distract people from worship but rather help them to concentrate. When you were saying St. Francis' hymn, did you think about the words or just the tune?

Let us now sing one more verse of it, and see if we can keep our attention entirely on what we are singing about, whether it is for us a hymn of worship, or whether it is an attempt to understand what worship meant to St. Francis.

It would be helpful if this assembly, or these assemblies, could be followed by some which explored in depth how people can best be helped to concentrate, whether by listening to words or stories, or by visual stimuli, by drama, by silence, for example.

LIBRARY

Brenda Watson

A School's Own Liturgy

There is much to be said in favour also of a school preparing its own simple liturgy with prayers from its own collection. This collection could include compositions by the children themselves, as well as some of the great prayers. It could be accompanied by art work so that visually it is very attractive, and it should have an introduction which puts it clearly into an educational perspective.

A possible introduction to such a school liturgy and collection of prayers might read as follows:

> Religion means a great deal to many people, and in school we try to learn more about it. One of the ways of doing this is by taking part in assemblies. This does not mean that all of us are religious; this is something each of us must decide for ourselves. But we all accept that we cannot think clearly about what we do not understand. So we take part in these assemblies in order to find out what it is like to be religious. We can relate this to the rest of our experiences to see whether or not it makes sense.
>
> We drew up this form of worship ourselves in the spring of ... We want it to be altered and added to each year. Please think about how it could be made better.

The advantages of such an approach are many:

(i) Distraction is a potent enemy of that quality of quietness and attentiveness which is at the heart of genuine worship. The variety or novelty of many assemblies therefore needs to be balanced by some which are always the same, and in which people can rest. They could perhaps be likened to the putting on of a well-worn glove.

(ii) Simplicity of preparation. Exciting or deeply moving assemblies may take a great deal of time and effort in planning, and therefore can only be occasional, but worship is something which, like good music, should be presented to children little and often for them to develop any real understanding of it. It follows that it is unrealistic to have elaborate preparation every time.

(iii) Children love repetition provided what is repeated is understandable, meaningful or beautiful. We do children a grave disservice not to introduce them to the language of prayer which they can, maybe years later, draw upon if they wish. They cannot draw upon what they have never received.

(iv) Such a liturgy and collection of prayers is an excellent way of establishing the school as a community. It would be most important that *all* the staff and *all* the children are involved in this, and that the liturgy and collection of prayers are open to amendment and development in the light of new experiences and people.

The liturgy should reflect the concern, and beliefs, most relevant to the school. A Church of England or Roman Catholic school could, for example, relate it to the liturgical year. A school in a strongly multicultural area should try to reflect this.

Notes

1 O'KEEFFE, B (1986) *Faith, Culture and the Dual System.* Lewes, Falmer Press, p. 76.
2 *ibid*, p. 80.
3 *Times Educational Supplement*, 14 June 1985.
4 The argument developed in the chapter takes cognizance of the debate over the educational validity of school worship in any form. For this see, for example, J. HULL, J. (1975) *School Worship — An Obituary*, London, SCM.
5 For fuller treatment of the themes of autonomy and nurture see my book on *Education and Belief* (1987), Oxford, Blackwell, chapter 2.
6 See, for example, ROBINSON, E. (1977) *The Original Vision*, Manchester College, Oxford, RERU.
7 Goldman's research based on an understanding of Piaget has been refuted. See, for example, Slee, N. (1986) 'Goldman yet again', *British Journal of Religious Education* spring 1986, 8, 2, pp. 84–93 who gives a very useful summary of a present-day critique.
8 Reported in the *Daily Telegraph*, 19 September 1986.
9 Old English *weorpscipe: weorp* 'worthy', *scipe* 'ship.'
10 O'KEEFFE, B. (1986) *op cit*, p. 86.
11 In the chapter on school worship in my book *Education and Belief* the importance of participation is further developed, and suggestion given of how integrity can be safeguarded.
12 John 4^{24}.
13 Karl Barth: commentary on *Epistle to the Romans — Romans* 1^{23f}.
14 O'KEEFFE, B. (1985) *op cit*, p. 86.
15 *The Times* 4 October 1986.
16 'Profile: Nadia Bakhsh' in *RE Today*, Autumn 1986, p. 10.
17 I owe this example to teachers attending a Farmington Institute consultation in October 1980.
18 Sarah Betts Rhodes' hymn in, for example, *Songs of Praise* No. 358.

19 The Saccidananda Ashram at Shantivanam in Tamil Nadu.
20 The number of possible variations is endless. A simple one to begin with might be 'Jesus, Jesus, Jesus Christ' or 'Holy, Holy, Holy God'.
21 A Muslim prayer recorded in an anthology compiled by HEDGES, S. G. (1970) *With One Voice* London REP, p. 8.
22 *ibid*, p. 13.
23 Singh D. (1969) 'The hymns of Guru Nanak', *The Sikh Courier*, autumn, p. 46.
24 HEDGES S. C. (1970) *op cit*, p. 49.
25 W. H. Draper's hymn based on the Canticle of Brother Sun, for example, *Songs of Praise* No. 439.
26 Singh D. (1969) *op cit*. p. 47.

7   *Religious Education After Swann*

Owen Cole

Introduction

No sooner had the *Swann Report's* views and recommendations on religous education become known than the then Secretary of State for Education, Sir Keith Joseph, stated that the government would make no alterations to the clauses of the 1944 Education Act. In these circumstances this chapter must be speculative to some extent. It cannot be assumed that Swann will influence the development of religious education, as perhaps the title of this chapter suggests.

The *Swann Report* is a brief way of referring to *Education for All*, a 773-page HMSO publication which appeared in 1985. It was the report of a committee chaired by Lord Swann, set up by the government, to enquire into the education of children from ethnic minority groups. Its most important recommendation is encapsulated in the report's title, education for life in a multifaith, multiracial, pluralist society and should have that society at the centre of its philosophy and practice in every part of Britain, not merely in areas where ethnic and religious minority groups live in large numbers.

Matters relating to religion and education are considered in chapter 8 *Religion and the Role of the School: Religious Education and 'separate' Schools Debate*. Attention is given to three interrelated issues, classroom RE, school worship, and denominational schools. Swann prefers to refer to the last of these as separate schools placing the emphasis upon the most feared aspect of what in the pages of the report turn out to be religious denominational schools. On the subject of the far more divisive independent and public schools, the report is strangely silent. Yet it is in these schools that many of those who will govern the country, run it as civil servants, control its education services, or influence it religiously as church leaders, are educated.

In this chapter the Swann Report will set the agenda of items to be discussed. Its premises, that the fundamental aims of and approaches to religious education will be the same wherever children are educated, is accepted as the only way forward in a small state in which there is considerable geographical mobility and a world which is contracting annually to be in reality a global village. However, though Swann indicated important issues, discussion will not be confined to comment upon its recommendation.

The Classroom

The Approach

One of the most important recent influences upon classroom RE has been Schools Council Working Paper 36, published in 1971[1]. Swann quite properly draws attention to it. Although its title was *Religious Education in Secondary Schools*, the approach to RE which it commended has become widely accepted in primary schools and in higher education. This is known as the phenomenological or undogmatic approach.

> This sees the aim of religious education as the promotion of scholarship in order to enter into an emphatic experience of the faith of individuals or groups. It does not seek to promote any one religious viewpoint but it recognizes that the study of religion must transcent the merely informative.[2]

Translated into simpler language and transformed to the classroom context, it means that the teacher and pupils stand back from making their own personal value judgements, set aside their own natural reactions — 'it's silly', or 'I don't see why they do this/believe that'. However, their restraint has to be balanced by a positive willingness to try to understand and engage with what is being studied.
'You may think it is silly, you may not be able to see why people do it — but lots of people do, you probably would if ... So let's try and find out why', is the response of the teacher and hopefully the class will go along with the suggestion. Education can be of two types basically. One is a method of communicating to children the skills and values of their parents and the adult community. There is value in this approach. All of us who drive cars, read or write, have been taught this response. But there is another way which can lead to

people inventing and designing cars, or writing creatively. This requires an approach to education which is exploratory. In theory this second approach is one which educators in Britain have chosen in the late twentieth century. It says, in theory because British society, of whom teachers form a part, is certainly as eager to look back with longing as it is to move forward in a spirit of risk — accepting adventure. Teachers are only members of that society. Those of us who are over 40 or perhaps 45 are the products of the first kind of educational process and, naturally, we teach what we learned in the manner we were taught. This is one reason for curriculum inertia, especially in the humanities subjects as taught in primary schools. A second is social pressure. Computers, new, or nearly-new mathematics, changes in science teaching, these are forced upon teachers by the demands of a competitive, industrial world. As most human beings are rather conservative they dislike such change reaching areas where it does not seem necessary — to include poems which do not rhyme, plays without a plot, history which is not chronologically structured or covers post-independence Africa or India, a religious education which introduces children to the facts that the world is multireligious and that even within Christianity there is diversity of forms and beliefs. All this is confusing. However, it is even more confusing to realize, at the age of 16 or 30, that your humanities education has failed to prepare you to live in the world as it is and is going to be, and this is becoming the experience of many young people.

In the classroom RE has changed and is changing for positive reasons, not because teachers are ashamed of being British and Christian, but because they cannot adopt different stances towards learning, adapted to different subjects, or if they can, they cannot impress them upon their pupils. 'Think', 'try to find out', 'use your intelligence', is what we encourage children to do in scientific and practical areas and we present them with almost unlimited horizons. We cannot require the same children to be schizophrenic or quiescent in the realms of values and beliefs, accepting what they are told to believe or do without question.

The phenomenological approach to the study of religion is going hand in hand with changing educational methods to produce a revolution in religious education. Instead of nurturing children into the national faith we are seeking to encourage children to understand — to understand what it means to be a Christain or a Muslim, to take religion seriously and have a commitment. There are those who caricature the new RE as being descriptive, a naming of the parts exercise (as though it was never such in the past!). As Working Paper 36 put it 'the study of religion must transcend the merely informative'. Somehow it must enable pupils to realize that religions are concerned with real and urgent issues, that they are studying something that matters. As with all such areas of life, there will seldom be an agreement of solutions. RE has to avoid communicating the untruth that religions present a common world-view.

Content

RE used to be concerned with teaching children Bible stories and perhaps the lives of great exemplars of the Christian faith. Today the debate is about whether there shall be any limit to the content of the syllabus and what criteria for inclusion or exclusion can be adopted. The Brent Agreed Syllabus of 1986 was drawn up by a conference on which ten faiths were represented. The implication is that all of these are to be found in Brent and all these faiths should be included in the syllabus. Even if RE was treated fairly, given as much time and resources as such comparable subjects as history and geography or biology, how could the ablest specialist, or group of specialists, do justice to all these faiths? Criteria for determining content and balance vary considerably. Clearly, if there are Muslim children in the school and locality, Islam will feature prominently in the syllabus. This should be obvious, though it is still possible to find schools where some faiths represented by large numbers of pupils, are ignored. Christianity, it is argued, should be taught in every British school, because of its historical and cultural importance. But should the attention given to it be greater in a Chichester comprehensive school than in one in Brent or Southall? In a multifaith school with 20 per cent children from Christian backgrounds, 50 per cent from Muslim and 30 per cent from Hindu, to keep the mathematics simple, should the religions be taught on a pro-rata basis? Just to make the issue a little more problematical, Anne Bancroft recently wrote a text book entitled *The New Religious World* which included Rastafarians, Hare Krishna, Unification Church, Mormons, Jehovah's Witnesses, Rajneeshis, Transcendental Meditationalists, and Baha'is. Where is the list to stop? At this point there is often an inclination to throw overboard the phenomenological approach and become subjective, using the vast range of religions as an excuse. The long-established and those regarded as wholesome are in; the new, especially if they seem to threaten the basic tenets of Christianity, or are maligned in the media, are out. Perhaps we have to rethink our approach. Historically the Bible has been replaced by Christianity and several other religions. If we sub-title religious studies 'an exploration of beliefs and values' we may be able to use the religions as exemplars, and find a place for such important stances for living as humanism and atheism. At a practical level things might remain little changed in primary and lower secondary schools but in the later years when such issues as suffering, or the purpose of life, are being investigated, it would permit the most insight-conveying or thought-provoking examples to be used rather than necessitating a catalogue of views.

The Teacher

Ultimately change in religious education, as in any other curriculum area, depends on the teacher. Teachers are no longer the figures of authority, arbiters of what is worth knowing and what is not, conveying knowledge in an authoritarian manner, that they once were. They are partners in learning. Here RE has some catching up to do. We still incline towards being didactic, defenders of the faith even if we don't think we should transmit it in a nurturing way any more. The revolution in RE requires us to become partners in learning, as we are elsewhere. 'Discover', 'find out', 'explore', are words as appropriate to the study of religion as to science or mathematics.

We might argue that the principal aim of religious education in schools within the public sector might be to enable pupils to understand the nature of beliefs and values by which people attempt to come to terms with life and the importance and influence which these have for the lives of believers.[3]

The Primary School

In the primary school, the popular way of teaching religious education is to combine it with other subjects in a topic. The subject-based timetable is being rejected in favour of integration, which corresponds to the way in which children learn. The topic or theme might be religion-centred, the focus being on festivals like Diwali, Christmas or a Muslim Eid. In preparing the theme, the teacher might draw a spider chart as a reminder of what curriculum aspects might be included. For example:

Eid ul-Fitr

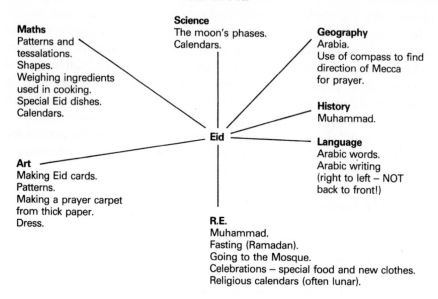

Maths
Patterns and
tessalations.
Shapes.
Weighing ingredients
used in cooking.
Special Eid dishes.
Calendars.

Science
The moon's phases.
Calendars.

Geography
Arabia.
Use of compass to find
direction of Mecca
for prayer.

History
Muhammad.

Eid

Language
Arabic words.
Arabic writing
(right to left – NOT
back to front!)

Art
Making Eid cards.
Patterns.
Making a prayer carpet
from thick paper.
Dress.

R.E.
Muhammad.
Fasting (Ramadan).
Going to the Mosque.
Celebrations – special food and new clothes.
Religious calendars (often lunar).

In a multifaith school with Muslim children in it, such a topic should require no justification. It enhances the self-respect of the Muslims and should develop the respect of other children for them.

In a monocultural, all white school, it could be a means of exploring the place of festivals in religion when Christmas might prove too familiar. It also provides an opportunity to widen horizons, not only in the area of religion.

Usually religion takes a less central position. For example, in a topic on journeys, geography would be much more the key subject area.

Journeys

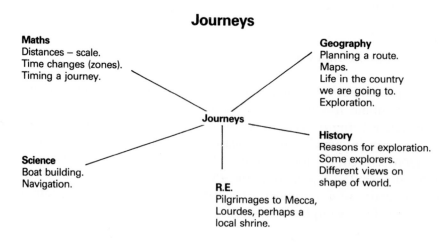

Maths
Distances – scale.
Time changes (zones).
Timing a journey.

Geography
Planning a route.
Maps.
Life in the country
we are going to.
Exploration.

Journeys

History
Reasons for exploration.
Some explorers.
Different views on
shape of world.

Science
Boat building.
Navigation.

R.E.
Pilgrimages to Mecca,
Lourdes, perhaps a
local shrine.

Art work and creative writing would obviously be important. For the teacher the difficulty is what to exclude. In an all-white school the pilgrimage to Mecca (Hajj) would be included because it is the most famous and most popular in the contemporary world. If a number of religions were represented in the class they could find out about one of their pilgrimages and tell all their class-mates about it. The purpose would be to discover why people go on pilgrimages and what they mean to believers.

In topic work a visitor to school would find model making or the use of religious artefacts (such as prayer carpets) having a place in religious education. 'Tell a story, then draw a picture' is becoming a thing of the past. The teacher is much less a story-teller than formerly. Religious stories have their place whether they be from the Bible or the Ramayana, but they need to be contextualized, given a setting in the experience of the children.[4]

The Secondary School

Changes in the secondary school where the subject is likely to be taught in isolation from other areas of the curriculum, have tended to be in content, the introduction of material from a variety of religions. However, the phenomenological approach presupposes that religions will be studied in all their facets. This means that besides the narrative element or study of scriptures, and a consideration of doctrines, children will also examine the ritual dimension, the place of religious actions, the study of what people do when they worship or go on pilgrimage, for example. They will also try to share the experiences of those who perform these actions or read a scripture, and what they experience deep down. Religions also have ethical teachings and social concerns, including a vision of the ideal society. These also will be examined.[5]

The change is most obvious when one looks at the approach to Christianity. The Bible has not disappeared, but it has been enhanced by studies of Christian worship, the Eucharist, the major festivals, Christmas in India, Africa, or South America, attempts to discover how Christians form their attitudes to the range of moral issues which face them, and what Christians believe. It will no longer be assumed that the white children in the class are Christians. The teacher will try to avoid saying 'we believe', or 'when you go to church next Sunday', but the aim will be that by the time pupils leave school, they will understand what it means in terms of beliefs, practices and commitment to be a Christian. If it were left here the charge could still be made that the aim of RE is to produce Christians, but not if the teacher is equally concerned that pupils should have a similar knowledge of Islam or what it means to be a humanist. Of course, it is still difficult to achieve these ideals. Almost all the material available for studying Christianity conveys the stereotype that it is white, British, and middle-class. Christian bodies could help the cause of religious studies by producing non-confessional material about Christianity in Africa, India, South America and other regions of the world, as well as black churches in Britain. At the same time it might be countering the racism which is often experienced among white British Christians by educating them in a realization of the fact that a large part of the Christian church world is not white and Anglican, and helping them to rejoice in the fact. Here I am not wishing to undo the work of the ecumenical movement which I have always actively supported, but it is becoming apparent that the success of its efforts in organizational terms could have resulted in a British church run by white middle-class men on behalf of white middle-class women. We may now be recognising that such a monochrome illusion would not be healthy and that diversity even within one religion can be stimulating and wholesome as long as it is not competitive.

In multifaith secondary schools, the thematic approach seems to be the most practicable one, despite some reservations which will be discussed later. These are most likely to focus upon such subjects as messengers or founders, scriptures, worship, festivals, pilgrimage, beliefs.[7] To these may be added socioethical themes taken from family life, for example, with able sixth-formers even some analysis of the vision of state and society which religions give. The undoubted value of the thematic approach is that it enables all pupils to be involved constantly, and their faith recognized. It is thoughtless and insensitive in multifaith schools to have a three-year study of Christianity followed by a term each on Hinduism, Islam and Sikhism. Some classes have six or more religions plus pupils lacking any religious commitment (post-Christian, post-Jew, or post-Muslim). In these situations, group work may be the only answer, but not necessarily with the Sikh children assembling a presentation on Guru Nanak. A mix has value if the purpose of the exercise is to acquire skills in studying religion, not only supporting boys and girls in the faith which they bring to school. Of course, such work must end with each group being given time to make an audio-visual presentation to the rest of the class.

Against these themes there are two points that must be made.

First, they can be disastrous if the appropriate methodology is not acquired. We are not trying to compare Jesus and Muhammad, the Buddha and Guru Nanak, in terms of better or worse, more successful or more humane. This must be clearly understood. Secondly, each has a different position in the religion and in Judaism and Hinduism there are not really persons in any way analogous to the four mentioned above. Also Islam does not regard Muhammad as the founder of that religion, that place belongs to God alone. It is unclear what is meant when Jesus is described as the founder of Christianity. The Sikh Gurus (not just one person) were messengers of God, but the Buddha was not, that religion being non-theistic. The same diversity is true of worship where it is easy for the impreession to be conveyed that women do not matter in Judaism or Islam, that worship is not important for Hindus, as many never go to the temple (forgetting that each home is a temple, as Hindu friends remind me). The relaxed atmosphere of much Jewish and Hindu worship can elicit from Christian observers the comment that 'they' don't take religion seriously. To these examples can be added others. However, in the hands of competent, professionally trained teachers, using reliable resources, the potential threats become possibilities for developing study skills and exploring the question — what is religion?

Public Examinations

Much of the destiny of secondary school RE is determined by the value which headteachers put on the subject and the requirements of public examinations. Although external political and religious influences upon schools and the curriculum can be harmful, particularly to RE, a point which will be taken up later, nevertheless, it does seem that if headteachers are unwilling to provide all their pupils with a balanced curriculum adequately resourced, which includes beliefs, values and the aesthetic realm of meaning, they have to be taken to task.

It is too early yet to offer much comment upon the GCSE. However, it must be remarked that although the National Criteria for the examination warn that syllabuses should be free from bias, every board has created a situation which makes it possible for all pupils to study only the Christian religion. No other religion is placed in this position of privilege with the exception of Judaism with the East Anglians and London boards. Here the two papers which candidates are required to sit could be studies of Judaism. It is surprising that the

Secondary Examinations Council (SEC) has endorsed this example of bias.

This is not to give support to Muslim views that Islam should have been permitted two papers.[9] It seems to be contrary to the concept of religious studies that any pupils can be regarded as having taken a course in it if they have studied only one religion, especially if it is their own. 'Who knows his own religion knows no religion'[10] is a statement possessing more than a grain of truth.

This argument has been lost temporarily, so has that for syllabuses which would go beyond the six religions to include something on methodology, approaches to the study of religion, for example. Hopefully, those who are catching their breaths after over-hastily preparing syllabuses, do not think that their task is over. As soon as they have revised some of the more badly structured syllabuses which have been approved, it is hoped they will try to push forward the frontiers of religious studies through the second generation of syllabuses.

Teacher Recruitment

Although religious studies is more than the teaching of world religions, the six traditions most strongly represented in twentieth-century Britain will provide most of the content of school syllabuses. Another reason for deploring the GCSE development is that they are scarcely likely to encourage people other than Christians to come forward to train to be religious study teachers.

The old race chestnut used to be, 'Would you like your daughter to marry a black man?' In terms of religious education it is now, 'Would you like your Christian child to be taught Christianity by a Hindu/Jew/Buddhist/Muslim/Sikh?' In passing, let me remind myself that we have never demurred at the idea of a Muslim child being taught Islam by a Christian! However, the answer to the last question must be that we would be perfectly happy for our Christian child to be taught Christianity by a Muslim, provided that the teacher was professionally trained, had a satisfactory knowledge of Christianity, was using reliable resources and, above all, was adopting a religious studies approach to the task. Eventually, we should arrive at the situation where a teacher is not distinguished by his/her beliefs or lack of them, but in the way we have to attract members of all six religions, Humanists, or those with no beliefs, to the work of teaching religious studies. We need their professional skills, faith and insight. Some GCSE boards consulted Muslims, Jews and others — some, I suspect, did not. The traditional arrogance of some westerners who think that they must know more than the Muslim or Hindu, accompanied by the notion, which the GCSE syllabuses could be seen to endorse, that RE is about Christians and for Christians, is unlikely to encourage members of the other five religions, or agnostics and humanists, to apply to colleges or universities to study religion, let alone wish to teach it.

School Worship

If the GCSE bias indicates that the debate about the openness of religious education continues, the requirement for a compulsory, collective daily act of worship, still a legal obligation, contradicts the religious studies approach.[11] It is perhaps for this reason that the greatest unease about school worship is found among specialist religious studies teachers in secondary schools.

Swann is fairly open in its attitude to school worship.

> With regard to the requirement for a daily act of worship in every county and voluntary school, we do not believe that this requirement can continue to be justified with the multiplicity of beliefs and non-beliefs now present in our society. We would not however wish to restrict the freedom of county schools to make provision for collective worship if it seemed appropriate and is acceptable to their pupils and parents.[12]

The Report recognizes that religious education is moving in a direction which makes it increasingly impossible to reconcile it with the idea of worship. However, from the passage quoted, it seems that Swann's reservations have to do with a change in society, in its religious habits, attitudes to religion and obvious pluralism. The real objections to worship are of a different kind. First, there is the religious one.

Any common sense definition of worship must include words which indicate response to belief in God. Worship is an act of faith. It seems wrong to assume such faith in the children and teachers who constitute our county schools. To continue to require children to worship can give the impression that anyone can do it regardless of personal belief. The result is likely to be that of cheapening commitment, faith and worship, something that should concern all believers, whatever their religion.

The second reason is educational. It has already been noted that religious education is now beginning to adopt the enquiring stance of the rest of the curriculum. Pupils are encouraged to think rather than passively accept. Worship, to some extent, does not share the approach of the rest of the curriculum. It is paradoxical to be open in the classroom, refusing to assume that there is a God and then expect pupils to affirm belief in him/her/it.

In the multifaith school the difficulty becomes even greater. To use masculine pronouns exclusively is to provide an inadequate statement about God for Hindus and, I would argue, Sikhs. To sing hymns is unacceptable to Muslims, whilst it is thoughtless to assume belief in God on the part of most Buddhists.

The requirements of the 1944 Education Act, relating to school worship are becoming increasingly difficult to justify and satisfy. Religious educationalists must be concerned where worship and classroom RE are linked, as in the Swann Report and the National Association of Head Teachers (NAHT) pamphlet[13], that criticisms of worship may threaten the subject, religious education. (No-one seems to have carried out research into the issue, but I sense that the linking of the two in children's minds, especially at secondary level, does the image of the subject no good at all). While the requirement remains, the best advice one can give anxious teachers is to adopt a 'Thought for the Day' approach. No hymns, no corporate repetition of The Lord's Prayer, but the use of religious readings, from scriptural and other sources, and the reading of a prayer, perhaps, accompanied by an invitation to the assembled school to reflect upon them. The believer's response will constitute an act of worship, but in such a way that the conscience of other pupils and the open approach of the school to education is not threatened. If the obligation to worship were abolished and assemblies were allowed to develop freely, they could contribute positively to the life of the school.[14]

Denominational Schools

As religious education becomes less confessional and moves more towards the position of the Durham Report which says 'to press for the acceptance of a particular faith or belief system is the duty and privilege of the churches and other similar religious bodies. It is certainly not the task of a teacher in the county school'[15] (a position which it is difficult to reconcile with an act of worship), denominational schools become increasingly anachronistic and less desirable. The paradox is this. Some parents and some religious bodies want an educational system permeated by religion. Their concern is not only for religious education and school worship. It is for the whole ethos of the school to reflect and exhibit the values and beliefs which they cherish. Other people, including members from all faiths, regard the retention or expansion of denominational schools as undesirable in a pluralistic society, partly because such schools can be divisive, but also because it implies an opting out rather than involvement in and positive acceptance of pluralism.

The Swann Report emphasizes the first kind of objection by entitling its discussion of the dual system, 'the Separate Schools Debate'. It recognizes that a major reason for Muslim pressure, in particular, to establish their own schools is 'the failure of existing schools in the past to recognize and respond to their concerns'.[16] It is all too true, sadly, that thoughtless and insensitive headteachers have adopted an assimilationist approach to religious minorities, not only ignoring them in curriculum therms, but even failing to respond to dietary needs.

However, Swann also recognizes that one of the reasons for Muslim concern is more fundamentally ideological. Namely, that there is a Muslim way of life which is threatened by the values of late twentieth-century western society.[17] However, it does not seem to perceive that the real issue is how far Britain is prepared to go along the paths of pluralism. Muslim denominational schools may be acceptable, but should this be extended to Muslim family law? Should other religions, as well as other Christian denominations, be officially represented in the House of Lords alongside the twenty-six Anglican Bishops? Here the issues lie beyond the scope of religious education and denominational schools, but they are not irrelevant. It has been known for schools teaching multifaith RE to keep to the traditional school meals which deny pluralistic values just as much as Christian assemblies do, and for a Jewish teacher to have to lose pay in order to observe Yom Kippur in an authority committed to a multifaith RE approach. Is pluralism to be no more than an intellectual concept?

Before leaving the denominational school issue, it is necessary to mention the research of O'Keeffe and Francis.[18] Each, looking at very different situations, suggests that Anglican denominational schools have lost their way. They are uncertain of their role in a secular society, they are even less confident how to respond to a pluralistic society. Very often, even if the governors or diocese have a policy, it does not have the unqualified support of teachers who would have taken a post anywhere. It is only by chance that some of them are working in denominational schools.

The European Declaration of Human Rights supports the creation of denominational and other forms of alternative schools. Anglicans, Roman Catholics, Jews and now Muslims — as well as other groups — have such schools and seem prepared to continue to invest in them.[19] They need not be ghetto schools as Swann tends to suggest, but there would seem to be a need for those responsible for such schools to ensure that they respond positively to a pluralistic society. The paradox of the Rochester Statement, produced by that Anglican diocese, which encourages schools to welcome Muslim and other pupils but sees no need to respond to their presence in curriculum terms, would seem to be educationally naive and socially and humanly intolerable.

The anxiety which many educationalists have concerning the role of denominational schools in a pluralist society is even greater when attention is turned to public and independent schools, for their influence is stronger. From these come many of our legislators and policy makers. Yet of these separate schools Swann makes no comment.

Envoie

This chapter has been concerned so far with the direction in which religious education is going. It would be rash to predict its destination. Perhaps I may be permitted to show some fears and hopes. First the anxieties.

The 1944 Education Act still remains in force. For some decades it has been relatively inefective. School religion has enjoyed a period of curriculum development unimpaired by it. There are signs ôf change. Sir Keith Joseph and other members of the goverment between 1979 and 1987 have given verbal support at least for education mainly to be in Christianity if not to be Christian education. Many specialists in the field of RE fear that they might do something to enforce their views. Religious education, especially failures to implement the clause relating to school worship, has sometimes been a target for religious groups, usually conservative Christians. However, hostility is not all from one quarter; the National Secular Society and some left wing politicians would like to abolish religious education as well as school worship altogether.

There is social pressure, too, for religious education to be used to propagate or endorse certain values, usually a simple Ten Commandments morality. These are seen as norms to which the nation aspires, and values upon which society is based, even if many of its teachers and other citizens have no intention of observing them personally.

No other subject is put at risk to the extent that RE is by the whims or deeply felt attitudes of a range of people from headteachers in education to county councillors, local clergy, parents or secretaries of state for education outside it. These pressures, sometimes imagined or potential, often real, could render any predictions about the future of RE inaccurate.

If these anxieties are set aside, even if adequate resources are denied the subject, the outlook is encouraging for those who favour the developments of the last fifteen-twenty years. Whereas in 1970 it was scarcely possible to find any religious studies courses which students training to be teachers could follow, now almost all courses are of that kind. The universities in their BA/BD programmes have much catching up to do and sometimes university PGCE provision in religious education does not bear thinking about, both at primary and secondary level, but the mass of BEd students who have had courses in religious studies are going forward able to teach the new RE. If their eagerness is encouraged and they are supported by headteachers, advisers and in-service courses, classrooms will change. At present there is a generation gap. Some over 35 are adopting the approach endorsed in this chapter. They are often self-taught, as I am. Those under that age have imbibed it as part of their preparation for teaching. The impact of their presence is slowly but inevitably being felt and will become dominant as they gain promotion and older teachers retire.

A question that has recently arisen is the school's responsibility for the spiritual development of pupils.[20] As teachers consider this, they need to be sure what they mean and do not mean. Those who wish to see the curriculum giving attention to spirituality are not supporting the retention of school worship. Some would even regard such collective acts as being harmful to spiritual growth or at least unhelpful. Nor are they equating spirituality with morality, and they are not claiming for religion an exclusive concern with the spiritual aspect of human personality. Perhaps spiritual is an inadequate word. It includes that which may motivate an artist in painting a picture, writing a poem, or creating a sculpture. It is more than feeling, it is an awareness of what might be described as the numinous. In worship and prayer, religious people seek to experience it, but nowadays many of them would not wish to confine the exploration of it to religion.[21]

Education can be a communication of information, a naming of parts, or can be the imparting of skills. If it is to respond to the total human personality it must be more than this. The aesthetic element must not be neglected when music, or literature, is being studied. So often it can be. As critical analysis grows, in the middle years and high school, appreciation diminishes. May one dare to say the same applies to science? Wonder has no place. In religious studies the spiritual lies in the experiential dimension of the religion; what is going on in the Hajj, what Christmas, Passover, arti, or the statue of the Buddha mean to the believer. This is the most difficult dimension to penetrate, yet it is the only one, ultimately, that matters. How to maintain openness without ignoring values, how to transcend the descriptive, seeking to help pupils perceive the aesthetic, without requiring them to interpret it through Christian or even religious eyes, is a task we have to address ourselves to in the eighties and nineties: all teachers, not just those interested in religions either academically or personally.

In looking at spirituality we have been asking what religious education should do for the individual. In summing up, we would want to say that it should provide him/her with the religious studies/ life skills of being able to set aside their own beliefs and attitudes and engage positively with those of other people in an attempt to understand them respectfully. It should help them to approach their own beliefs and values, whatever they are, in the same way. It should equip them to explore life in such a manner that if they wish to turn religious studies into a personal quest, they may do so, though it is not the aim of the subject to provide pupils with a variety of religious choices or invite them to select one, or even require them to participate in a search for meaning. With the rest of the curriculum it enables them to reflect upon the question — who am I?

Whether there should be social aims or not is a matter of debate. Some regard the study of religion as something purely academic. However, if schools have a social purpose to equip people for life in a democracy in the late twentieth century, for example, RE must recognize the contribution it can make towards developing an understanding of, and a respect for, the beliefs of others, and the part it can play in helping pupils to be informed citizens of the world of tomorrow.

Those teachers responsible for life skills programmes or courses in personal and social development, should recognize that religious studies has much to offer in terms of methodology and concern with ethics and social issues. Often it connives at its own exclusion by being dogmatic and prescriptive, or being perceived as such by teachers who were on the receiving end of that kind of religious education.

Religion, for good or ill, and whatever our personal attitudes to it, is still a potent force in the world. It has influenced history and art, science and politics, and continues to do so. It invites people to reflect upon themselves and seek some kind of vision of society. It is a proper subject for study in its own right as well as providing those who undertake it with important academic skills. If these kinds of reasons are put forward convincingly and transmitted into real aims in the classroom by those who teach religious education, its future should be healthy, for it should command the respect and support of all who are concerned for education in the fullest sense of that word. However, in seeking allies and advancing the claims of the subject, we must be wary of the temptation to take part in special pleading. The only justification for the study of religion in education at any level must be educational.

Notes

1 *Religious Education in Secondary Schools*, Schools Council Working Paper 36, Evans/Methuen Educationals (1971) appeared mid-way through the Schools Council RE Project based on the University of Lancaster (1967–73). It was very much influenced by the Director of the Project, Professor Ninian Smart.

2 *ibid*, p. 21.

3 This is a modification of the aims of the Hampshire Agreed Syllabus of 1978, *Religious Education in Hampshire Schools*, p. 8. This is one of the important documents on religious education, but it does tend to confine meaning, purpose and the area of exploration to the religions. The aim expressed here seeks to enable the study to go beyond the religions, though including them, of course.

4 For examples see *Paths to Understanding*, and *Following the Paths*, (Macmillan) the Hampshire handbooks. Articles in *Child Education* or *Junior Education* frequently serve as a reminder that the desire to reduce RE to Bible story-telling is not dead. It seems to be based on the fact that the Bible is naturally inspiring or intelligible, and the comfort teachers gain from using explicit religious material. It also requires little effort.

5 These dimensions of religion can conveniently be found in SMART, N. (1969) *Religious Experience of Mankind*, London, Collins (with many subsequent reprints).

6 BRITISH COUNCIL OF CHURCHES (1986) See *Educational Principles in Religious Education*, London, British Council of Churches. The Chichester Project, directed by John Rankin, has published many books following this approach through Lutterworth press. Details may be

obtained from the Lutterworth Press, 7 All Saints Passage, Cambridge, CB2 3LS.

7 See the SOLE, O. and MORGAN, P. (1984) *Six Religions in the Twentieth Century* London, Stanley Thorne/Hulton. Also GCSE syllabuses of London and East Anglia Group A, Midland B and Northern B are thematic.

8 A convenient summary of all the syllabuses was published as a supplement in *RE Today*, spring 1986.

9 *Islam and the GCSE Examination in Religious Studies*, Islamic Academy, 23 Metcalfe Road, Cambridge, CB4 2DB, 1986.

10 MULLER, F. M., (1973) *Introduction to the Science of Religion*, p.16. Muller actually wrote 'He who knows one knows none'. See SHARPE, E. J. (1975) *Comparative Religion*, London, Duckworth, 1975, chapter 2.

11 The clause (25) of the 1944 Education Act relating to school worship reads:

Religious Education in County and Voluntary Schools General provisions as to religious education in county and in voluntary schools

(1) subject to the provisions of this section, the school day in every county school and in every voluntary school shall begin with collective worship on the part of all pupils in attendance at the school, and the arrangements made therefor shall provide for a single act of worship attended by all such pupils unless, in the opinion of the local education authority or, in the case of a voluntary school, of the managers or governors thereof, the school premises are such as to make it impracticable to assemble them for that purpose.

(2) Subject to the provisions of this section, religious instruction shall be given in every county school and in every voluntary school.

(3) It shall not be required, as a condition of any pupil attending any county school or any voluntary school, that he shall attend or abstain from attending any Sunday school or any place of religious worship.

(4) If the parent of any pupil in attendance at any county school or any voluntary school requests that he be wholly or partly excused from attendance at religious worship in the school, or from attendance at religious instruction in the school, or from attendance at both religious worship and religious instruction in the school, then, until the request is withdrawn, the pupil shall be excused from such attendance accordingly.

(5) Where any pupil has been wholly or partly excused from attendance at religious worship or instruction in any school in accordance with the provisions of this section, and the local education authority are satisfied:

   (a) that the parent of the pupil desires him to receive religious instruction of a kind which is not provided in the school during the periods during which he is excused from such attendance;

   (b) that the pupil cannot with reasonable convenience be sent to another county or voluntary school where religious instruction of the kind desired by the parent is provided; and

(c)   that arrangements have been made for him to receive religious instruction during school hours elsewhere, the pupil may be withdrawn from the school during such periods as are reasonably necessary for the purpose of enabling him to receive religious instruction in accordance with the arrangements: provided that the pupil shall not be so withdrawn unless the local education authority are satisfied that the arrangements are such as will not interfere with the attendance of the pupil at school on any day except at the beginning or end of the school session on that day.

(6)   No directions shall be given by the local education authority as to the secular instruction to be given to pupils in attendance at a voluntary school so as to interfere with the provision of reasonable facilities for religious instruction in the school during school hours; and no such direction shall be given so as to prevent a pupil from receiving religious instruction in accordance with the provisions of this section during the hours normally set apart for that purpose, unless arrangements are made whereby the pupil shall receive such instruction in the school at some other time.

(7)   Where the parent of any pupil who is a boarder at a county school or at a voluntary school requests that the pupil be permitted to attend worship in accordance with the tenets of a particular religious denomination on Sundays or other days exclusively set apart for religious observance by the religious body to which his parent belongs, or to receive religious instruction in accordance with such tenets outside school hours, the managers or governors of the school shall make arrangements for affording to the pupil reasonable opportunities for so doing and such arrangements may provide for affording facilities for such worship or instruction on the school premises, so however, that such arrangements shall not entail expenditure by the local education authority.

12   DEPARTMENT OF EDUCATION AND SCIENCE (1985) *Education for All*, (The Swann Report), London, HMSO, chapter 8, section 5.3, p. 497.

13   NAHT (1985) *Religious Education in Schools*, London, NAHT.

14   Many useful suggestions are to be found in Griffin, W. (1984) *Exploring Primary Assemblies*, London, Macmillan. See also BRITISH COUNCIL OF CHURCHES (1985) London, British Council of Churches for a discussion of interfaith worship. At the time of writing the RE panel of the British Council of Churches Committee for Relations with People of Other Faiths is producing a booklet on school worship.

15   *The Fourth R* (The Durham Report on Religious Education) London SPCK (1970) paragraph 217, page 103. This important document explains the nature and purpose of RE as generally seen on the eve of the Lancaster Schools Council project (1969–73). *Views on RE*, Religious Education Council of England and Wales (1981), comprising statements by twenty-three national bodies on the purpose of RE indicated a

widespread support for this attitude and a positive recognition that RE has to do with understanding the nature of religion.

16 DEPARTMENT OF EDUCATION AND SCIENCE (1985) *op cit*, chapter 8, section 2–5, p. 503.

17 *ibid*, sections 2.5 to 2.19 passim pp. 503–14.

18 O'KEEFFE, B. (1986) Faith, Culture and the Dual System, Lewes, Falmer Press, and FRANCIS, L. J. (1986) *Partnership in Rural Education*, London, Collins.

19 During 1986 the Bishop of Durham, the Right Reverend Dr David Jenkins, questioned the relevance of denominational schools to the educational needs of the present time. See especially *Times Educational Supplement*, 25 July 1986. See also *The Guardian*, 9 July 1986, where twenty-three other people question the system of subsidizing denominational schools out of taxes.

20 Ursula King considered this issue in *Religious Education: Transcendence and Liberation*, in *Celebration and Challenge*, CEM, 1984. See also WEBSTER, D. (1984) Religious education and a rediscovery of the spiritual: A pathless path' *News and Events*, York RE Centre, Summer; and WEBSTER, D. (1985) Commitment. Spirituality and the classroom', *British Journal of Religious Education, autumn*.

21 Humanist friends sometimes regard the kind of concern with spirituality which is mentioned above as a new kind of confessionalism of a claim of religious imperialism. To avoid confusion and find a place for such elements as awe, wonder, beauty and mystery in many areas of the curriculum, not just in religious studies, perhaps we might confine spiritual and spirituality to our religious vocabulary, using aesthetic when the meaning is broader (see PHENIX P. H. (1964) *Realms of Meaning* New York McGraw Hill, pages 247–9).

8   Church Schools in Service to the Community

Geoffrey Duncan

I recall that shortly after writing his book *The Sacred Canopy*[1] the American sociologist Peter Berger felt it necessary to produce *A Rumour of Angels*[2] to counter any inference readers of the former work might have drawn to the effect that the author was concerned with promoting atheism. Bernadette O'Keeffe's *Faith, Culture and the Dual System*[3] could be perceived as an ammunition store for those who would argue that Church of England schools have had their day. Indeed, such an inference has already been drawn by Owen Cole who has written, 'I am becoming increasingly unconvinced of the value of the dual system. Personal experience, supported by the findings of ... Bernadette O'Keeffe ... raise strong doubts in my mind.'[4] O'Keeffe's editorship of this present work is, I understand, an indication that she herself does not believe that her earlier work has to lead to a position such as the one indicated by Owen Cole. In advocating a continuing role for church schools in this chapter, I must emphasize that my presentation is largely impressionistic, based not on first-hand research but, like Owen Cole's chapter from which I have just quoted, drawn from personal experience and reflection.

In response to a question from the floor during his talk to the North of England Education Conference in 1985, Professor Charles Handy said that in his view one of the main justifications of voluntary-aided schools was that their degree of independence and autonomy (compared with county and controlled schools) enabled them to be in the van of innovation and courageous experimentation. Such a perspective echoes the call in a church publication[5] a year or so earlier for the Church of England to return to the role of pioneer in education, to promote new initiatives, rather than simply defend the *status quo*; the exciting prospect before us is that 'seeking and finding goals and objectives which match our own time may recover for the

Church's endeavour in education an earlier role of 'pioneer'.[6] Any discussion of present and future practice in church schools in a multicultural, multifaith society will inescapably have to be conducted in a context that perceives the tension between on the one hand conservative functions of an established church and its agencies, noted by so many sociologists of religion and, on the other hand, the potential to innovate that nevertheless can also be noticed. This syndrome was neatly illustrated during a General Synod debate in February 1985 on the role of bishops, who were seen as having a leading, stimulating role but, as the Archbishop of Canterbury candidly observed, at the same time having an almost inescapable conservative role. Many of the comments by headteachers in *Faith, Culture and the Dual System* reflect this tension.

One wonders if there is significance in the fact that any biblical concordance has far more references to 'walls' than 'bridges'. Walls are normally built to exclude, protect, defend, often in the context of a perceived threat. Bridges usually imply going out, improving communication, promoting enterprise, in the context of confidence. Retreating armies blow up bridges. Walls can, of course, be less defensive and fulfil less of an excluding function if they are generously interrupted by welcomingly open doors. The analogies that form the sub-title of this book could well be applied to a Church of England approach to the provision of schools in the maintained system: some walls, certainly, to reflect the conservative part of the tension, to fulfil the 'domestic' role where appropriate, to preserve and affirm the Christian foundation of its schools; but also doors to allow the service to the community role to be implemented, to allow the 'openness' pole of the openness/commitment tension to be represented.

But how many doors and how wide are they to be opened? There are those, mainly of a Jewish, Roman Catholic and to some extent Muslim (at least those who are currently arguing for Muslim-aided schools) persuasion who can present a case for schools, whose main commitment is nurturing in the faith, that denies that these must necessarily be divisive for society.[7] (One must try to avoid stereotyping: there are Roman Catholic schools with a high percentage of children of other faiths and at least one Jewish school with a substantial minority of Christian pupils, the head of which delights to surprise people at meetings in December by announcing that he must go to check that the arrangements are going well for his school's Christmas Carol service!) Within the Church of England there are voices that promote the nurture of the faithful approach. Dr Leslie Francis, for example, shows signs of becoming disillusioned with the traditional 'service to the community' function of Church of England schools and is appearing to favour the traditional Roman Catholic model or at least the model of a school for Christians on an ecumenical basis.[8] There are signs that many are finding the latter model an increasingly attractive one, not only as a response to an increasingly multifaith society but also to what is perceived as an increasingly secular one. There are some Church of England schools that, while happy to receive children of other faiths, are not willing to make any concession to or recognition of faiths other than Christianity, at least as far as the school's worship and religious education is concerned.

It is probable that schools that take such a 'hard' line are very much in the minority. My impression, supported I think by *Faith, Culture and the Dual System*, is that there is another minority of schools that is very much in the business of affirming and recognizing other faiths, while the majority are somewhere within a broad middle spectrum, feeling unhappy with a 'hard' line on both practical and moral grounds but also fearful of betraying their Christian foundation.

Those who look to the Roman Catholic/Jewish or ecumenical model concerned primarily with 'nurture' as a basis for aided schools supported by the Church of England have yet to show they have fully thought out the implications, not least the likelihood of a very patchy distribution of Church schools throughout the country. In particular one wonders what their future would be in the inner cities where, we are told, often barely 1 per cent are churchgoers. One even wonders how viable such schools might be in rural areas: one of the apparent advocates of this model, Dr Leslie Francis, has himself painted a not very encouraging picture of rural Anglicanism as a solid basis for Church schools.[9] To be fair, Dr Francis, in the paper to which I referred earlier, does recognize that the development of a system of ecumenical Christian aided schools 'would depend upon the churches creating national and area structures to assess the local needs and structures' but gives no grounds for being confident that a distribution any more rational than the present one would result. For example, he does not really address himself to the admissions policies to be pursued by such schools: will they insist upon the application of rigid criteria based on parents' religious background or will they also cater for children whose parents, while not practising Christians themselves, want a Christian-based schooling for their children? Unless they become 'exclusivist' schools it is difficult to see how they will escape many of the dilemmas faced currently by aided church schools and find themslves developing a 'service to the community' rationale after all.

Apart from a couple of passing references to the multifaith nature of British society, Dr Francis, in his paper, is overwhelmingly preoccupied with searching for appropriate schooling in a secular society. He gives little guidance for schooling in areas where there is a substantial proportion of adherents of other faiths no one of which is strong enough to set up an aided school but who might prefer a sensitive Church of England school to one with a secular foundation, other than to suggest that controlled status might be appropriate in such circumstances. Should the Church of England really turn its back on the opportunity for providing such a service? Whilst it claims to be a national church (and even if it should ever give up such a status) should the opportunity for its aided schools to provide a service and a witness with an element of stability in areas the population of which can swiftly change its characteristics be lightly discarded? As I have written elsewhere,[10] the service to the community role should not be abandoned too readily. Difficult as it may be to hold the tension between a school's Christian foundation and the need to serve a population that is largely non-Christian, such a model still has much mileage in it.

An expansion in the number of Christian or joint (for example, Joint Anglican/Methodist and Joint Anglican/Roman Catholic) schools has its attractions and there is doubtless scope for this. Again, it is unlikely that there is the potential for a wholesale adoption of this model or that it will help resolve the question of the most suitable form of schooling to serve the children of non-Christian faiths in areas where the Christians form a substantial proportion of the population. In any case many of the existing joint schools are very much concerned with a service to the community role. Insofar as joint schools successfully demonstrate how it is possible both to be true to one's own religious foundation and to cope with, profit from and rejoice in living at close quarters with difference, they should be in position to fulfil Professor Handy's vision of voluntary schools being on the borders of experimentation. Indeed, in years to come they may come to be seen as providing helpful lessons for schools of explicitly multifaith foundation. (Although such schools were called for some years ago in a radical Roman Catholic publication,[11] their imminent arrival is not very likely. But who knows? Perhaps in the not very distant future some group of people may bring about such an innovative venture within the maintained sector.) It is, incidentally, worth noting that although the first joint school was established some fifteen or so years ago, since when many others have emerged, at the time of writing there has been no published research on them, certainly not any that evaluates their role as innovators and experimenters. In other words, I certainly see a future for joint or ecumenical schools but not for those devoted to a Christian nurture function without a service to the community role. I find myself wondering if Owen Cole, who invokes Leslie Francis's work as well as Bernadette O'Keeffe's to reinforce his disillusionment with aided schools, would welcome Dr Francis's model of an ecumenical school.

There is probably little that can be done to modify the position of those schools whose governors take the 'hard' line towards other faiths, based on an exclusivist theology. Some may at present be functioning apparently successfully on the basis of receiving children from other faiths in the spirit of Christian love but having nothing to do with those faiths, even denouncing them as 'evil', but one has to wonder how hong it will be before such a model is seen as intolerably patronizing and educationally unsound not least to the extent that it imposes a conflict on children between what their parents should stand for and what their school and its teachers proclaim. I believe that the arena for debate must be with those schools in the broad middle spectrum and it is such schools that are still in large measure calling for guidance. I drew attention to this in the short discussion paper I wrote in 1984[12] and a similar observation is made in *Faith, Culture and the Dual System*.[13] We really are by and large being very slow in disseminating examples of good practice as one of the best ways of offering guidance.

And examples of good practice on the part of Church schools involved in multicultural education there certainly are. One such was briefly described in a recent National Society publication[14] and we must make sure other examples are publicized. I am pleased to see that the latest SHAP Handbook[15] contains an article on another Church of England aided school that rejoices in serving a multifaith pupil population, that aims to affirm other faiths without denying its Christian foundation, among whose educational objectives are those that try to round off the pupils' religious education 'with a multifaith exploration of significant religious issues which ... encourage pupils "to develop what they have learned, and also to break new grounds by tackling some of the ultimate questions that men and women have asked through the ages"' and help them 'recognize that a religious stance in life is still a valid option in this last quarter of the twentieth century'. The article concludes that 'if at the end of the day Christian, Muslim, Hindu and their agnostic or atheist counterparts, can grasp hands in friendship and understanding ... then we would consider that our time and efforts have not been wasted'. Indeed not, and although county schools can and do attain these objectives, church schools should be able to guarantee more firmly that the objectives will be pursued in an environment where religion can be expected to be taken seriously.

It seems to me that before Church schools can, however, begin to 'deliver', they (governors, teachers, the wider Christian community on which to a greater or lesser extent they depend) generally need to do more to work out their aims and objectives in two main respects. Firstly this should involve thrashing out a rationale (theological, educational and practical) for a service to the community role appropriate for the setting in which the school is placed. Secondly I believe governing bodies and staffs will increasingly have to reflect on, work out and clarify their attitude regarding other faiths; although such a challenge will have a particular urgency for schools admitting children of other faiths, in the closing decades of this century and beyond all schools will need to understand how any education that claims to prepare children for life (including living among, understanding and having some idea of how to cope with difference) will have to address itself to this area. Church schools with their professed understanding of the importance of belief/faith systems should be well placed to implement such an approach, so long as the heavy hand of the conservative predisposition commented on earlier does not stifle any initiatives in this direction.

The fear has been expressed by Leslie Francis that the net result of the service to the community role of Church schools is, or eventually will be, to water down their distinctiveness, particularly if it is done in the context of recent National Society and General Synod calls for partnership within the maintained system.[16] There is certainly the danger that certain perceptions of the application of partnership to relationships with local education authorities could have this effect. I would claim, however, that a Christian rationale for a sevice to the community role quite different from that feared by Dr Francis, is possible if it contains two important, traditional Christian elements: a prophetic perspective and a sense of vision. (The two elements are of course very closely related; there can hardly be any prophecy without *forth*-telling). Indeed, a convincing case for the former element has been made by Dr Francis in the very paper in which he questions the 'general service' role of church schools.

Basically he outlines some of the traditional arguments against church schools (that they are divisive, elitist, unfair to the rest of the maintained system, guilty of indoctrination and take Christian pupils and teachers out of the rest of the schools system) and argues that if and when such features are present they would stand condemned by the prophetic conscience. My understanding of prophecy is that amongst other things it includes a perception, grounded in faith with a discernment of the divine will, that relates current practices to discerned trends, that comments on current practices in the context of the direction in which society appears to be heading. One thing that appears to be generally agreed by commentators on the social scene is that, whereas 'difference' has always been with us, to some extent in the past it could be held at bay. Over the last couple of decades, however, and increasingly so during the next, in a shrinking world of greater mobility, more effective communication and transportation systems and ever more pervasive mass media, difference of one sort or another will be omnipresent. As *Faith, Culture and the the Dual System* observed, we have a pretty poor record in coping with diference or pluralism within Christianity itself[17]. How are we to cope with the diferences of race, faith, life stance and so on that are being and will be experienced? I hear a voice of prophecy certainly asking what we are doing to keep children rooted in something firm and stable in what could be a bewildering morass of variety. But I also hear the voice of prophecy asking the educational system what it and any of its agencies, particularly in the context of this essay on church schools, are doing to help prepare its children for difference and to give them positive, constructive options of coping with it to the benefit of the general good and to the ideal of diversity in unity. That these two voices produce a tension is undoubted, but the prophetic voice I increasingly hear is the one that asks if church schools mainly for Christians (rather than provided by Christians) in the closing years of this century and beyond are the best means of facing up to the challenges and opportunities of difference. Dr Francis's appellation of current British society as 'post-Christian' seems to me to beg many questions, as I shall try to indicate when I suggest the lines along which a sense of vision might develop. One such line, though, is the direction which theology may be taking in the years ahead, and here I echo Dr Francis's insistence 'that the integrity of the churches' involvement in education demands that the necessary underlying choices should be firmly based on theological decision'.

There are already many signs that theology will in the future have to become increasingly involved in and concerned about other faiths. Whether or not his own particular position is too relativist for many people's tastes, Alan Race has argued for the development of a theology of other faiths as a matter of increasing urgency.[18] In a review of another person's reflections on Christianity and other faiths, Race observes 'Witness without superiority and with a readiness to learn from others becomes the new understanding of the Christian mission ... We should think of this not as the selling of the Christian past, more as the celebration of a new direction in Christian existence'.[19]

What a General Synod Board of Mission and Unity Report has described as a 'journey through unfamiliar territory, which interfaith dialogue is for most of us'[20] will doubtless involve people going off in different directions: there will be the 'building walls' approach already seen by those Christians who support the private fundamentalist 'accelerated Christianity' schools; there will be some church-aided schools that will try to hold the line by making little or no concession to other faiths, either in the total curriculum offering or their admissions policies; it is quite likely that eventually at least a few aided schools will be founded by faiths other than those that have hitherto done so probably first by Muslims; there may be developments along the lines of the Christian ecumenical schools advocated by Dr Francis. But there should still be scope for Church aided schools to be in the van of providing a service to the community, despite many non-Christian elements in the community. Such a role should certainly serve the strivings for a theology of other faiths: 'Theological reflection ought not be undertaken in the abstract. It must engage with the experience of those whose lives are daily caught up in interfaith situations.'[21]

Far from urging the abandoning of the service to the community role, it is possible to query whether it has ever really been practised — at least in an altruistic way, with no vestige of vested interest, however unconsciously self-interest may have been wrapped up. I take Robert Waddington's point that there is a possible danger in over-emphasizing the philanthropic service to the community at the expense of building a truly Christian ethos in the school in that the suffering servant image might be prostituted and turned into mere subservience.[22] However, I think the Church of England and particularly its schools are still some distance from being in this danger. Bernadette O'Keeffe reminds us of the policy of the founders of the National Society together with their way of dealing with oversubscription.[23] But one has to question the degree of Christian or Anglican altruism in such an approach. It was after all put forward before the shock of the 1851 Census so that assumptions about the faith and practice of the majority could be thought to enable people to perceive such a policy as being fairly safe. There was also doubtless an element of conviction that the responsibility for educating children, even if many were non-Anglican, could not really safely be left in other hands. A service to the community role surely can receive a theological rationale, not least by application of the 'Golden Rule', 'Always treat others as you would like them to treat you'. (Mt 7.12). As A. E. Harvey comments, 'Jesus' teaching is not prudential at all, but an absolute principle: this is how you are to treat others — regardless!'[24] However unlikely a scenario it might be Christians could possibly profit by pondering on how they would like their children treated if they were living in a country where Christianity was a minority faith and many of the available schools had been founded by a non-Christian religion.

There is, indeed, potentially a great danger in abandoning the service role. The argument about the priest's role put forward by Hooker and Lamb in their recent book on Christian ministry could well be extended to other agents of the church, including schools. 'If their role is seen primarily as internal to the church then there is a danger that the whole life of the church will come to be self-serving, concerned only with the interests of a diminishing band of religious enthusiasts, the rump of a national church'.[25] The authors themselves contend that Christian ministry is in fact implicitly evangelistic.[26] Be that as it may I find much support for altruistic service from their reminder that 'friendship and love must be offered for their own sakes, without the intention of using them for any purpose outside themselves ... love must indeed have its own integrity. If it is 'used' for anything beyond itself it ceases to be love and becomes something else.'[27] I suppose they are right to imply that one always hopes for a response from love but the crucial point is surely, as they go on to argue, that one cannot predict what the response will be, nor control the results which flow from it.

I can best describe my vision of a Church school fulfilling a sevice to the community role by means of an anecdote. A few years ago I visited a Church of England aided middle school serving a mainly Muslim population, a school going through the early stages of wondering just what it, as a Christian foundation, was doing in such a situation. The headmaster invited me to meet one of his former pupils, a girl who had gone on to high school where she had acquired several 'O' levels but whose conservative Muslim parents had decided that she was to go no further with her education but wait until they arranged her marriage. In the meantime the girl returned to her old Church of England school where she acted as a sort of unofficial liaison officer between the school and Muslim parents. From the meeting I gained some idea of the internal struggle that some Muslim girls experience: part of them feeling they could and should take their education further, the other part of them not wanting to be disloyal to their parents. My other reflection was based on the thought that I would like that girl and other children of non-Christian faiths to think back on their Church of England school as a place where they received a good education in a place provided by and largely staffed by Christians who appeared to have no other motive than to serve the children in their charge, certainly with no proselytizing motive and no denigrating of the children's faith. Or is this vision too sentimental?

I hasten to add that my work does not allow me to underestimate the practical difficulties faced by Church schools serving children a majority of whom follow a faith other than Christianity. Difficulties faced in one diocese have been outlined in an article 'Up to summat in Bradford' by the Diocesan Director of Education.[28] *Faith, Culture and the Dual System* also discusses many of the difficulties and I shall not repeat them here. Although some of the problems may provoke, and indeed have provoked, *ad hoc*, crisis-management, it must be recalled that church schools (and not only church schools) have often been faced with unprecedented situations. I recall meeting the head of a Church of England aided school who had first joined the staff of the school in the late 1940s. He reminisced about how many of the boys used to go across the road to the church to sing in the choir; many of the girls joined the Girls Life Brigade at the church. The head himself was particularly interested in music and, as an assistant teacher, his great ambition was to become head and build on and extend the school's and church's joint musical activities. Within two years or so of his becoming head the neighbourhood drastically changed character with over 90 per cent of the school's popplulation being Bangladeshi Muslims. In his late fifties, towards the end of a professional career spent in very different circumstances, all the head's reserves of adaptability, resourcefulness, sensitivity and imagination were put to the test, not least in the matter of school worship with the challenge of providing worship that did not lead to the Muslim parents exercising their right of withdrawing their children. I mention this not to be uncritical and unaware of the church at all levels and of individual church schools often reacting too slowly or inadequately to the demands of a new situation but to remind some critics of the demands faced by individual schools and their staffs and governors and of the commendable efforts made by many to respond to them.

While my vision remains, Christians such as Leslie Francis and

Owen Cole question the traditional role of church schools and there has recently been a resurgence of voices doing so outside the church. The Swann Report gently called for a review of the 1944 Education Act's provisions for the dual system.[29] Correspondence in *The Guardian*[30] put the issue more sharply. Understandably frightened by the Northern Ireland situation and alarmed by a movement to set up a Muslim aided school, members of the National Secular Society argued that the abolition of voluntary aided schools was the most pressing issue in education, the nettle that most needed grasping. I have also seen copies of correspondence in which an official of a teachers' union opposes a proposal for a church aided school to serve an inner city, multifaith area on the grounds that county schools are inherently more suited to such a task.

Whilst one can fully sympathize with any determination to avoid replicating the divisiveness evident in Northern Ireland, and even if one believes (though it is open to debate) that the educational system there is a major contributory factor, there has been little beyond assertion to substantiate the fears that the English and the Welsh voluntary aided school system must lead to similar divisiveness and intolerance, even if there is a modest extension of the system to other faiths. One wonders if those who see the abolition of voluntary aided schools as 'the most urgent nettle to be grasped'[31] have fully thought out the probable or at least possible effects of such a move. Have they considered the possibility that there could be a substantial increase in the number of private schools proclaiming a religious allegiance? Indeed Owen Cole expresses reservations (as I do) about 'the emergence of (private) Christian schools of doubtful merit' at the same time that he admits his doubts about the dual system.[32] I fear that the abolition of the dual system could lead to a proliferation of private Christian schools.

Without sympathizing with the philosophy of contemporary Americans who are currently using similar language, there is a large proportion of the population who are uneasy with what they perceive as secular humanist values and assumptions increasingly infiltrating educational theory and practice. Although they have by no means given up their commitment to the county schools system, many Free Church people are worried that the RE and worship provisions built into the 1944 settlement are proving to be of questionable worth and, to put it at its least, opposition to church schools by Free Church people is much less than it used to be. An increasing number of people are also coming round to appreciate some merit in a system which, by being diversified, puts some limit on the part of centralist tendencies at governmental or local education authority level. However ' post-Christian' a society we may be, such people constitute a significant proportion of the population.

These are, however, all somewhat negative factors. There is potential — often realized, though, as *Faith, Culture and the Dual System* indicates, with scope for greater realization — for the great majority of Church of England aided schools to become a very suitable agent for reconciliation and the promotion of a rounded education. There will always doubtless be some church schools that will reject any such model as will also some individual Christians, Muslims and secularists. I have elsewhere quoted the Rev Kenneth Cracknell of the British Council of Churches for his view that, notwithstanding his Northern Ireland experience, church schools may be appropriate for a multifaith population.[33] A similar opinion is expressed by Hooker and Lamb in their recent book. In their chapter on 'The church school and other ministries' and indeed elsewhere in the book, the authors suggest that 'many in our society need a "healing of memories"' and that 'our children too need to be initiated into shared understandings, and it is at least possible that in this process people of other faiths can be creative partners, recalling us to things we might otherwise neglect.'[34] Many would see a valid multicultural approach to education as one that both honours and recognises cultural roots but also *transcends* the cultures of all concerned, the latter aim assuming greater importance when preparing for the twenty first century and an even smaller world.

No category of school will gain unanimous support but it is a tenable vision to see Church of England schools as having the potential with others to hold together people of many of the philosophical and faith sections into which society forms itself. A church school can, although it involves a tension, both promote a liberal education (liberal in the sense that it practises critical openness and abjures indoctrination) and to that extent satisfy many of a humanist disposition, and at the same time affirm the faiths of those who eschew a secular humanist stance. Of course there will be some atheists/agnostics for whom the religious element will be too strong and who will only be satisfied by a completely secular foundation. There will also be people committed to a religious position for whom the religious element will be too watered down. So be it. But there are grounds for believing that many parents see a place for a school that strives to retain a place for worship and RE other than in a dispassionate phenomenological way, that has as one of its main aims to affirm the children's respective faiths but also to help them see beyond their own faith, that in its practice witnesses to the view that 'in a society which generally preaches a secular materialistic ethic particularly through the media and commercial activity, some form of positive discrimination in favour of the religious dimension of life is required in curricular provision in schools'.[35]

In offering this vision of a possible context within which Church of England schools might find a bridge-building and pioneering role, in addition to the practical difficulties to which I have already referred, I see looming the overarching question of whether the church as a whole will be willing to support such an approach — in terms of providing the necessary resources and in terms of offering 'psychological' or moral support at all levels, from the 'person-in-the-pew' at parish level to those in positions of power and responsibility within the structures of church government.

On the question of resources I reiterate a point I have made elsewhere: 'any "partner" wishing to retain an institutional presence in the maintained system of schooling ... in addition to being able to contribute someting distinctive, must also be able to provide the professionalism, expertise and sophistication required to make an effective contribution to an increasingly demanding educational arena.'[36] I believe it is difficult to overstimate this challenge. To the above list I would add the need for coordination, both to enable some sort of strategic approach to be applied but also to make best use of very uneven distribution of resources. Some inner city areas where the multifaith challenge and opportunity are most pressing have very limited resources at parish level to put into their schools; perhaps the only hope for such schools to survive is for them to become in effect diocesan schools. Often the small proportion of churchgoers in such areas will need some convincing that it is proper to put financial and other effort into a church school that serves few if any Christian pupils and does other in the religious sphere than 'teach Christianity' and provide Christian worship. 'The Church at all levels has to make its mind up if it wants to continue with and provide the necessary means for church schools as part of its response and contribution to the changing world.'[37]

Even where there are some resources available there will be those Christians who will need to be persuaded that they are not 'selling the pass' in supporting church schools which provide the sort of service advocated in this chapter. Two private members' questions listed (but not reached) for the February 1987 General Synod meeting illustrate the psychological reservations that some people will feel. One question, for example, asked 'what steps are being taken to bring (Mus-

lims) to an acceptance of Jesus Christ as the only Saviour of the
world?' Another asked if there were any plans 'to monitor the
teaching of religious education in Church of England schools, with
special emphasis on biblical teaching instead of multifaith religious
teaching? In a sermon that would appear to have little sympathy with
the implication of this latter question, the Bishop of Willesden neatly
encapsulates the tensions involved and the adaptability of mental
approach required of those involved in education within a multifaith
setting. The quote I offer is a fitting reminder that whatever the likes
of me may write about the potential of church schools as bridge
builders in the present and future society, the teacher in the classroom
is the key figure. To be a Christian teacher, particulary one in a
Church school 'requires gifts of sensitivity and imagination which are
not easily learned. It is a different task to the earlier one of keeping
God alive in indifferent times' (though in many respects such times are
still with us), 'that required stubborn and persistent courage and faith.
The torch has now to be passed on to those having different gifts,
those who are called to explore faiths unfamiliar to them and who
have the skill to take their pupils with them as they learn together in
unfamiliar territory.'[38]

Bishop Butler comments that not all are called to be such explorers and he sees a role for those who will concentrate 'upon witnessing
to the truth claims of our faith, and in the case of Christianity to the
claims of Jesus Christ ... the final word of God to his creation.' I
would want to add the qualification that notwithstanding those who
make such a stand, the overall atmosphere and climate within the
Church will have to be one that encourages and affirms the work of
the 'explorers', if church schools in a pluralist society are to have
much of a future. I have agreed with Bernadette O'Keeffe's viewpoint
that 'A redefinition of the church's approach which will take account
of both the realities and the just demands of all sections of British
society today remains a pressing need.'[39] After all, as Bishop Butler
reminds us, the stakes are high, for any form of Christian witness
must be one that does not give 'ammunition to the religious, political,
and racist bigots in our society who have their own agenda and are
always ready to misuse the scruples of good and conscientious men
and women, and play on the fears of the battered and bemused'. This
whole context provides a wonderful opportunity for Christian service
and witness and, I am convinced, the 'explorers' in their bridge-
building work will not be selling the truth claims of their own faith
short.

Much work remains to be done by those engaged in work connected with Church of England schools. *Faith Culture and the Dual System* revealed many of the gaps. Church schools will also always experience some tension in serving a 'multifaith', 'post-Christian', 'secularist' society (whichever term suits your fancy) and will also at times have to wrestle with ambivalence and ambiguity. Here surely they will be mirroring the great Church of which they are part, for tension, ambivalence and ambiguity are never far from the surface for the Church of England — and indeed from life itself! The potential — and in many cases the practice — is there. After all although there was institutional inactivity regarding multicultural education in 34 per cent of church secondary schools and 43 per cent of church primary schools in Bernadette O'Keeffe's survey,[40] perhaps this implies that 66 per cent and 57 per cent respectively were at least doing something in this regard!

In a recent General Synod Miscellaneous Paper[41], its Board of Education suggest that continuing involvement in multicultural education is an 'inescapable imperative'. It later commented that in the context of an actually and potentially divisive, controversial arena, the Church 'should be in the middle of it, to serve the cause of justice certainly but also often to reconcile, to help hold together what might otherwise fragment in bitterness and conflict, to show how opportunities can be grasped and the positive brought out'. If Church schools do not and cannot contribute to such ends, I would not want to support their continuing existence; it is in the belief that they can and do that the General Synod Board of Education strongly advocates a role for Church schools and colleges in a pluralist society, a standpoint affirmed by the General Synod during the 1985 debate on Positive Partnership.[42]

Notes

1 BERGER, P. L. (1967) *The Sacred Canopy — Elements of a Sociological Theory of Religion*, New York, DoubleDay.

2 BERGER, P. L. (1971) *A Rumour of Angels*, London, Pelican Books.

3 O'KEEFFE, B. (1986) *Faith, Culture and the Dual System*, Lewes, Falmer Press.

4 COLE, W. O. (1987) 'Muslims and British education: A western non-Muslim view, paper presented to a conference at Homerton College, Cambridge, 20 March. 1978.

5 THE NATIONAL SOCIETY (C OF E) FOR PROMOTING RELIGIOUS EDUCATION (1984), *A Future in Partnership*, London, The National Society (C of E) for Promoting Religious Education, p. 54.

6 O'KEEFFE B. (1988) 'On the margins of education: Finding a dimension

of belief in GREEN, T. and BALL, S. J. (Eds) *Inequality and Progress in Comprehensive Education: A Reconsideration for the 1980s*, London, Croom Helm.

7 HALSTEAD, J. M. (1986) *The Case for Muslim Voluntary-Aided Schools*, Cambridge, The Islamic Academy.

8 FRANCIS, L. J. (1986a), *Church and School, a Future for Christian Education*, Abingdon, Culham College Institute for Church Related Education.

9 FRANCIS, L. J. (1986b), *Partnership in Rural Education*, London, Collins.

10 DUNCAN, G. (1986) *Faith for the Future*, London, The National Society (C of E) for Promoting Religious Education, p. 76.

11 Catholic Commission for Racial Justice, (1978) *Notes and Reports No. 1*, August. See also CATHOLIC MEDIA OFFICE (1984) *Learning from Diversity*, London Catholic Media Office, p. 65.

12 DUNCAN, G. (1984) *Schools and Multicultural Education*, London, General Synod of the Church of England Board of Education.

13 O'KEEFFE, B. (1986) *op cit.*

14 DUNCAN, G. (1986) *op cit*, see chapter 8.

15 COMMISSION FOR RACIAL EQUALITY (1987) *The SHAP Handbook on World Religions in Education*, London, Commission for Racial Equality. See the article by Rev. P. Shepherd p. 30.

16 FRANCIS, L. J. (1986a) *op cit*. See THE NATIONAL SOCIETY (C OF E) FOR PROMOTING RELIGIOUS *op cit*.; and THE NATIONAL SOCIETY (1985) *Positive Partnership*, London, The National Society.

17 O'KEEFFE, B. (1986), *op cit*, p. 108.

18 RACE, A. (1983) *Christian and Religious Pluralism*, London, SCM Press, p. ix.

19 Review in *Theology*, July 1986 London, SPCK, p. 328.

20 GENERAL SYNOD (1984) *Towards a Theology for Inter-Faith Dialogue*, London, CIO Publishing, p. 35.

21 *ibid*, p. 1

22 NATIONAL SOCIETY (1985) *op cit.* p. 65.

23 O'KEEFFE, B. (1986) *op cit*, p. 29.

24 HARVEY, A. E. (1979) *The New English Bible Companion to the New Testament*, Oxford and Cambridge University Presses, p. 40.

25 HOOKER R. and LAMB C. (1986) *Love The Stranger*, London, SPCK, p. 2.

26 *ibid*, p. 9.

27 *ibid*, p. 62.

28 *Crosscurrent*, 15, October 1984, London, The National Society.

29 DEPARTMENT OF EDUCATION AND SCIENCE (1985) *Education for All* (The Swann Report) London, HMSO.

30 Correspondence in *The Guardian* during July 1986.

31 Letter in *The Guardian* from A. J. Ayer and others, 9 July 1986.

32 COLE, W. O. (1987) *op cit.*

33 Duncan, G. (1984) *op cit*, p. 59.

34 HOOKER, R. and LAMB, C. (1986) *op cit*, p. 98

35 *A Future in Partnership op cit*, p. 81.

36 National Society (1984) *op cit*, p. 74.

37 *ibid*, p. 76.

38 Sermon preached by the Rt. Rev. Tom Butler in St. Margaret's Westminster, on 16 September 1986.
39 O'KEEFFE, B. (1988) *op cit*.
40 O'KEEFFE, B. (1986) *op cit*, p. 148.
41 General Synod (1986) *Multicultural Education. A Report by the Board of Education G. S. Misc 254*, December, London, General Synod Board of Education.
42 *ibid*, p. 9.

9 Five Items for the Policy Agenda in Church Schools

Robert Burgess

In the popular imagination the term 'church school' is often seen as synonymous with a Victorian building standing in the shadows of the local Anglican or Catholic church. Originally, these were all age schools that provided education for the children in the parish. However, they have been replaced and modified in the twentieth century as old, inadequate buildings have been removed and new schools have been constructed within and beyond the parish. Church schools are provided at primary and secondary level and offer facilities that are broadly similar to their county school counterparts (cf. Firth, 1977; Burgess, 1986a). In 1986, 34.9 per cent of primary schools belonged to the churches and 15.3 of per cent secondary schools (see table 1).

Table 1 *Number of county schools and church schools in England and Wales: January 1986*

PRIMARY SCHOOLS		SECONDARY SCHOOLS	
County primary	12725	County secondary	3432
Church of England	4827	Church of England	238
Roman Catholic	1880	Roman Catholic	446
Jewish	15	Jewish	5
Methodist	34	Methodist	—
Other	68	Other	165
TOTAL	19549	TOTAL	4286

Source: Department of Education and Science Statistics Branch: personal communication.

However, alongside these schools in the state sector, it is important to recall that all the major churches, Catholic, Church of England, Methodist and the United Reformed Church have their own schools in the independent sector. While there are only 2272 church independent schools it is evident from only a brief glance in *The Public and Preparatory Schools Year Book* that many of these schools have the support of those who are highly placed in the hierarchy of their respective church. For example, many independent schools with an Anglican foundation have a bishop as chairman of the school governors as well as considerable representation by clergy. Indeed, the General Synod of the Church of England recently remarked:

> Many private schools employ chaplains. Many schools in the private sector invite bishops to their prize days and confirmations, and clergy to preach, conduct retreats and take part in festive occasions, or to be involved in the management of the schools.

The report continued by commenting that many bishops, clergy and lay people, but especially bishops

> spend a disproportionate amount of their time at the schools attended by 6 per cent of the population of the country, and rarely visit the schools which educate the other 94 per cent (GSCE, 1985, p. 313)

Such remarks automatically point to the way in which church schools directly contribute to social division within education (see the chapter by Ball in this volume). However, following the recommendation of the report from the General Synod, this chapter will focus on the state schools.

Church schools not only cover a range of denominations but also a variety of age ranges and stages. In addition, some ecumenical schools have been established and considerable pressure has come from the Muslim community who want to establish voluntary aided schools in the same way as the major Christian churches (Harrison, 1986). Furthermore, in common with county schools, the members of church schools have also been confronted with such problems as falling rolls, redeployment, school amalgamation and school closure. The result is that Church schools and voluntary aided status has been at centre stage in recent years. With the publication of *Faith in the City* (GSCE, 1985) there have been further debates about voluntary-aided schools and their status. Finally, remarks from prominent churchmen, such as the Rt. Rev. David Jenkins, Bishop of Durham (Jenkins, 1986; Lodge, 1986) has helped to keep the subject of the church school in the popular press.

Church schools include voluntary-aided and voluntary-controlled establishments that were granted special status under the terms of the 1944 Education Act. Indeed, Rick Rogers states

> Around a third of all state schools are run in part by religious
> bodies. These are in the main the voluntary schools. Two
> thirds of those schools are Church of England — the rest are
> Catholic, Jewish or Methodist. Of every five children, one is
> being taught in a denominational or Church school. (Rogers,
> 1981, p. 27)

But who controls these schools? Under the terms of the 1944
Education Act voluntary-aided schools have two-thirds of their
governors appointed by the voluntary body itself. While it is the
voluntary body that provides the school premises and is responsible
for external maintenance and repairs, 85 per cent of these costs are met
by the DES and all running costs in terms of equipment and teachers'
salaries are provided by the LEA. It would appear, therefore, that we
need to look elsewhere to examine the influence of voluntary bodies
on schools. In particular, the Anglican report *Faith in the City*
recommended a review of

> diocesan policies for church schools on admissions criteria and
> other issues such as religious education and worship, equal
> opportunities and community education. (GSCE, 1985, p.
> 315)

Some of these issues such as admissions criteria are considered
elsewhere in this volume (see the chapter by Ball). It is, therefore, the
purpose of this chapter to take up some of these policy issues by
examining the management of church schools, the appointment of
staff, the curriculum and community education, over which church
schools have considerable autonomy (O'Keeffe, 1986; Burgess, 1983
and 1988). Finally, we shall briefly consider the role of evaluation in
keeping other issues on the policy agenda under review. In considering these issues, evidence will be drawn from reports and studies
that have been published in recent years as well as published and
unpublished case study material from my own study and restudy of a
co-educational Roman Catholic comprehensive school that I called
Bishop McGregor School (Burgess, 1983 and 1987a) where I have
examined several of these issues including school management,
appointments procedures, and curriculum matters.

Some Management Issues

We have already noted the way in which governors in voluntary-
aided schools have direct control over such matters as admissions,

appointments and aspects of the curriculum. Indeed, Tirrell (1969) points to the areas in which voluntary school governors have control. Furthermore, a training course for governors in voluntary-aided Roman Catholic schools also provides some clues to their areas of responsibility. After two background sessions on the dual system the course covers the following issues:

Finance and Buildings
(a) Responsibility for
    — Building schools
    — Capital cost
    — Alterations
    — Repair and maintenance
(b) Sources of income
(c) Contribution to costs
    — LEA
    — DES
(d) Procedures

Governors and Staff Relationships
(a) Employer/employee relationship
    — Contract of engagement
    — Payment of salaries
    — Grades and promotion
    — Training and career development
    — The headteacher
    — Departmental heads
    — Quality of teaching
(b) Appointments
    — Shortlisting
    — Interviewing
    — Redeployment
    — Involvement of Diocesan Schools Commission and LEA

Governors relationship to parents and pupils
(a) Admissions policy
(b) Publication of performance
(c) School discipline
(d) Consultation and dissemination of information
(e) Providing a Catholic education
    — Curriculum
    — Liturgy
    — The School Chaplain

(Extract from Voluntary-Aided School Governors Course in Merton LEA, 1984)

In part, this syllabus provides some guidance on the areas for which governors are directly responsible and which are often devolved to the headteacher. But, we might ask: How does the headteacher transmit these issues to staff and pupils?

Studies of voluntary schools (cf. Burgess, 1983; McLaren, 1986) have pointed to the importance of worship within the school and the way in which the ritual conveys meanings to teachers and pupils. For example, under the terms of the 1944 Education Act it is laid down that

> the school day in every county and in every voluntary school shall begin with collective worship on the part of all pupils in attendance.

On the basis of my observations in a Roman Catholic comprehensive school I found, in common with O'Keeffe's work in Church of England schools (O'Keeffe, 1986), that the acts of worship could be classed as Christian with hymns, prayers and addresses that were used to convey information about the organization of the school, and about the rules and routines that were established. In addition, the symbolism associated with acts of religious worship helped to remind participants about the religious 'community' within which it was assumed they were participants. However, the use of such occasions to transmit the Christian faith raises a number of issues that have been summarized by O'Keeffe (*ibid*). First, do such acts of worship suggest that the church is only concerned with its own followers? Secondly, is dialogue between Christians and other faiths reduced to a one-way process? Thirdly, how can the aims of worship be explored in an area of mixed belief? Indeed Cracknell and Lamb (1984) have summed up these issues in the following terms:

> What is the proper form for a school assembly in a multi-religious school or even in an all white school which wishes to be sensitive to the multi religious society it is part of? How can the integrity of every conscience be respected while introducing children to the fundamentals of worship? (p. 17)

However, the Bishop of Durham has taken these issues further as he argues that the act of worship is now questionable in church schools. In particular, he asks:

(1) What right in civil liberties or in Christian religious terms

have we to impose a Christian act of worship in a pluralistic society?

(2) What effect do indifferent and confused acts of worship have on innoculating children against developing their religious sense?

(3) When is society going to face up to how there is to be a common commitment to serious matters of worth and worship in a pluralistic society, which includes various religions and various varieties of 'non-religion'? (Jenkins, 1986, p. 1)

Such questions have confronted many teachers and headteachers already as the Swann Committee (DES, 1985) reported that

> Given the multiplicity of beliefs now present in society, it is not surprising that we have received much evidence about the difficulties generated by the 1944 Act for a daily act of collective worship and the provision of a particular form of religious education. We therefore believe that the government, in consultation with religious and educational bodies, should look afresh at the relevant provisions of the Act to see whether alterations are called for after an interval of forty years. (p. 773)

However, it is not only through school assembly and acts of public worship that the headteacher conveys a Christian ethos but also through the appointment of teaching staff and the organization of the curriculum to which we now turn.

The Appointment of Staff

The governors of voluntary-aided schools are responsible for the appointment of teachers and more recently for their redeployment. Indeed, teachers in voluntary-aided schools have contracts with the governors who are their employers. Furthermore, in cases of appointments, redeployments and disciplinary procedures, the local authority acts in an advisory capacity. However, aided schools, wherever possible, follow the patterns and procedures of local authorities in the appointment and redeployment of teachers. For example, the Catholic Archdiocese of Birmingham have indicated to governors that it is important to cooperate with LEAs in the redeployment of teachers, to avoid overstaffing. However, they point out:

If we do not cooperate with the local education authority in solving these problems

(a)   some of our schools will be overstaffed while neighbouring schools are understaffed — an imbalance which is quite unacceptable.

(b)   At a later date as the problem intensifies it might well occur that some teachers in the overstaffed schools may be made redundant. It might be to the advantage of such teachers to transfer to a more stable situation as the opportunity arises.

It is this pattern of cooperation between local authority and church authorities that is mirrored in the staff procedures. But we might ask: to what extent do the governors of church schools follow the policy of the local authority in which they are located? Indeed, we could go further and ask: do church school governors know about the policies of their local authority?

In the course of my second study of Bishop McGregor School I have been engaged in research on teacher appointments. The authority in which the school is located has adopted an equal opportunities policy. On this basis advertisements for posts carry the statement:

We welcome applications from men and women regardless of disability, race or marital status.

Yet in the two years in which I studied appointments procedures this policy was rarely explicitly discussed apart from one occasion when governors checked with the headteacher whether they could be prosecuted under equal opportunities legislation as men were appointed to positions that had previously been held by women.

All appointments at Bishop McGregor School were made by a Staffing Sub-committee that consisted of a parish priest who chaired the governors, two or three (depending on their availability) foundation governors who were appointed by the church rather than the LEA, the headteacher and a local authority adviser. The local authority was therefore always in a minority and always in the position of 'guest' in a church school; a position that the chairman of governors often jokingly reminded advisory staff about.

Some attention was devoted to the appointment of women staff; especially where promotion was concerned, but this issue was usually raised by women governors. However, to say that women supported women is to oversimplify the issue. Furthermore, advisers from the local authority were often witnesses to discussions that were in clear breach of local authority policy and equal opportunities legislation. Among the topics that were openly discussed in my presence were:

(a) the possibility of ending maternity leave with a clear signal from some governors that they would be prepared to sign petitions that set out the case for such action;

(b) the domestic responsibilities of particular candidates for posts, especially where child care was concerned;

(c) the possible sexual preferences of a particular candidate for a post whom it was considered might be homosexual given the individual's style of haircut, age and unmarried status.

Clearly, such evidence points to problems in appointments procedures. Yet it is too easy to pillory the governors of this church school or, indeed, the governors of all church schools. The evidence that has been assembled points to processes that have occurred in a church school and might occur in a county school. Such evidence points to a series of issues that need consideration. First, that appointments committees are given sufficient information so that they are clear about local education authority policy. Second, that special attention be given to equal opportunities; especially as far as appointments and appointments procedures are concerned. Indeed, it might be argued that this is more important in church schools where, given the traditional role given to women in the Anglican and Catholic churches, there is a danger that women will not only be underrepresented, but also underrepresented in 'top' positions such as head, deputy head, head of house or year and head of department. In these circumstances, this will influence the messages that are transmitted to pupils about the roles that men and women hold in society; it will be part of the hidden curriculum of schooling that forms part of the curriculum package to which pupils are exposed.

The Curriculum

When interviewing pupils in Bishop McGregor School I often asked the question 'what do you feel is distinctive about McGregor?' Among the most common answers was a direct reference to religion. Indeed, pupils often made direct comparisons with county schools located in the same geographical area where they argued their friends were not exposed to so much religious education through school assembly and through religious education classes. Yet this oversimplifies the situation by making the assumption that

Christianity is only directly transmitted through the classes provided in religious education. My evidence from Bishop McGregor School would suggest otherwise. For example, the head attempted to make religion a central focus in school life and school routines. Each year he issued a paper to his staff entitled 'Religious cycles in the school year' in which he argued that the liturgical cycle should be integrated with the school curriculum. In particular, he maintained:

> various events of the church's year do come annually and should be reflected in our joint worship, informal religious education lessons and informally in other subjects where this can be done.

The paper went on to explore the way in which church festivals at Harvest and Christmas could be used as a focus for music and drama, while Lent could be used as a time when teachers and pupils could celebrate the Passion and death of Christ through the Lenten charities collections that were organized by house heads who were the key participants in the pastoral team.

All members of the pastoral team in the local authority concerned were seen to be important in the establishment of discipline and order but in McGregor School they were also responsible for dealing with problems of moral order as the headteacher indicated in further particulars for the post of house head that he expected holders of such posts to

> play a very important part in the moral and social education of their house pupils.

House heads within McGregor School were, therefore, responsible for welfare, attendance, discipline, uniform and progress as well as moral education. A situation that was summed up by the head when he stated that the job involved:

> responsibility for the pastoral care, social and academic welfare and discipline of each child within the house. [The head of house] is expected to be involved in the implementation of agreed school policy and play a major role in helping to plan future school policy.

In addition, all holders of such posts had to be committed Christians and practising Catholics; a situation that resulted in houses being a series of strong bases from which Catholic education could be promoted, not only through the affective curriculum, but also through the introduction of school wide policy which would be permeated by religion. The work of these senior teachers was subject to criticism from their colleagues as

> their job did not involve 'real' teaching. David Peel (Head of the Geography Department) summed it up by saying 'If you're a head of house you just check to see that all your kids are in uniform and that you have enough chairs for dinner sittings and your job's done'. George Jackson (Head of the English Department) considered the job involved 'Looking after the Children of Mary'. (Burgess, 1983, p. 60)

Even among the staff room cynics, note was taken of the relationship between religious and moral education and the transmission of values through school wide policy and through the affective or pastoral curriculum. However, for these teachers the 'real work' involved introducing pupils to subjects.

But does the religious ethos of a school influence subject teaching? While governors in church schools may look for 'the committed Christian' to take appointments, they may have to settle for individuals who are sympathetic to the Christian faith. In this way, religious values and convictions may be transmitted through the subject curriculum especially in areas such as home economics, child care, sex education and science. One area of the UK in which religion can be clearly examined in relation to the subject curriculum is Northern Ireland where Catholic and Protestant schools co-exist. Here, a study by Murray and Osborne (1983) found that in general, girls in Catholic schools were more often involved in arts and humanities subjects rather than physical and biological sciences; a situation that they argue may rest on the values of the Catholic church (cf. O'Brien, 1966). Indeed, they state:

> As the value system of the Roman Catholic church is often supposed to foster a more traditional view of the female role, this stereotyping may be more marked in the voluntary schools. These same values may also lead to a higher proportion of girls in voluntary schools leaving at 16 rather than staying on at school to prepare themselves for higher education and a subsequent career, and this in turn would tend to lead to a lower proportion of 'A' level passes within the voluntary system. (Murray and Osborne, 1983, p. 126)

In addition, they also point to problems associated with physical and staff resources concerning science and craft subjects. First, they argue that voluntary schools have problems in fully providing the specialist facilities and equipment for these subjects. Secondly, they argue that there is a problem in recruiting staff with qualifications in science subjects given that less pupils leave voluntary schools with science 'A' levels that will enable them to acquire degrees in these subject areas. While their data apply to Northern Ireland, it is still important for the church school to consider

(a)   the balance of subject provision between the arts and the sciences;

(b)   the provision of equal opportunities for girls and boys;

(c)   the extent to which values and attitudes permeate the subject curriculum.

One area in which the latter subject is important concerns questions of culture and the multicultural curriculum. Evidence from Ball and Troyna (1987) and O'Keeffe (1986) points to a lack of serious concern on the part of church schools to multicultural education. Ball and Troyna indicate that in a study of one local education authority their data point to the ethos and values of church schools being at the centre of the stage. They conclude:

> On the one hand were those teachers who felt that the celebration of cultural diversity contradicted the notion of religious unity which constituted the *raison d'être* of the school... On the other hand there were those teachers who felt that the promotion of tolerance and understanding for all cultures was best tackled through the established religions, Christian ethos of the school and not by the introduction of multicultural education. (Ball and Troyna, 1987, pp. 20–1)

As a consequence, Church schools may constrain the diffusion of multicultural or anti-racist education even when they are located within LEAs that promote such policies. The members of church schools must therefore consider the following issues:

(a)   the extent to which their procedures and policies deny black and white students equal access to education;

(b)   the extent to which the curriculum reflects the cultures from which the pupils are drawn.

Both these issues are crucial if the church school is to play a key role in overcoming problems associated with social divisions in schooling and the school curriculum. For example, who has access to schools will influence the composition of the pupil population and have direct implications for curriculum content. Nevertheless, regardless of intake, all white schools need to consider the ways in which they can offer a multicultural curriculum if their pupils are to be adequately prepared for life in a multicultural society. For example, Catholic schools who have high proportions of white pupils need to consider the cultural origins of these pupils — from Ireland, Poland, Italy and other European societies. In this respect, a curriculum that is based on a selection from culture should not simply be established around British culture but the cultures of the societies from which pupils are drawn and the multicultural society of which they are members. For some schools this has meant considering the relationship between the curriculum and the community; a further policy issue to which we now turn.

The Curriculum and the Community

In recent years a developing theme among educationalists and social scientists has been the role of the community school within the comprehensive network (Cowburn, 1986; Hargreaves, 1982). The idea of the community school has a long history that is rooted in the village colleges of Cambridgeshire in the 1920s but is now also established in several urban authorities such as Coventry and Manchester and also in Leicestershire. Yet as David Hargreaves (1982) has remarked, the term 'community' lacks precision with the consequence that the term community school covers a broad range of activities. He divides changes and developments in community schools into four models:

1   The promotion of a community within the school where there is increased democratization within the school; especially between teachers and pupils. It is, therefore, marked by a high degree of pupil participation.
2   Participation in the school by the outside community which results in increased parental involvement and community participation on the governing body. In its weak version Hargreaves argues this will mean parental involvement but 'the strong version of this reform, parent-governors are but the first step in a process of *community control* of the secondary school'. (*ibid*, p. 115)
3   The school as a community centre where school premises are located in buildings that are shared with libraries, swimming baths, and leisure facilities. Here the artificial

divisions between schools, further education classes and adult classes are broken down.

4   A situation where not only structures are changed but also the curriculum. Here the reform is focused on new options. In its weak form it may involve a package of 'community studies', while in its strong version a major part of the curriculum can be organized around community themes and interests.

A brief examination of these four models might lead us to the conclusion that church schools already possess some of the key attributes of community schools with direct parental involvement in the school and where members of the 'community' (in this case the parishes) are formally represented on the governing body. Certainly, there is potential for the church school to become a community school. However, there are a series of problems that have to be directly confronted:

1   What constitutes 'the community' for the church school? Is it merely those people who are members of the Anglican or Catholic churches that are linked to the school or is it far broader?
2   If parents are to be involved in the school governing body, does this merely point to maintaining the status quo?
3   Will community involvement mean just the Christian community or all those living within the locality of the school?
4   What does community involvement in the curriculum mean in this context?

Members of many church schools are currently considering the possibility of community college status or in some cases have become community schools (cf. Mitchell, 1985; Burgess, 1986b). Taken in one direction, it can be used as a conservative force to endorse the *status quo* by merely drawing on parent groups. A second model may result in breaking down artificial divisions between school and community but where community is narrowly defined in terms of the parishes to which the school relates. A third model holds the potential for the church school to go beyond the boundaries of its parishes and to seek participation by all who live in the geographical area within which it is located. It is this model that would seem to hold the greatest potential for the church school as it can overcome the problems associated with intake and access that have been discussed by O'Keeffe (1986) and by Ball in this volume. Certainly, if this approach is taken, we shall see dual use of facilities by adults and pupils and the potential will be there to broaden the curriculum so that the church school may respond to the society in which it is located. However, as with any changes of this order, it is important that the situation should be monitored so that the relationship between the church school and educational provision can be kept under review.

Evaluation

The focus of the discussion so far has been upon some current practices in church schools and in turn the processes associated with them. In particular, emphasis has been given to some of the contradictions in current practice and to some issues that members of church schools need to discuss. Often discussions may take place within department meetings and in school-wide meetings but there is a lack of systematic evidence of current practice. In these circumstances we might ask: how might the members of a church school monitor the policies and practices in the areas we have examined?

In recent years there has been increasing interest in evaluation and self-evaluation procedures being used by school staff. It is, therefore, this issue that should also be placed on the policy agenda. But what counts as evaluation? In a recent discussion Malcolm Skilbeck warns of the dangers of overlooking some of the

> simple truths about evaluation, not least the normal human tendency to reflect upon experience, to assess the value of one's actions and intentions, and to relate consequences to aims. (Skilbeck, 1984, p. 1)

At one level, therefore, evaluation is part of the day-to-day activities that are conducted by the members of any school. However, it also involves the use of specific theories, concepts and methods. It is research based but is not an end in itself as the research is linked to development and forms of action. In this respect, we can examine a range of evaluation strategies including the check lists and monitoring procedures advocated by some local authorities (cf. the ILEA document *Keeping the School Under Review*, ILEA, 1976) to schemes of school self-evaluation (cf. Simons, 1984 and 1987). It is the latter model that is of interest to us here with its focus on teachers working together or in collaborative relationships with outside researchers (cf. Pollard and Woods, 1987; Burgess, H. 1987; Burgess, R. G. 1987b) where teachers use methods of observation, interview, diaries and diary-interviews to examine their own activities and that of their colleagues (cf. Burgess, 1985; Woods, 1986).

The issues that we have particularly identified as important items for the policy agenda could be examined using strategies of self-evaluation. At first glance, it may appear that these issues are the province of particular groups: the school governors, the headteacher, the senior management team and teachers drawn from a particular department. Indeed, some of the issues might mistakenly be regarded as the concern of those teachers within the Religious Education department. However, the issues that have been identified relate to the 'ethos' of the school and, therefore, it is argued it is important for all teachers to be involved in obtaining knowledge that can be used to evaluate and refine school policy. In conducting such an exercise Eraut (1984) has noted that the members of a school need to consider the following:

1 What issues and questions should be placed on the agenda and on which evidence should be sought?
2 What evidence will be collected and from whom?
3 Who owns the evidence that is collected? Who will have access to the evidence and how will it be handled?
4 To what extent will the evaluation be used as a review, as a problem solving exercise or as a guide to future decisions?

It is with these questions in mind that we turn to four areas that could be the subject of evaluation in church schools.

Appointments

Among social and educational research reports we have very little evidence on the processes associated with school appointments procedures (cf. Burgess, 1988), although we have an account of national trends that has been obtained from statistical data that are collected by the DES (Byrne, 1978; Deem, 1978; Burgess, 1986b). In particular, special attention has been given to the lack of women in senior posts relative to their numbers in the English educational system. But how might such an exercise be conducted in a school? Here, a group composed of local authority advisers, school governors and teachers drawn from different levels in the school hierarchy should conduct a monitoring exercise. Among the data that need to be collected are:

(a)   Numbers of posts advertised, the terms of the appointment, the job description involved.

(b)   The composition of the appointments committee.

(c)   The procedures adopted by the committee — the use of written evidence (application forms and references), the use made of questions to candidates and the process of discussion.

Data of this kind will allow the members of a school to have access not only to the patterns of recruitment but also to the way in which the procedures that are used assist or impede the appointment of particular groups.

Worship

Often it is assumed that the dominant character of worship within a denominational school will reflect the religious group. But what do we know about worship and assembly within the church school? A further cross-school group might therefore monitor the assemblies that are held during a term with special reference to the following issues:

(a)   Who conducts the assemblies?

(b)   What form do the assemblies take?

(c)   What is the content of the assemblies?

(d)   In what ways are religion and ritual used?

Such questions will assist teachers to consider the extent to which the pattern of worship within their institution adequately prepares pupils for a pluralist society, the way in which values are transmitted and the relationship that is implied between the sacred and the secular.

The Curriculum

It is the relationship between religious belief and other areas of the school curriculum that is often the subject of debate. But there are a series of fundamental issues of curriculum management that Light (1984) considers need to be examined. The key issues are:

(a)   Determining aims and targets.

(b)   Devising programmes whilst considering the constraints of policy and resources.

(c) Implementing programmes.
(d) Controlling, monitoring and reviewing programmes.
(e) organizing the school for effectiveness.

While these constitute important areas of curriculum management, it is also essential for features of curriculum design and implementation to be considered as part of the evaluation exercise. In terms of design and implementation special consideration needs to be given to the pastoral, as well as the academic, curriculum, to teaching style as well as content and to the model that is implicit within a curriculum programme. Here again, an evaluation group might consider the extent to which religious belief influences the form and content of the school curriculum as discussed by Hirst (1985) and the extent to which pupils have access to a range of knowledge that would properly equip them for a plural society. But we might ask: what resources are used? Here we might turn to consider the community.

The Community

We have already noted the way in which some commentators have pointed to the importance of using the community as an essential resource in the design and implementation of the curriculum. A group concerned with evaluating the role of the community in school might therefore consider:

(a) The extent to which there is a shared use of resources by adults as well as pupils.
(b) The extent to which members of the community are involved in (i) the school; and (ii) the curriculum.
(c) The influence of community involvement in the school.'

With these questions in mind we might successfully shift towards an evaluation of the use made of church schools by the locality and the extent to which teachers use the community as a resource.

Conclusion

In this chapter five issues have been examined that need to be placed on the policy agenda of the church school. As such this will involve governors, teachers, parents and members of the locality in which the schools are placed entering into dialogue and debate about the purpose of the church school and the way in which such schools relate to the state. Already the Bishop of Durham has raised some questions about the future of state aid to schools run by a particular church when he asks:

(1) Ought the state to support educational establishments, one purpose of which is, or may well be, religious indoctrination and discrimination?

(2) Do we want, both on humane and prudential citizenship grounds, and on grounds of the Christian understanding of the way God acts in love and freedom for reconciliation, to see the multiplication (with state support) of schools which in terms of society at large will be inevitably 'sectarian'? Is this the right or proper way for parents or communities to attempt to pass on their religious identities? (One may also ask, in the light of experience so far whether it is very likely to be a successful way).

(3) Might not the strong Christian concern that education should be kept open to the worshipful, the moral and the riches and love of God and, also that education should not be diminished by a dull pragmatism, a rigid utilitarianism or a distorting ideology be most effectively promoted by supporting all Christians and other concerned persons who work in or around education in their fight for and against these various things right across the board and in all schools? (Jenkins, 1986)

Clearly, there is much to be done by all who are concerned with church schools and with Christian education to think through these issues not only in relation to their own school but also in relation to school and society. For in analyzing the position of church schools in society we also need to analyze the influence of the churches on equality of educational opportunity in all schools if artificial social and religious divisions are not to be established in a society that is no longer united by a Christian culture.

References

BALL, W. and TROYNA, B. (1987) 'Resistance, rights and rituals', *Journal of Education Policy*, 2, 1, pp. 15–25.
BURGESS, H. (1987) 'Collaborating in curriculum research and evaluation' in

POLLARD, A. and WOODS, P. (Eds) *Sociology and the Teacher*, London, Croom Helm.

BURGESS, R. G. (1983) *Experiencing Comprehensive Education: A Study of Bishop McGregor School*, London, Methuen.

BURGESS, R. G. (1985) (Ed) *Issues in Educational Research: Qualitative Methods*, Lewes, Falmer Press.

BURGESS, R. G. (1986a) 'Changing concepts of secondary education' in MASON, T. and LANCASTER, B. (Eds) *Life and Labour in Twentieth Century Coventry*, Coventry, Cryfield Press.

BURGESS, R. G. (1986b) *Sociology, Education and Schools: An Introduction to the Sociology of Education*, London, Batsford.

BURGESS, R. G. (1987a) 'Studying and restudying Bishop McGregor school' in WALFORD, G. (Ed) *Doing Sociology of Education*, Lewes, Falmer.

BURGESS, R. G. (1987b) 'Examining classroom practice using diaries and diary interviews' in POLLARD, A. and WOODS, P. (Eds) *Sociology and the Teacher*, London, Croom Helm.

BURGESS, R. G. (1988) 'Points and posts: A case study of teacher careers in a comprehensive school' in GREEN, T. and BALL, S. J. (Eds) *Inequality and Progress in Comprehensive Education: A Reconsideration for the 1980s*, London, Croom Helm.

BURNET, J. F. (1975) (Ed) *The Public and Preparatory Schools Year Book*, (published annually), London, A & C Black.

BYRNE, E. (1978) *Women and Education*, London, Tavistock.

COWBURN, W. (1986) *Class, Ideology and Community Education*, London, Croom Helm.

CRACKNELL, K. and LAMB, C. (1984) *Theology on Full Alert*, London, British Council of Churches.

DEEM, R. (1978) *Women and Schooling*, London, Routledge & Kegan Paul. *Education Act* (1944), London, HMSO.

ERAUT, M. (1984) 'Institution-based curriculum evaluation' in SKILBECK, M. (Ed) *Evaluating the Curriculum in the Eighties*, London, Hodder and Stoughton.

FIRTH, G. C. (1977) *Seventy Five Years of Service to Education*, Coventry, Coventry, Coventry Education Committee.

GENERAL SYNOD OF THE CHURCH OF ENGLAND (1985) *Faith in the City*, Report of the Archbishop of Canterbury's Commission on Urban Priority Areas, London, Church House Publishing Company.

HARGREAVES, D. H. (1982) *The Challenge for the Comprehensive School*, London, Routledge & Kegan Paul.

HARRISON, S. (1986) 'Swann: The implications for schools', *Journal of Education Policy*, 1, 2, pp. 183–95.

HIRST, P. H. (1985) 'Education and diversity of belief' in FELDERHOF, M. C. (Ed) *Religious Education in a Pluralistic Society*, London, Hodder and Stoughton.

INNER LONDON EDUCATION AUTHORITY (1976) *Keeping the School Under Review*, London, ILEA.

JENKINS, D. (1986) 'Comments on the future of church schools', (mimeo) (9 September).

LIGHT, T. (1984) 'Evaluation in school curriculum management' in SKILBECK,

M. (Ed) *Evaluating the Curriculum in the Eighties*, London, Hodder and Stoughton.

LODGE, B. (1986) 'The death that will bring life', *The Times Educational Supplement*, 19 September, p. 10.

McLAREN, P. (1986) *Schooling as a Ritual Performance*, London, Routledge & Kegan Paul.

MITCHELL, G. (1985) 'Croft Church of England Community Primary School, Leicestershire' in RENNIE, J. (Ed) *British Community Primary Schools: Four Case Studies*, Lewes, Falmer Press.

MURRAY, R. C. and OSBORNE, R. D. (1983) 'Educational qualifications and religious affliation' in CORMACK, R. J. and OSBORNE, R. D. (Eds) *Religion, Education and Employment: Aspects of Equal Opportunity in Northern Ireland*, Belfast, The Appletree Press.

O'BRIEN, J. (1966) 'Science and Catholic education', *Catholic Teacher's Journal*, 9, pp. 16–17.

O'KEEFFE, B. (1986) *Faith, Culture and the Dual System: A Comparative Study of Church and County Schools*, Lewes, Falmer Press.

POLLARD, A. and WOODS, P. (1987) (Eds) *Sociology and the Teacher*, London, Croom Helm.

ROGERS, R. (1981) 'Denominational schooling', *Multiracial Education*, 10, 1.

SIMONS, H. (1984) 'Issues in curriculum evaluation at the local level' in SKILBECK, M. (Ed) *Evaluating the Curriculum in the Eighties*, London, Hodder and Stoughton.

SIMONS, H. (1987) *Getting to Know Schools in a Democracy: The Politics and Process of Evaluation*, Lewes, Falmer Press.

SKILBECK, M. (1984) (Ed) *Evaluating the Curriculum in the Eighties*, London, Hodder and Stoughton.

DEPARTMENT OF EDUCATION AND SCIENCE (1985) *Education for All* (The Swann Report) London, HMSO.

TIRRELL, L. B. (1969) *The Aided Schools Handbook* (2nd edn), London, National Society SPCK.

WOODS, P. (1986) *Inside Schools*, London, Routledge and Kegan Paul.

10 Theological Reflections

Stewart Sutherland

Within any society are to be found microcosms which differ in size from one another and in scale from the society of which they are part, but which, nonetheless, reflect with a sharp and intense light some of the complexities of that society. This is true of schools specifically and of the educational system more generally. It would be interesting but not directly relevant to pursue the implications of this claim over a wide range of issues. The discipline of this chapter must be to reflect upon the ways in which the subtleties and in some contexts uncertainties of theological discussion can be illuminated by, or can illumine, the issues which the educational system of our country faces in the detailed relationships of the classroom.

Teachers, parents, pupils and headteachers are drawn together in our state schools by the contingencies of age, career development and address. In any society this is bound to result in a degree of tension and adjustment. Whether the tension is creative or disruptive will depend upon a number of factors, one of which is the degree of homogeneity of aspiration, intention and motivation between the respective parties. One consequence of this is that schools are particularly sensitive indicators of change within certain areas of society, and particularly of those changes which question accepted patterns of goal-setting and means of achievement.

To be fairly, but I hope helpfully, simplistic, successful classroom activity presupposes some agreement upon what is considered educationally valuable, and upon how to achieve that. Behind this of course, lies the question of what the point of education is and the answer to that question will include a declaration of what one considers to be of fundamental value for human (individual and social) flourishing, and of the role which education can play in helping individuals and societies achieve this.

Even in periods of comparatively even-tenored change these issues must be kept under regular revue. The urgency of the discussion could, or should, reflect the speed and proportion of changing perceptions within a community of how to answer these very basic questions. At one end of the spectrum, the questions hardly come up at all: at the other end social and quite probably political discussion and chaos will reign. Healthy societies will find themselves between these two extremes, and perhaps it is worth recording at this stage that I would regard a degree of change as a sign of health rather than the reverse. Neither do we already live in the best of all possible worlds, nor are we immune to changes outside of our control. Both of these factors combine to support the view that a degree of change is both inevitable and desirable.

The classroom is our microcosm and this chapter will focus upon the changes perceived with sharp clarity by teachers who work in schools whose real environment is multicultural, and upon the particular problems which this poses for those engaged upon religious education, not least if they are based in 'church schools'.

There is one initial point of illumination for those whose field is 'education' or 'theology'. Neither of these areas of intellectual endeavour has, ready to hand, a theory which will provide an appropriate framework for finding adequate answers to the questions which face teachers with such immediacy. 'Education' and 'theology' are not great intellectual monoliths. Rather they are interacting areas of enquiry through which we try first to help formulate and reformulate practical questions and then to begin to answer them. The process, however, is and must be firmly interactive. This shows most obviously in our present discussion by the way in which very fundamental questions of theology are raised pointedly by the teacher who is genuinely puzzled about the appropriate form of religious education, or school worship in a class which is both multicultural and multifaith. The problems are even more complex if one raises the role of a church school in a neighbourhood which has changed by patterns of immigration to one in which the vast majority of children belong to Muslim or Sikh communities. Neither the theologian nor the educational theorist has an off-the peg answer ready to dispense.

Changes in society which demand reflection and action stemming from that show themselves at very early stages in the classroom. In that sense the classroom is a microcosm which in the detailed urgency with which practical questions demand answers (what is the content of the RE lesson tomorrow, or the form of the school assembly the day after?) forces the pace of theological and educational reflection.

Of course, we should not be over-surprised that 'even' theology does not have pre-packaged answers to all practical questions. That it should have could only be expected by those who would see it as ossified in insulated isolation from the empirical world. The real test of theology, or of educational theory for that matter, is that it should be rich enough in resources to respond positively to new forms of interrogation from the community which it seeks to serve.

It would be useful to recall three of the major elements of change in our society which are central to the topic of this chapter, and which provide the testing grounds variously for theology and educational theory. Each in its own way tends to relegate to a past age the negotiated consensus of the clauses of the 1944 Education Act which bear on our discussion.

The first is that the place of the church, and indeed of many institutions in our society, is subject to significant reassessment. That this is so need not be a matter for pessimism, indeed possibly the reverse. However, there is a complex of ideas and terms whose shifting relationships and meanings illustrates well some of the issues. The days are gone in which it could be confidently affirmed that

> By 'religion' I mean 'Christianity', and by 'Christianity' I mean 'the Church' and by 'the Church' I mean 'the Church of England'.

Equally the expression 'a Christian country' is less confidently used and less clearly defined when it is used. There are two obvious consequences of these changes. The first is that we may be encouraged to look elsewhere to see where there are lessons to be learned about how to cope with multicultural and multifaith environments. The second is that the rationale of the idea of an 'Established Church' is bound to be reassessed. What happens in schools will clearly not settle the question of the future of the Established Church, but how the established church reacts to the changing face of schools (including voluntary-aided or church schools) will doubtless have a bearing on the broader question.

The second major change which defines the context of our discussion is that there is a decline in the obvious marker of traditional Christian commitment — church attendance — and along with that a much more overt and public attachment to a plurality of views, religious and secular. Inevitably this has resulted in a diminution in the, perhaps apparent, but nonetheless powerful, former consensus on the type of belief framework which informed public policy in these matters. RA Butler did have to seek consensus in the drafting of the 1944 Education Act, but the consensus was not about belief-systems. That, by and large, could in general outline be taken for granted. The consensus concerned rather the political and financial stakes which the various Churches would be prepared to accept. A common set of aspirations, intention, and motivation could be assumed. Or at least it could be assumed that there would not be significant widespread rejection of such an assumption. This could not be said today and no doubt that would be the basis of some firm ecclesiastical opposition, should a major reconsideration of the 1944 Act be canvassed.

The third area of change of most dramatic significance for the central topic of this chapter is the growth of large urban areas which have multicultural and multifaith populations. There are large immigrant communities, increasingly now second generation immigrants with a varied set of cultures, and often adherents of religious traditions which are major world religions other than Christianity. There is certainly no developed theology of education at hand to offer guidelines in this situation. Granted also the speed of change within Britain in this respect it is not surprising, although neither is it a matter for satisfaction, that theology and educational theory are reactive rather then anticipatory in their response to the questions set by teachers in church schools.

All of this provokes for theology and the churches on the one hand and for educational theory and the schools on the other, a series of questions in which practice and decision-making are inextricably bound up with concepts and language of a highly general nature. In the second half of the chapter I shall reconsider some of these questions in more detail.

There are two models for the role of church schools in multicultural and multifaith environments, which together depict the extremes of a spectrum of theologies. The first is to view the church school as the model of a missionary evangelical church which carries the teaching of the church to children. The second is to view the church school more on the pattern of a serving church which provides, on one missionary pattern, the equivalent of the services of a mission hospital.

The justification for the former to be provided by taxpayers' contributions is hard to find. Educationally also it is suspect, although not all would accept this view. There is no doubt, however, that it would cause much dissension in multifaith communities if this is what the nearest 'state' school offered. The latter, however, does seem to be a much more acceptable model, not least because there is much evidence that church schools provide a good education which is attractive to many who do not have church connections.

There are many implications of following the latter course. One central point which I shall not discuss is selection policy. The question of the role of religious worship and assemblies becomes particularly pointed and I shall turn to this shortly. The final thorny issue which I shall mention is the question of whether voluntary-aided status should be granted also to proposed Muslim, or Sikh schools, for example. My answer here is affirmative, but I should like to add one or two further comments.

The first is that any voluntary-aided school be it Christian, Muslim, Jewish or whatever, must conform to the standards laid down by Her Majesty's Inspectorate. Indeed this applies to any school, whether public or private sector. The more subtle point here relates to the interface between educational openness and religious commitment. I comment on this further below.

There are in addition two more practical points. Always — and Christian church schools have not uniformly avoided this danger — there is a risk of creating a ghetto mentality or approach to education. There are many good social reasons for weighing this point very seriously in considering any particular application for voluntary-aided status. The related point concerns the questioning of continuing demand for such schools and again 'best estimates' would have to be made of the shifts in perception as increasingly the immigrant communities which show most interest in such proposals become second and indeed third generation British citizens. However, this is to do no more than signpost practical issues which require detailed analysis in the context of accepting the general principle.

An important general question which belongs to the discussion of the nature of education is whether education includes nurture, and if so, to what extent. The question becomes even more difficult and complex when one places it in the context of nurture (? religious ? spiritual) within a multifaith community.

The answer to the question however, is that education does inevitably include nurture. This is not the sum total of what education is, but the younger the child the more difficult it is to deny the fact that the bonds of dependency and support which are characteristics of the structures of nurture are structural elements of the classroom relationship. If this is so, then it is important to raise the related questions of the significance of multifaith and multicultural contexts for educational practice.

Undoubtedly a most difficult area here can be identified by the terms 'religious' or 'spiritual' nurture, and lest we dismiss these terms too readily, it would be wise to recall the definition of aims offered by the 1944 Education Act;

> ... and it shall be the duty of the local education authority for every area, so far as their powers extend, to contribute towards the spiritual, moral, mental and physical development of the community by securing that efficient education throughout these stages (of primary, secondary and further education) shall be available to meet the needs of the population of their area.

Our question now becomes that of how, in an area where the population is multifaith and multicultural, a school might contribute towards spiritual development.

There seem to me to be two main possibilities here which we might consider. The first is very specific, the second is more general. On the one hand one might equate spiritual nurture with, in the Christian community, something like 'denominational' nurture. This is to see spiritual development as primarily related to a particular group or community. Thus spiritual nurture for Anglicans would take one form, and for Roman Catholics or Presbyterians rather different forms. There are obvious analogies if one transfers the issue to, say, Muslim or Sikh groups.

There are good reasons for pressing this point, for undoubtedly the younger the child the more important it is that any form of nurture must belong to relatively specific structures. The 'ocean of Being *qua* Being' does not provide the possibilities of response to a 7-year-old which are the great strength of stories about Allah, Jehovah or God. Equally in so far as the prescriptions in the 1944 Act concerning worship bear on the idea of spiritual development or nurture — and what else could they bear on educationally? — then the particular patterns of specific traditions are bound to be the points of reference. Up to a point at least religious or spiritual nurture must be particular. It is precisely this which poses problems of increasing complexity in multifaith contexts, but before turning to these, I should like to outline an alternative, but less specific face of religious or spiritual development.

The view of a possible form of spiritual development which I find more congenial — though doubtless because I am no longer 7 years old, nor do I have to teach 7-year-olds — is one which focuses upon the broader questions of how we perceive ourselves and the world in which we live. Thus I count it essential to any form of religious or spiritual development that we learn to see ourselves as part of a world which is a world '*sub specie aeternitatis*'. That is to say, that we refuse to see ourselves as nothing but contingent specks of matter drifting briefly in time and space. The exposition of such a view belongs and has been offered elsewhere, but central to it is the affirmation that human beings can form purposes, goals and intentions, and with varying degrees of success try to achieve these. Such goals express and indicate human preoccupations with values and the intelligibility of such a view is central to though not completely definitive of the idea of spiritual development or nurture.

Of course, it is easier to think of forms of religious nurture which can be shared acceptably in multifaith communities and schools which are of the latter (more general) rather than former (more specific) type. But this would be to dodge the educational question of what is appropriate to young children, as well as the philosophical and theological one of how the generalities of talk of viewing the world '*sub specie aeternitatis*' can be grounded in human language and experience. Thus I do think that it would be disingenous to allow the appropriate elements of education to focus on the latter solely, to the exclusion of the former.

If this is so a whole host of questions arise, of which two are particularly central. Can one hope to foster spiritual development without in fact engaging in indoctrination? Is it possible to avoid indoctrination without crippling the capacity for belief? The two are closely related, but in commenting upon them I can do no more than offer a few signposts to the way ahead.

The answer to the first of these two questions has to do not with the specific acts of worship nor with the particular religious stories told to the 5 or 7-year-old, but with the context in which these take place, and the context in which the 7-year-old becomes in due course a 16-year-old. The essential element, if indoctrination is to be avoided is the encouragement to ask questions. This presupposes an 'openness' on the part of the teacher and the school which must parallel the openness and open-ended nature of, for example, the teaching of science. It should be as natural to ask exploratory questions in religious education as it is in scientific or historical education. Of course there are subtle differences, but equally there are close analogies. Stories about Jehovah are not open to testing in quite the same way as stories about the origin of the species are, but in both cases the credibility of the stories is an issue which if ignored is bad educational practice. The art of nurture and the skill of development is the timing, the pace and the balance of question and affirmation in each case.

This is why my second question 'is it possible to avoid indoctrination without crippling the capacity for belief?' will preoccupy many. The sign posts towards an answer to this question are two in number. The first is that in history, in literature, in the sciences, questioning is the cornerstone of understanding and reasonable beliefs are based on understanding. The second sign post is the very strong tradition to be found in Christianity and in other major religions that insists not simply that avoiding indoctrination is compatible with nurturing belief, but that it is a condition of full religious development. However, it must be admitted that there are traditions, again within Christianity and other major religions which would deny this in practice and sometimes in precept. The question which is then defined and which would require much more than one chapter to analyze, is whether it is the case that only certain forms of Christianity or indeed of any world religion are compatible, and which allow the possiblity of retaining the Butler Act's reference to 'spiritual development'.

This leads, however, to the final question which I propose to raise, and which belongs to the following context.

It might be conceded that perhaps 'questioning' and 'openness' have an important role in spiritual development, but that the care necessary to define such a role can only be exercised in the detailed focus upon how this is dealt with in *one* religious tradition. There are, however, major difficulties in raising these matters outside the confines of a basic *shared* religious tradition. If the questioning is part of a common purpose of refining *the* tradition, then one can see how this may be done and how it has been done. Surely, however, we are in a radically new situation of many traditions, at least embryonically, being present in the classroom.

Am I not avoiding the point that believers have beliefs? They believe that these beliefs are true. *Ipso facto* they disagree with others. Is this a situation in which there is a place within a multifaith classroom for the subtleties of the pattern of spiritual development at which I have hinted? That is the question of whether into this complex situation can be built the further concept of tolerance. Once again the classroom is the microcosm for society at large. If we cannot solve this problem there, then the prospects for a multicultural and multifaith society are severely constricted.

My assertion, rather than argument, is that there is a difference to be drawn between the private beliefs to which we may be passionately or moderately committed, and the constitutional position which we hold with regard to the position of others and of the nature of a state educational system. Part of what religious or spiritual development is will be measured in the ability of growing children to embody this as part of their inheritance as citizens. In part this is to make a value judgment about the kind of society which we must become, but in part it is to describe one of the conditions of such a society. The sensitive question with which I conclude this short essay is whether *all* forms of belief which are found under the general headings of, say, 'Christianity' of 'Islam' can have a place in the type of school system implied in this chapter.

Notes on Contributors

Dr Muhammad Anwar is Director of Research at the Commission for Racial Equality.

Professor Syed Ali Ashraf is Director-General of The Islamic Academy, Cambridge. He is also a Member of the Faculty of Education, University of Cambridge.

Professor David Aspin is Professor of Education at King's College London.

Dr Stephen Ball is a Lecturer in Urban Education at King' College London

Dr Robert Burgess is Senior Lecturer in Sociology at the University of Warwick.

Dr Owen Cole is Head of Religious Studies at West Sussex Institute of Higher Education.

Geoffrey Duncan is Deputy Secretary and Schools Officer of the National Society and Schools Secretary of the General Synod Board of Education.

Maurice Hobbs is a member of the Birmingham Community Relations Council's Education Panel. He was a member of the Swann Committee Sub-group on Teacher Education.

Dr Bernadette O'Keeffe is a Senior Research Fellow at King's College London.

Professor Stewart Sutherland is Principal of King's College, London, and was Professor of History and Philosophy of Religion from 1977 to 1985.

Dr Brenda Watson is Director of the Farmington Institute for Christian Studies.

Index